"Any curious and intelligent person can learn a great deal about our planet and ourselves by reading this book about ways of using sunlight."
—THE WHOLE EARTH CATALOGUE

THE SUN IS

our most important natural resource—it's abundant, nonpolluting energy—if only it could be stored and concentrated!

DIRECT USE OF THE SUN'S ENERGY

Up until his recent death, Dr. Daniels was the leading American authority on Solar Energy. He spent many years studying the possibilities of converting the sun's rays into mechanical and electrical power with the purpose of suggesting ideas and areas for research into providing low-cost sources of energy.

DIRECT USE
OF THE
SUN'S ENERGY

Farrington Daniels

BALLANTINE BOOKS • NEW YORK

Library of Congress Catalog Card Number: 64-20913

ISBN 0-345-25938-6-195

This edition published by arrangement with
Yale University Press

Manufactured in the United States of America

First Ballantine Books Edition: February 1974
Seventh Printing: February 1977

Cover photograph courtesy of Freelance Photographers Guild

Contents

Tables

Illustrations

Foreword

The direct use of sunlight to supply the basic human needs for energy is of primary importance to man's continued survival on earth, for the stored fuels, fossilized or organic, are being consumed at an incredible rate. Only green plants are able to convert the sun's energy into fuel and food for animal needs, but the amounts thus produced, large as they are, cannot keep pace with the requirements after the stored supplies of fossilized fuels—coal, oil, and gas—have been consumed.

This conversion ability of green chlorophyll-bearing plants, as in past ages, to form organic compounds is nature's solution to the problem of capture and storage of energy. It remains for scientists to develop photosynthetic processes suitable for commercial development on an enormous scale—a complex but not insoluble problem.

Another approach is to devise efficient physical equipment to utilize directly the heat energy from the sun's rays on a practical low-cost basis. This field has already received much attention but the results to date have not been too encouraging. Professor Daniels has given many years to a consideration of all aspects of the problems associated with the direct transfer of solar energy. His studies have involved extensive experimental programs and conferences with scientists all over the world. It is indeed fortunate that his results and conclusions are now made available in this most timely volume of *Trends in Science*—a project of the Yale Chapter of Sigma Xi and the Yale University Press.

GEORGE A. BAITSELL

Winter Park, Florida
February 1964

Preface

The purpose of this book is to interest scientists and engineers in undertaking research on the direct use of the sun's energy. The book is expanded from a Sigma Xi lecture delivered at Yale University in April 1960, and from an earlier Sigma Xi lecture tour in 1951, and it is based in part on the author's research program on solar energy during the past decade.

Research in the field of solar energy use is unique in several respects. First, it cuts across many different sciences and branches of engineering—physics, chemistry, meteorology, astronomy, chemical engineering, mechanical engineering, and electrical engineering. Often an area between different fields of science that has been neglected becomes a fruitful field of research. Solar energy research is an example.

Second, it holds promise of leading rather soon to benefits for human welfare. Scientists formerly took little thought of the social and political impact of their work—but all this has been changed since they developed nuclear energy and made atomic warfare possible.

Third, it can be carried out in small laboratories with inexpensive equipment. Expensive nuclear reactors, atom smashers, and wind tunnels are not required, nor is it necessary to master highly specialized techniques such as the handling of radioactive materials.

The author has visited scientists in many of the nonindustrialized countries where abundant sunshine is available and fuel is expensive, and he has been asked frequently, "What research can we undertake in solar energy which might help our country?" This book is an attempt to answer this question and to point out the array of challenging problems in both pure and applied science that await scientists and engineers in the study of solar energy utilization. In an effort to interest readers who are not specialists in solar energy, many engineering and technical details have been minimized, but an attempt has been made to give a comprehensive bibliography where these details can be found.

Four international symposia on solar energy use have been held recently and it is therefore appropriate at this time to survey the present status of the many different ways in which solar energy can be used directly, to summarize present trends and opportunities in research, and to gather together the latest references so that others can build on the efforts which have gone before.

Until recently solar energy research has not been given much financial support, but now with the need for power in space vehicles the United States government is supporting large efforts in the use of solar energy in outer space; some of it will find application on earth.

The author desires to express his deep appreciation to Dr. Warren Weaver and to the Rockefeller Foundation, which has supported generously the research program on solar energy utilization for the past nine years at the University of Wisconsin. The grant has made possible the exploration of many of the ideas described here and is designed to emphasize helping the economically less-developed countries. The author is indebted also to the Guggenheim Foundation, which supported his work in its earlier phases. He is pleased to acknowledge the efficient help of Mrs. Irene Frey in typing the manuscript and of Mr. Harry A. Schopler in preparing many of the figures.

F. D.

Madison, Wisconsin
January 1964

CHAPTER I

Introduction

All our food and fuel have been made possible by the sun through the photosynthetic combination of water and atmospheric carbon dioxide in growing plants. If the world's supply of fuel were evenly distributed there would be a sufficient amount everywhere for present use. But if the earth's population increases at its present rate and if all people achieve the standard of economic development which the quarter of the world's population now industrialized enjoys, there will not always be an adequate supply. Plans should be made now to develop substitutes for combustion fuels—coal, oil, and gas. These fuels have become so vital to modern civilization that research for new sources of heat and power is long overdue.

All our machines have been developed to operate with heat engines or with electricity generated from heat engines or water power. In large units the power is cheap, but in small units of from 1 kw to 500 kw, operated by Diesel engines in isolated areas, the power is relatively expensive—5¢ to 15¢ per kwhr. The upkeep and repair of the Diesel engines and the high cost of transportation of petroleum fuel over poor roads contribute to these high costs. In large power stations electricity is cheap at the bus bar of the power plant but it becomes expensive after distribution over large rural areas to many small consumers. Because atomic energy is essentially a weightless fuel, the cost of its transportation is negligible, but atomic energy can be produced only in large, expensive units and accordingly there is still a high cost of distribution through power lines.

Solar energy requires neither transportation of fuel nor distribution of electricity because it can be produced in small electrical converters wherever the electricity is to be used. For heating and cooling also the direct use of the sun eliminates the need for transporting fuel and conveying power over long distances. These advantages tend to offset

1

in part the present high cost of any device that will convert the sun's energy into electricity and the serious handicap in the storage of power required by the intermittency of sunlight. In some cases, then, it is practical to consider the use of solar devices even though they are more expensive than those that consume fuel.

One of the important characteristics of our present civilization is that we are concerned for the welfare of others—for our descendants and our neighbors. We are aware as never before of the living conditions in other parts of the world, and the industrialized countries are eager to help the nonindustrialized countries become more productive and achieve a higher economic level. More mechanical or electrical power would be a very effective means of help. Though the industrialized countries do not seriously need more fuel now as the nonindustrialized countries do, they are in a good position to give important practical help through research and development of means for using solar energy. Fortunately even the smaller countries with little experience in scientific research and engineering and with small financial resources can undertake both basic and applied research in the use of solar energy.

The rapidly developing countries are eagerly looking for new sources of industrial power. Some are expecting too much too soon, and it is important to emphasize that education and research and the spirit of public service are more important than kilowatts. If however it is a question of "water or no water" or "power or no power," no price is too high to pay. Solar energy is a hopeful source, especially in sunny, rural areas, though it cannot compete with conventional sources of energy where these are abundant, or in cloudy climates, or in large cities where the amount of available sunlight is too small to supply the power needs.

The question may properly be asked: "Will the need for solar-generated power be only temporary?" Conventional fuel-powered electric generating systems with their transmission lines and power grids are expanding rapidly and will eventually cover the earth. But there are now 2 billion people in the world without electricity and it will be a long time before they can be served. Moreover, in communities of small rural users widely distributed the cost of distribution of conventional electric power will continue to be so great that solar energy may perhaps be competitive.

Already there is a specific case that might be considered.

Twenty thousand wells are needed for pumping water in Pakistan to rinse salt deposits out of irrigated lands which have become agriculturally unproductive because of water-logging and excessive accumulated salinity. It would be natural to turn to electric pumps with large, efficient electric power plants and a network of transmission lines. But if practical solar pumps can be developed soon enough, they might well be considered, in spite of the considerably greater cost of power production, because they would eliminate the long, expensive power lines.

The immediate urgency for research in solar energy is for use in the economically less developed countries. The long-range need for research in solar energy is in the highly industrialized countries, because the fossil fuels will not last indefinitely and will certainly increase in cost. There is now a temporary excess of petroleum production, but within five years the domestic supply of petroleum in the United States is expected to continue to rise, pass its peak, and begin to decline. More petroleum will have to be imported. The present rate of petroleum production in the world is about 7 billion barrels per year, and the world's proven reserves are about 300 billion barrels, which would last less than half a century at the present rate of consumption. But since the rate of consumption is bound to increase rapidly, par-ticularly in those large areas of the world seeking to in-dustrialize as fast as possible, shortages may be expected within a half century. New reserves, far beyond the 300 billion barrels, will continue to be found in the future as they have in the past, but eventually fuel will become so expensive to recover that new sources of energy must be found to supply a world which will have become ever more dependent on abundant fuel.

Solar energy research has been neglected. In the indus-trialized countries fossil fuel is abundant (or they would not be industrialized), and there is little private incentive for solar research. Neither has there been need for govern-ment support. In the nonindustrialized countries in sunny areas there have been few resources in funds and technical manpower and little knowledge of the potentialities of solar energy. If a small fraction of the resources and efforts now directed toward atomic energy and space science were di-rected toward use of solar energy, a great deal of progress could be made. There is no gamble in solar energy use; it is sure to work. It has been demonstrated that solar energy will heat, cool, convert salt water into fresh water, and generate power and electricity. The problem is to do these things cheaply enough to compete with the present methods based on fuel, electricity, animal power, or manpower in any given locality. The competition is difficult because of the low intensity of radiant energy in sunlight and the interruptions of night and cloudy weather. It is hoped that intensive work by many scientists and engineers in many countries will solve the problems and make solar energy useful in some areas of the world now and in many areas in the future.

The direct use of the sun's radiation is not new, but we have new materials to work with, such as inexpensive transparent sun-resistant plastics and semiconductors of high purity. We have new ideas in science, accumulated experience in engineering, and a broader knowledge of world-wide opportunities and needs. Thus it is important to re-examine all the ways in which science and technology can help to make direct use of the sun practical.

GENERAL BIBLIOGRAPHY

The scientist or engineer who desires to look over the field in search of an interesting or useful project may study the following general bibliography, which is largely based on the international symposia of the past decade. (Specific references will be given in later chapters when the research opportunities in the several different solar energy applications are discussed.)

1. *Proceedings of Space Heating Symposium*, Cambridge, Massachusetts Institute of Technology, 1950.

2. *Solar Energy Research*, ed. F. Daniels and J. A. Duffie, Madison, University of Wisconsin Press, 1955.

3. *Applied Solar Energy Research: A Directory of World Activities and Bibliography of Significant Literature*, ed. E. J. Burda, Menlo Park, Calif., Stanford Research Institute, 1955.

4. *Proceedings of the World Symposium on Applied Solar Energy, Phoenix, Ariz., 1955*, Menlo Park, Calif., Stanford Research Institute, 1956.

5. *Wind Power and Solar Energy: Proceedings of the New Delhi Symposium*, Paris, UNESCO, 1956.

6. United Nations Dept. of Economic and Social Affairs, *New Sources of Energy and Economic Development*, New York, United Nations, 1957.

7. *Transactions of the Conference on the Use of Solar Energy: The Scientific Basis*, Tucson, University of Arizona Press, 1958.

8. *Dictionary of World Activities and Bibliography of Significant Literature,* Tempe, Ariz., Association for Applied Solar Energy, 1959.

9. *Applications Thermiques de l'Énergie Solaire dans le Domaine de la Recherche et de l'Industrie: Symposium at Mont-Louis, France,* Paris, Centre National de la Recherche Scientifique, 1961.

10. Research Frontiers in the Utilization of Solar Energy, in *Proceedings of National Academy of Science,* 47 (1961), 1245–1306; *Solar Energy* (previously *Journal of Solar Energy Science and Engineering*), 5, special issue. Sept. 1961.

11. United Nations Dept. of Economic and Social Affairs, *New Sources of Energy and Energy Development,* U.N. Conference on New Sources of Energy, Rome, 1961. New York, United Nations, 1964. E/3577/rev. 1. Doc. ST/ECA/72.

12. *Proceedings of Advanced Study Institute for Solar and Aeolian Energy,* Sounion, Greece, Greek Atomic Energy Commission and the Hellenic Scientific Society of Solar and Aeolian Energy, 1961; ed. A. G. Spanides, and A. D. Hatzikakidis, *Solar and Aeolian Energy,* New York, Plenum Press, 1964.

13. *Solar Energy* (previously *J. Solar Energy Sci. and Eng.*), Tempe, Ariz., Solar Energy Society, starting in 1957.

14. Zarem, A. M., and Enway, D. D., *Introduction to the Utilization of Solar Energy,* New York, McGraw-Hill, 1963.

15. Perrot, M., *L'Energie Solaire,* Fayard Bilandela Science, Paris, 1963.

CHAPTER 2

History

EARLY EXPERIMENTS

In 1774, Joseph Priestley concentrated the rays of the sun onto mercuric oxide and collected the gas produced by the heating. He found that in this gas a candle burned much more brightly than in air and that a mouse lived longer in a given volume of this gas, which seemed to be air "in a much greater perfection." Thus oxygen was discovered. These findings enabled the great French chemist, Lavoisier, to propound the correct theory of combustion as caused by combination with oxygen. Also in 1774, an impressive picture was published of Lavoisier standing on a platform near the focus of huge mounted glass lenses, carrying out laboratory experiments with the focused sunlight.

In 1872, in the cloudless desert of North Chile, a solar distilling operation covering 51,000 ft² of land was built to provide fresh water from salt water for use at a nitrate mine. Over troughs of salt water, slanting roofs of glass plates served to transmit the sun's rays and reduce the infrared radiation emitted, thus heating the water. The vaporized water condensed on the air-cooled underside of the glass roof and ran down into channels. This plant operated effectively for 40 years, until the nitrate mine was exhausted. A remarkably large-scale application of solar energy, it produced up to 6,000 gal of fresh water per day.

At an exhibition in Paris in 1878, sunlight was focused onto a steam boiler that operated a small steam engine and ran a printing press (see Fig. 1).

1. Solar steam engine, Paris, 1878.

In 1901 at South Pasadena, a large focusing collector in the form of a truncated cone developed 4½ hp using an area of 150 ft² hp⁻¹ (see Fig. 2).

From 1902 to 1908 H. E. Willsie and John Boyle built four solar engines in St. Louis and in Needles, California. One 6-hp and one 20-hp engine operated on water and sulfur dioxide.

In 1907 and 1911 near Philadelphia, F. Shuman developed solar steam engines of several horsepower which pumped water (see Fig. 3).

In 1913 near Cairo, Egypt, F. Shuman and C. V. Boys built a large solar engine, of over 50 hp (see Fig. 4), with

2. Solar steam engine, Pasadena, 1901.

long parabolic cylinders that focused the solar radiation onto a central pipe with a concentration ratio of 4.5 to 1. It pumped irrigation water from the Nile River.

One of the earliest attempts to store solar-generated power was made by J. A. Harrington in New Mexico nearly half a century ago. He focused sunlight onto a boiler and ran a steam engine that pumped water up 20 ft into a 5,000-gal tank, from which it ran down through a water turbine

3. Solar steam engine with flat-plate collector, Philadelphia, 1907, 1911.

4. Solar steam engine, Cairo, 1913.

operating a dynamo and small electric lamps that lighted a small mine day and night.

With the exception of C. G. Abbott's activity, little took place in the development of solar power during the next 30 years. Abbott exhibited at an International Power Conference in Washington in 1936 a ½-hp solar-operated steam engine and in 1938 in Florida an improved ⅕-hp engine with a flash boiler.

From 1941 to 1946 F. Molero developed solar steam engines at Tashkent in the U.S.S.R.

These and other developments of solar power are summarized by Jordan and Ibele[1] and by Robinson.[2-4] None of the early solar-operated devices survived competition with cheap fossil fuels, with the exception of solar water heaters, developed chiefly in Florida. The developments of solar energy uses after 1950 are described in the later chapters of this book.

For millennia man has used solar radiation in agriculture. While solar instruments were being devised, a tremendous development in agricultural research and in the improvement of the efficiency of storing solar energy in the form of food was also going on. Some attention likewise was directed toward basic research on the process of photosynthesis in growing plants. The efficiency of chemical energy storage in algae, under ideal conditions in the laboratory, has been found to be as high as 30 per cent of the radiant energy absorbed. Ordinary agricultural plants, as will be shown later, store only about 2/10 of 1 per cent of the energy received from the annual sunshine. In the direct use of the sun, without the intermediate step of growing plants, it is possible to convert several per cent of the solar radiation into mechanical or electrical energy and a much larger fraction into heating, cooling, and the distillation of water.

Perhaps the first substantial support for basic research in the direct use of sunlight came from the Cabot Fund given to the Massachusetts Institute of Technology and to Harvard University about 30 years ago. Pioneering work was carried out on house heating, flat-plate collectors, and photochemical possibilities. An important symposium on house heating was held in 1950.

In 1949 at the centennial meeting of the American Association for the Advancement of Science, in Washington, one session was devoted to sources of energy including atomic energy and solar energy. The potentialities and the economic difficulties in the direct use of the sun's energy were pointed out by the author at this meeting[5] and in 1950 they were further emphasized through publications and a Sigma Xi lecture tour.[6]

Active practical developments in the direct use of solar energy were carried out in the United States in the 1940s by Dr. Maria Telkes and by Dr. George O. G. Löf, both of whom did some of their work at M.I.T. A grant from the Guggenheim Fund and substantial support from the Rockefeller Foundation, starting in 1955, have been responsible for a considerable program of research at the University of Wisconsin on the use of solar energy with particular emphasis on applications in the nonindustrialized countries.

With the exception of the researches cited and work on the solar distillation of salt water supported by the Department of the Interior, very little attention was given to the use of solar energy before the mid-1950s by the government or by the universities of the United States.

This summary of early work in solar energy use has been concerned chiefly with American scientists. There was also active work in the U.S.S.R. starting a decade ago, under the direction of V. A. Baum, and in India at the National Laboratory of Physics in New Delhi. It should be mentioned that in 1952 a rather pessimistic report was issued by British scientists concerning the direct use of solar energy, particularly in the English climate. Nevertheless H. Heywood in England has been active in this field.

SOLAR SYMPOSIA

Within the past decade, several international symposia have led to an active and rapidly increasing interest on the part of scientists and engineers, and of the general public as well, in the direct use of the sun's energy. In fact there is danger that the layman may expect too much too soon without realizing the great difficulties involved in collecting the very low-intensity sunlight. There is a long road of research, involving many tests, before solar energy can compete economically with conventional fuels.

A symposium on space heating was held in 1950 at M.I.T. (Chapter 1, Ref. 1). Symposia on solar energy were organized by the American Academy of Arts and Sciences[7] and the Ohio Academy of Sciences.[8] In 1953 a symposium on solar energy utilization was held at the University of Wisconsin with support from the National Science Foundation. Most of the scientists who had been active in this field were invited. The thirty participants discussed their findings informally. Progress was reported in the fields of solar cooking, heating, cooling, saltwater distillation, steam engines, thermoelectrical and photovoltaic conversion, photochemistry, and mass culture of algae. The papers were fully discussed and attempts were made to evaluate possibilities for success in the various branches of solar energy use. The results of this symposium were published (Chapter 1, Ref. 2) with an added chapter by J. A. Duffie which reviewed the patent literature on solar energy.

In 1954 UNESCO and the Indian Government sponsored a symposium on solar energy and wind power in New Delhi. The proceedings (Chapter 1, Ref. 5) stressed social and political implications as well as technical possibilities in the use of solar energy. Following the conference, representatives of the Indian government took the thirty scientists by plane to the semiarid regions of northwest India, showed them the dry agricultural land, the water under the surface, and the abundant sunshine, and asked, "Can't you do something to help us?"

In 1955 two conferences in Arizona were organized under the newly formed Association for Applied Solar Energy (now the Solar Energy Society). The first was a conference at the University of Arizona, at Tucson, which stressed basic research in solar energy. The proceedings were published in 1958 in a 900-page volume (Chapter 1, Ref. 7) and provided a complete background of basic information on the use of solar energy. The second conference in Phoenix immediately following this, the World Symposium on Applied Solar Energy, was organized with the help of the Stanford Research Institute. These proceedings were published in 1956 in a volume of 300 pages (Chapter 1, Ref. 4) and give a good general survey and analysis of the practical and economic problems in different parts of the world. The conference and symposium were attended by 900 registrants, 130 of whom came from 36 countries outside the United States. A solar engineering exhibit held in conjunction with the symposium displayed examples of solar devices, including many working models.

In 1958 Professor Felix Trombe organized an international symposium at his Laboratoire l'Énergie Solaire at Mont-

Louis, Pyrénées Orientales, France, emphasizing the thermal aspects of solar energy in research and industry (Chapter 1, Ref. 9). The excellent solar furnaces at this laboratory were an important feature of the program. Also, in 1958 a solar conference was held in Los Angeles.[9]

In April 1961 nine papers, including one from Baum of the U.S.S.R. and one from Tabor of Israel, were presented at a symposium organized by the National Academy of Science in Washington on research frontiers in solar energy utilization (Chapter 1, Ref. 10). At this symposium economic restrictions were disregarded, and an attempt was made to bring out new ideas and encourage research on solar energy that might find practical application in the future.

The Social and Economic Division of the United Nations organized a large symposium on practical ways of using the energy from the sun, the wind, and the earth's underground heat. The conference was held in Rome in August 1961 and attracted 500 scientists from over 50 countries. It pointed out to the representatives of the nonindustrialized countries what help they may expect from solar energy in the future, and informed the scientists and engineers of the industrialized countries what limits of costs and technological competence for operation must be met in the newly developing countries. The great need for small sources of power and heat in isolated areas where conventional power and fuels are unavailable or very expensive was stressed. All the symposium papers were preprinted and the entire ten-day session was used for discussions. All phases of applied solar energy except agriculture were considered, and the dozen sessions on different aspects of solar energy were summarized by rapporteurs and also were preprinted and distributed. All these papers are being published by the United Nations.

Also in 1961 a two-week summer seminar on solar and aeolian energy was held at Sounion in Greece. It was sponsored by NATO and the Greek Atomic Energy Commission and arranged by the Hellenic Society for Solar and Aeolian Energy. There was a close exchange of ideas between the solar scientists, who were eager to make their researches useful, and those scientists who were looking for ways of using the sun to improve their countries' social and economic conditions. The informal sessions were concerned with all applications of solar energy, prominent among which were the generation of electricity, the large-scale use of solar water heaters, and the production of power from methane obtained from the formation of algae (Chapter 1, Ref. 12).

At the United Nations Conference in Rome in 1961 the social and economic aspects of solar power were discussed as they might be imagined to affect the development of the nations seeking rapid industrialization. It is interesting to contemplate other imaginative conferences. We may note that no similar conference was held at the turn of the century when automobiles were being developed. Perhaps less thought was given then to the social sciences and long-range planning. If such a conference had been held no one would have been able to foresee the enormous influence that gasoline-engined vehicles were to exert within half a century. They have of course completely revolutionized movement of people and freight, developed suburbia, and transformed rural life. Our hypothetical symposium of 1900 might have concluded that automobiles would never be important on farms because of the "free" food for horses, or in crowded cities because of the lack of parking areas. It is always difficult to foresee the changes that will be brought about by new developments in science and engineering, including possible progress in solar energy use.

Another hypothetical situation has been suggested by Dr. V. A. Baum of the U.S.S.R. Suppose that, during a continuous ice age which covered the coal deposits, a civilization near the equator had developed engines and heating and cooling devices operated by the sun. When the ice retreated and coal was discovered and suggested as a means of doing the world's work, would there have been objections? "This would not be nature's way. The burning of coal would pollute the atmosphere, and truly the coal would be much more valuable as a source of chemical products."

Or we might imagine a conference in the distant future when the shortages of coal, oil, and gas are felt. Our descendants might well blame us for our wasteful extravagances in the use of these most important natural resources. They might say, "You consumed gasoline in 200-hp engines simply to carry one person to his office and back. You talked about the folly of burning for fuel cow dung which should be used for fertilizer, yet you burned the limited supply of organic fossil fuel that should have been used as raw material for making petrochemicals. You used it not only for concentrated energy in engines at high temperatures but even for low-temperature operations such as cooking, heating and cooling of houses, and distillation of water that could often be as well done by the sun, thereby saving more of the coal, oil, and gas for us."

SOLAR ENERGY SOCIETY

In 1954 the Association for Applied Solar Energy, now named the Solar Energy Society, was organized in Phoenix, Arizona, with a board of directors from Arizona and elsewhere and an advisory council of solar scientists from around the world. This society now has over 800 members. It encourages the development of solar energy uses by publishing a journal and a news magazine, and in 1955 it organized a notable world symposium attended by a thousand people. The society maintains a complete library and information center available to visitors and those who write for information.

Such facilities and particularly *Solar Energy* (previously the *Journal of Solar Science and Engineering*) are valuable in drawing together the workers in the many different disciplines that contribute to advances in solar energy. Physicists, chemists, meteorologists, biologists, chemical engineers, mechanical engineers, and other specialists are familiar with the literature in their own fields but unacquainted with important contributions to solar energy applications in other fields. They all profit by being able to turn to one central source that covers all the related sciences and branches of engineering with respect to the application of solar energy.

REFERENCES

1. Jordan, R. C., and Ibele, W. E., in *Proceedings of World Symposium on Applied Solar Energy*, Phoenix, Ariz. 1955. Menlo Park, Calif., Stanford Research Institute, 1956, pp. 81–89.

2. Robinson, N., in ibid., pp. 43–61.

3. Robinson, N., *A Report on the Design of Solar Energy Machines*, NS/AZ/141, 1953, Paris, UNESCO.

4. Robinson, N., *A Brief History of Utilization of the Sun's Radiation*, 1953, Jerusalem, Actes de Septième Congrès, International d'Histoire des Sciences.

5. Daniels, F., Solar energy, *Science, 109:* 51–57. 1949.

6. Daniels, F., Atomic and solar energy, *American Scientist, 38:* 521–48. 1950.

7. Sun in the service of man, *American Academy of Arts and Sciences, 79:* 181–326. 1951.

8. MacNevin, W. C., The trapping of solar energy, *Ohio Journal of Science, 53:* (5): 257–319. 1953.

9. Fisher, J. H., *An Analysis of Solar Energy Utilization,* WADC Technical Report 59–17, Vols. 1 and 2, Wright Air Development Center, ASTIA Document no. AD 214611, 1959.

CHAPTER 3

Solar Radiation

Solar radiation is customarily measured in langleys per minute. One langley is equivalent to 1 calorie of radiation energy per square centimeter. Most meteorological stations of the world report the solar radiation in terms of total langleys received on a horizontal surface at ground level. The intensity varies with geographical location, time of day, season, clouds, and dust, from zero to about 1.5 cal cm^{-2} min^{-1}. One langley of solar radiation per minute (1 cal cm^{-2} min^{-1}) is equivalent in the British thermal units to 221 BTU ft^{-2} hr^{-1}.

Assuming solar radiation of 1 langley min^{-1}, a square meter receives 10,000 cal min^{-1} or 10 kcal min^{-1}. A house roof of 100 m^2—equivalent to a square nearly 33 ft on a side, containing 1,076 ft^2—receives a million cal min^{-1}. With an average of 1 langley min^{-1} for 500 min per day (which is slightly more than 8 hr, or a third of the 24-hr day) the 100 m^2 roof receives, in bright sunshine, 5×10^8 cal or 500,000 kcal day^{-1}. This is equivalent in heat to burning a man's weight in coal or a 14-gal tank of gasoline. If converted to electrical energy with an efficiency of 10 per cent it is equivalent, on the average, to 7 kw and to 56 kwhr while the sun is shining.

In order to receive *heat* at the rate of 1 kw from the sun's radiation it is necessary to obtain 14.3 kcal min^{-1}. At 1 langley this requires a receiving surface of 1.43 m^2 or 15.4 ft^2. If the solar radiation is used to produce electricity with 10 per cent conversion, 14.3 m^2 or 154 ft^2 of solar radiation will be needed. Considering larger units, theoretically, 1 acre of sunlight could give 280 kw of electrical power while the sun is shining, if the conversion of solar energy to electrical energy is 10 per cent efficient; and a square mile could give 180,000 kw of electrical power. It must be emphasized that these calculations are on a basis of 8 hr of sunshine. If the power is to be used continuously day and night a heavy additional investment for energy storage is needed, and the average kwhr for a 24-hr day must be divided by 3 or more.

The solar energy received in several different areas of the world, and expressed in different units, is summarized in Table 1.

Radiation of 1 langley min^{-1} is a reasonable average value to take for a tilted surface under a cloudless sky. If the radiation is only half a langley min^{-1} all the values of the table should be divided by 2. For a reasonable maximum radiation of 1.4 langley received on a clear cloudless day with a tracking solar collector maintained at right angles to the sun's rays, all the values of the table should be multiplied by 1.4.

VARIATIONS IN SOLAR RADIATION

Solar radiation at the earth's surface. The solar constant is 2.0 cal cm^{-2} min^{-1} as received in the outer space around the earth above the atmosphere. The solar radiation on the upper atmosphere is 2.4×10^{15} kcal min^{-1} or 1.7×10^{14} kw. This varies only within a range of 3.3 per cent as the elliptical orbit of the earth brings it closer to the sun and then farther away. Of this solar radiation a considerable portion is reflected back into outer space from the atmosphere and the tops of clouds, some is absorbed or scattered by molecules, but more is scattered by water droplets in clouds and by dust particles. As a result of these phenomena the 2 cal cm^{-2} min^{-1} of solar radiation falling on the outer atmosphere is materially reduced, so that by the time it reaches the surface of the earth it is between 1.5 and 0 cal cm^{-2} min^{-1}. Part of this radiation may come directly from the sun, but sometimes as much as 10 per cent of it comes as scattered light even when the sun is unobstructed by clouds. In cloudy weather the total radiation is greatly reduced and most of the light that gets through may be scattered light.

Solar energy received on flat-plate collectors includes both direct and scattered radiation, but the scattered radiation does not contribute to the solar energy caught by a focusing collector.

16   Direct Use of the Sun's Energy

TABLE 1. Quantities of Solar Energy Received by Different Areas when the Average Intensity of Radiation is 1 cal cm⁻² min⁻¹

area	langleys	kcal min⁻¹	kcal day⁻¹*	BTU hr⁻¹	kw (heat)	hp (heat)
1 cm²	1.0	0.001	0.500	0.238	7.00×10^{-5}	9.39×10^{-5}
1 ft²	929	0.929	464	221	0.065	0.087
1 m²	10^4	10	5.0×10^3	2380	0.700	0.938
100 m² (roof)	10^6	10^3	5.0×10^5	2.38×10^5	70.0	93.8
1 acre	4.05×10^7	4.05×10^4	2.02×10^7	9.64×10^6	2.83×10^3	3.79×10^3
1 km²	10^{10}	10^7	5×10^9	2.38×10^9	7.00×10^5	9.38×10^5
1 mile²	2.59×10^{10}	2.59×10^7	1.3×10^{10}	6.15×10^9	1.81×10^6	2.42×10^6

Conversion factors: 1 kcal = 1,000 cal; 1 BTU = 0.252 kcal; 1 kw = 14. 3 kcal min⁻¹; 1 hp = 0.742 kw; 1 ft² = 929 cm²; 1 acre = 43,560 ft². A complete list of conversion factors is given in the Appendix.

*Assuming 500 min day⁻¹ of solar radiation.

In the solar radiation striking the outer atmosphere the distribution of energy among the different wavelengths is essentially that of a perfect radiator, or "blackbody," heated to 6,000° C, as shown by the dashed line in Figure 5. A typical distribution at the earth's surface is indicated by solid line. The X-rays and ultraviolet light less than 2,000 Å in wavelength are absorbed by oxygen and nitrogen, and most of the radiation from 2,000 to 3,000 Å is absorbed by ozone in the outer atmosphere. There are prominent absorption bands in the red and infrared from the passage of the light through carbon dioxide which is quite constant in quantity at 0.03 per cent in the atmosphere, and through ozone and water molecules which vary greatly in concentration. The absorption by water occurs with both water vapor and condensed droplets of water. The droplets not only absorb the longer rays but also scatter some of the solar radiation of short wavelengths.

A thorough study of diffuse solar radiation and means of estimating diffuse radiation from total radiation has been reported by Liu and Jordan,[1] together with radiation data for several stations in the United States.

A report was made by a Committee on Applied Solar Energy of the Radiation Commission of the International Association of Meteorology and Atmospheric Physics[2] in

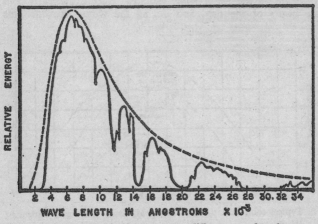

5. Relative intensity of solar energy at different wavelengths.

an effort to ascertain means of reporting solar radiation data that would be useful to solar scientists.

Further information on solar energy distribution and measurement is available.[3-9]

Position of the sun. When the sky is clear the solar radiation striking a horizontal surface is greatest at the equator at noon. Here the sun's rays pass straight through the atmosphere and on to the receiver with a minimum length of passage through the air. At all latitudes the sun moves from east to west and sweeps through an arc of 15° every hour. In the early morning and late afternoon the rays pass obliquely through a longer path in the atmosphere, which results in more absorption and scattering. The radiation intensity depends on the hour of the day, the day of the year, the latitude of the earth at the point of observation, and the clarity of the atmosphere.

In the northern hemisphere the sun is highest in the sky on June 21 and lowest on December 21. The midpoints are at the equinoxes, March 21 and September 21. In the southern hemisphere the sun is highest on December 21 and lowest on June 21, with midpoints again on March 21 and September 21.

Figure 6 gives a solar record on a horizontal surface on clear rays close to December 21, March 21 (or September 21), and June 21 taken at Madison, Wisconsin, latitude 43° N. It shows the lesser solar radiation during the early and late hours of the day, and during the winter season. This

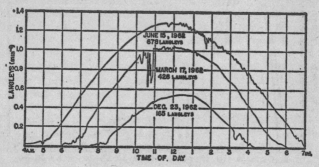

6. Typical solar radiation records at Madison, Wisconsin. Latitude 43° N.

lower radiation is due to the more slanting angle with which the solar radiation strikes the horizontal surface, to the longer passage of light through the atmosphere, and to the fewer hours of sunlight in the winter time. The decrease in radiation caused by passing clouds which frequently cover the sun is shown in a typical record in Figure 7.

The transmission of solar radiation is discussed by Fritz[10] and the importance of sky radiations by Drummond.[11] Moon gives useful standard radiation curves,[12] and Hand gives full radiation data at a selected place and time.[13]

Inclination of the receiver. As already stated, the official records of solar radiation usually refer to heat energy re-

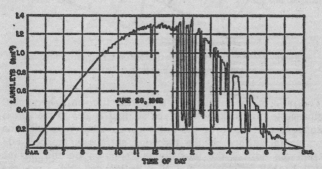

7. Effect of passing clouds on solar radiation.

ceived on a square centimeter of a horizontal surface. It is much less in the early morning and in late afternoon than at noon time, and the radiation north and south of the equator is less than at the equator.

The loss of intensity caused by the radiation striking the horizontal receiver at an oblique angle can be greatly reduced by tilting the receiver. The maximum radiant energy cm^{-2} is obtained if the receiver is rotated continuously and tilted in order to be always at right angles to the sun's rays, as shown in Figure 8. The planes of the dotted lines, at right angles to the sun's rays, always intercept the same amount of radiation. The area of a horizontal plane, given by the full lines, has to be larger in order to receive the full amount of radiation. The radiant energy cm^{-2} on a horizontal plane is less because the cross section of 1 cm^2 of solar radiation intercepts a smaller area than when it hits a plane obliquely.

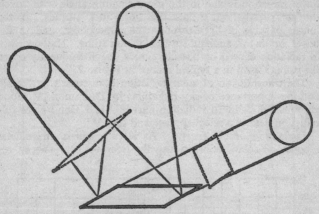

8. Energy received per square centimeter on a horizontal surface and a surface at right angles to the sun's radiation.

The ratio of the intensity of solar radiation on a horizontal surface to that striking a surface at right angles to the sun is equal to the cosine of the angle of the sun's rays with the horizontal surface. If the receiving surface is inclined 60° from the normal the intensity of radiation on the surface will be half as much, and if it is inclined 45° from the normal the calories received per minute will be 70.7 per cent as much, because the cosine of 60° is 0.500 and the cosine of 45° is 0.707.

Tilting the solar receiving surfaces from the horizontal position to be more nearly at right angles to the sun's rays is a considerable improvement. In areas of very large latitude where the sun is close to the horizon in winter a stationary vertical collector can receive much more solar radiation than a horizontal collector.

The increase in radiation received on a normal surface over that received on a horizontal surface is shown in Figure 9, where the two records are given for a clear day late in October in Madison, Wisconsin, at latitude 43° N. At this latitude and time of year the radiation received cm^{-2} on a normal surface is more than twice as much as that on a horizontal surface.

A convenient circular sun-angle nomograph[14] is available

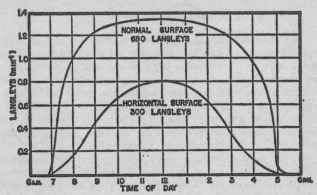

9. Radiation received on a normal surface and a horizontal surface in late October at Madison, Wisconsin. Latitude 43° N.

for the rapid calculation of solar radiation intensity and the effect of the sun's position in the sky.

In some applications of solar energy it is necessary to take account of the radiation that comes up from the earth. This is of two types: first, solar radiation reflected from the ground or particularly from snow or water, and second, long-wavelength infrared radiation emitted by the warm earth at ground temperature to the colder sky. The reflected sunlight is known as the *albedo* and is an important factor in solar heating in certain locations. Important new data are now being collected from the earth satellites concerning the total energy reflected and radiated from the earth into outer space.

The infrared radiation emitted to the colder sky, depending on the location and meteorological conditions, can amount to the order of 0.1 cal cm^{-2} min^{-1} (20 BTU ft^{-2} hr^{-1}). It is greatest in clear weather and becomes small when the surface of the earth is blanketed with clouds, which have temperatures not much below that of the earth's surface. In the Chilean desert and elsewhere, in spite of hot sunny days, it is possible to freeze water by loss of energy through radiation to the night sky. It is a matter of common observation that when the temperature is near freezing the formation of frost is greatly facilitated by the absence of clouds.

Measuring Instruments

The solar radiation at any time, or over a period of time, can be estimated roughly from the solar constant 2.00 cal cm^{-2} min^{-1} at the outer edge of the earth's atmosphere, provided that suitable corrections are made for the angle of the sun's rays with the earth and for absorption and scattering by the atmosphere, taking into account the length of the path which the rays take through the air masses. Several formulas have been proposed for making these estimates; prominent among them that of Ångstrom.[15]

Direct measurement is more reliable, and the meteorologists have been active for many decades perfecting instruments and recording solar radiation. They have established international organizations and set up cooperative programs such as the International Geophysical Year and the World Meteorological Organization. The accuracy of measurement required has been a matter of considerable debate. It is possible to obtain some solar radiation measurements, using great care, with an error of less than 1 per cent, but it is difficult to obtain them with less than 3 per cent error. Commercial instruments are readily available which give daily totals with less than 5 per cent error and instantaneous readings with less than 10 per cent error. There are 700 stations in the world that record continuously the total solar radiation, including both direct and scattered, on a horizontal surface; many of these are in Europe. About 100 stations in the world record radiation received on a surface kept at right angles to the sun. Blanco estimates[16] there are perhaps 2,000 stations in the world that record the number of hours of sunshine.

Meteorologists have been eager to cooperate with solar scientists and to find out what kind of records they need. Unfortunately, in the arid and semiarid regions of the world there have been few good solar radiation records; and these are just the regions with the most sunshine, the least fuel, and the greatest need for developing solar devices. For accuracy, many meteorologists believe that records over a 10-year period or an 11-year solar cycle are necessary, but in some areas it will not be practical to wait this long and limited direct experimental measurements and less accurate calculations will have to suffice. In clear-weather areas, short-term averages are adequate.

The instruments for measuring and recording the sun are of several types ranging in cost from $25 to $1,000. They may be classified in several different ways. Some give instantaneous readings and others give integrated readings over periods of an hour or a day. Some measure the total radiation and others only the direct radiation. Measurements are made on a horizontal, vertical, normal, or inclined surface. The principles used in the operation of different types of instruments include thermoelectric measurement of the rise in temperature on a black solar receiver, balancing the heat with a measured electrical Peltier cooling, direct calorimetric measurement; evaporation of a measured volume of liquid, photovoltaic measurements, photographic measurements, and photochemical actinometers. There is still opportunity for the development of new and more convenient instruments.

An important instrument is the Eppley pyroheliometer (Epply Laboratories, Newport, R.I.), which is widely used, principally in the United States. It has a thermocouple of copper–constantan junctions on the back of a horizontal blackened metallic receiver 3 cm in diameter, heated by the sun. The cold end is connected to a white or silver outer ring which reflects the solar radiation and remains at the ambient temperature, and the receiver and ring are covered tightly with a hemisphere of glass. The thermocouple is connected to a recording potentiometer. Langley and Abbott of the Smithsonian Institution developed early pyroheliometers, the construction and performance of which are described by Hand.[17] In early work Abbott calibrated this type of solar recorder with a flowing-water calorimeter. In still earlier work Langley used the bolometer, in which the resistance of one arm of a Wheatstone bridge is increased by the solar heat.

The Eppley normal-incidence pyroheliometer is arranged to give the radiation as measured at right angles to the sun's rays under conditions which exclude scattered radiation. The thermopile receiver is mounted in a blackened tube with shields; the ratio of its width to its length is 1 to 10, thus subtending an arc of 5° 43′. It is adjusted until a small hole in the front ring gives an image of the sun on a spot marked on the rear ring.

Another excellent instrument of the thermopile type is the Moll-Goczynski solarimeter (Kipp and Zonen, Delft, Holland).

In order to measure only the scattered radiation the receivers of these instruments may be shielded from the direct solar radiation by a disc which moves to keep the receiver always in the shadow or with a ring so positioned to the sun that throughout the day the direct rays never fall on the black receiver. The difference between this reading and the reading of the unobstructed receiver gives a measure of the direct solar radiation.

The Robitzsch bimetallic recorder works by unequal thermal expansion on two sides of an arm which moves a recording pen. It does not require electrical connections. The Bellani distillation instrument (Meteorological Laboratory, Davos, Switzerland) is used in some weather-recording stations for measuring the solar radiation over a period of hours or a day. In it pure alcohol in an enclosed glass vessel is vaporized by the solar radiation and condensed as a liquid, the volume of which is easily measured in a graduated tube. The Campbell-Stokes spherical lens is widely used for automatically recording the hours of sunshine on a strip of paper. The sphere acts as a lens throughout the day regardless of the position of the sun and burns the paper when the sun is shining.

A simple calorimetric instrument for measuring the total daily solar radiation has been developed by Heywood.[18] The horizontal blackened metal receiver of 20 cm^2 is soldered to a thick-walled copper tube filled with 420 cc of water and set into an evacuated thermos bottle. The receiver is covered with a hemisphere of glass. A rise in temperature of 1° in the water is produced by radiation amounting to 23 cal cm^{-2}. A cresol thermometer gives a maximum and minimum reading each day. A simple, inexpensive radiometer has been developed also by Suomi,[19-21] in which the solar radiation is absorbed by a blackened surface in a highly insulated box of plastic foam with transparent plastic windows. The temperature of the black surface rises quickly and is measured with a thermometer.

Photovoltaic cells such as photographic exposure meters are convenient and give precise readings, but they respond only to the visible sunlight and not to the infrared radiation which comprises over half the total. For many purposes they are satisfactory when properly calibrated. Silicon solar cells (Hoffman Electronics Co., Evanston, Ill.) connected to a galvanometer or milliameter are effective and inexpensive. A description of this type of solar meter is given by Schoffer[22] and by Selcuk and Yellott.[23] The silicon solar cell responds up to 1.1 μ, with maximum intensity recorded at 0.9 μ. The solar radiation extends to 1.9 μ with maximum intensity at 0.5 to 0.7 μ. With suitable calibration it gives results in close agreement with the Eppley radiometer.

For many purposes the knowledge of the total solar radiation for the day is sufficient. The Bellani and Heywood instruments give this integrated value. To obtain an integrated value for the day with an Eppley or other continuously recording radiometer it is necessary to carry out tedious planimeter readings on the charts, and the results are not accurate when complicated with clouds. Accordingly, integration devices have been developed for finding the total radiation over a period of time with the help of electrical circuits like those described by Schoffer.[22,24] The silicon cells do not require an amplifying circuit, and the movement of the printed paper and integrating mechanism is accomplished with electric batteries. Moreover the silicon cells are not much affected by temperature.

A device for direct observation of the shadowing effect of local building and trees at different times of day has been useful for architectural planning.[25] These shadowing obstructions are observed in a concave parabolic mirror which is semitransparent, and their images can be viewed against underlying charts.

Photochemical actinometers have not been used for measuring solar radiation, but they might well be considered for long exposures of hours and several days, particularly when it is desirable to know the amount of radiation in the short-wavelength region of the visible or ultraviolet. The uranyl-oxalate actinometer[26] is a standard for this purpose; for each molecule of oxalic acid decomposed, 1.75 photons of light below 4,400 Å are absorbed. The amount of oxalic acid decomposed is measured by titration with a standard solution of potassium permanganate. Other photochemical reactions responsive to other regions of the spectrum might be considered also.

The problem of determining the distribution of energy among different wavelengths in absolute units under different atmospheric conditions has not yet been satisfactorily solved.

For measuring intense solar radiation from focusing collectors a calorimetric method is useful.[27] The calorimeter (see Fig. 10) consists of a circular copper can of about 550-cc capacity with an opening for a 0.1° thermometer

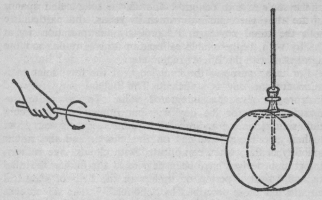

10. Calorimeter for focused radiation.

and with a long insulated handle. It is insulated except on the blackened front face and circular shields are attached to measure the radiation incident on circles of different diameters. Five hundred cc of cold water is added from a half-liter volumetric flask, the thermometer and stopper are inserted, and the calorimeter handle is rotated vigorously to stir the water and assure a uniform temperature. After the thermometer is read, the calorimeter is carefully held stationary at the focus of the collector with the help of a support, for exactly 60 sec or other recorded time interval that will give a rise of 8 or 10° C. The calorimeter is withdrawn and quickly rotated to assure uniform temperature and the thermometer is read. The radiation received by the calorimeter is calculated by multiplying the temperature rise by the heat capacity of the water and the copper. The measurements are made easily and quickly, and one filling with water suffices for two or more measurements before the rate of cooling becomes appreciable. More accurate measurements of focused radiation are made with a flowing-water calorimeter in which the inlet and outlet temperature and the rate of constant flow of water are measured.

GEOGRAPHICAL DISTRIBUTION
OF RADIATION

As indicated in the preceding section, the solar radiation varies greatly with the length of the day, with the angle of the sun's rays to the ground, with the length and quality of the atmosphere through which it passes, and particularly with the cloud coverage. Accordingly the radiation varies greatly with the geographical location, the altitude, and the weather. Figure 11, adapted from the U.S. Weather Bureau,[28] shows lines for the average number of sunshine hours on a horizontal surface throughout the world.

A wealth of information on weather in the United States including some data on solar radiation has been collected and summarized by Visher.[29] Figure 12, adapted from Visher, gives the normal annual number of hours of sunlight visibility in the continental United States. The range is from 2,200 hr in the northeast to 4,000 in the southwest. Figures 13 and 14, also adapted from Visher, give respectively the number of langleys day[-1] in the United States east of the Rocky Mountains for June 21 and December 21. Other data are available, such as the per cent of possible sunlight recorded in different areas, the number of daily hours of sunshine in winter and summer, and the number of clear days.

Table 2 summarizes solar radiation in a few selected regions of the United States.

It must be emphasized that the data given in these maps and tables, and almost all data reported in langleys by weather stations throughout the world, apply to the radiation received on a horizontal plane. This is much less than can be obtained with a tilted surface, particularly in winter, as already explained.

Caryl[30] found that in Arizona the solar radiation between 9 A.M and 3 P.M. on a surface facing south and inclined 45° from the horizontal varied only from 13,000 langleys in the month of January to 19,000 langleys in March and September.

TABLE 2. Solar Radiation in Langleys (1 cal cm[-2]) Per Day on a Horizontal Surface

	December	March*	June
New York and Chicago	125	325	550
Southern California and Arizona	250	400	700
Florida	250	400	500
Nevada	175	400	650

* September radiation is close to that of March.

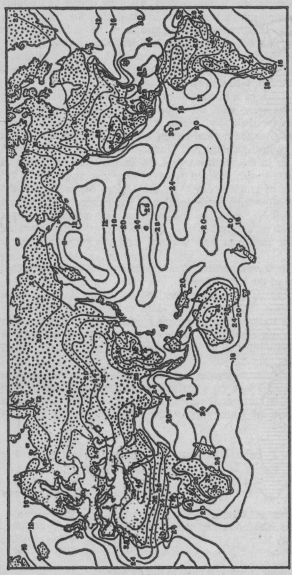

11. Worldwide distribution of solar energy in hundreds of hours per year. [Adapted with permission from *Solar Energy*, cover, *1*, no. 1 (1957).]

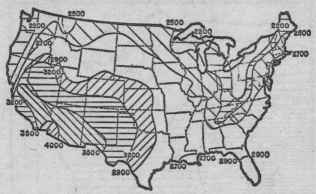

12. Annual number of sunshine hours in continental United States. [Adapted with permision of the Harvard University Press from Visher's *Climatic Atlas of the United States* (1954), p. 177.]

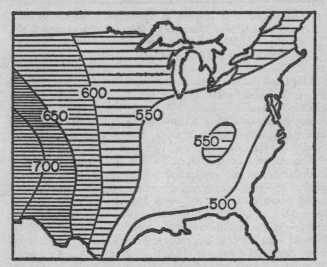

13. Solar radiation, in langleys, in the United States east of the Rocky Mountains on June 21. [Adapted with permission of the Harvard University Press from Visher's *Climatic Atlas of the United States* (1954), p. 183.]

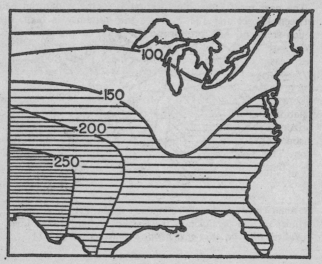

14. Solar radiation, in langleys, in the United States east of the Rocky Mountains on December 21. [Adapted with permission of the Harvard University Press from Visher's *Climatic Atlas of the United States* (1954), p. 183.]

Maps and detailed solar energy radiation data are available for some other parts of the world such as Australia,[31] Canada,[32] Arabia,[33] India,[34,35] Japan,[36] and South Africa.[37] A comprehensive atlas is now being published which will summarize, with the help of maps, most of what is now known concerning the solar radiation in all parts of the world.[38]

The regions of the world where solar energy is most available for direct application are discussed by Ward.[39] In general the greatest amount of solar energy is found in two broad bands encircling the earth between 15° and 35° latitude north and south. In the best regions there is a minimum monthly mean radiation of 500 langleys day⁻¹ and a monthly overall variation of less than 250 langleys day⁻¹. These regions are on the equatorial side of the world's arid deserts. They have less than ten inches of rain in a year. In some of the countries more than two thirds of their area is arid land, and there is usually over 3,000 hr of sunshine a year, over 90 per cent of which comes as direct radiation. These areas are well suited for applied solar energy.

The next most favorable location is in the equatorial belt between 15° N and 15° S. Here the humidity is high, the clouds frequent, and proportion of scattered radiation high. There are about 2,300 hr of sunshine per year and very little seasonal variation. The radiation is from 300 to 500 langleys day^{-1} throughout the year, and there are few successive days of low radiation.

Between 35° and 45° at the edge of the desert areas the radiation can average 400 to 500 langleys day^{-1} on a horizontal surface throughout the year, but there is a marked seasonal effect and the winter months have low solar radiation. This seasonal variation can be greatly minimized by tilting the receiving surfaces to face the sun.

The regions north of 45° N and south of 45° S are limited in their year-round direct use of solar energy. One might think of the Arctic and Antarctic regions as hopeless for solar energy utilization but in the summer season they may be quite important. Some of the Antarctic records show long days that receive 700 langleys of solar radiation. which is extraordinarily high. Of course in the winter time there is no opportunity to use solar devices. Where heat and power come only from gasoline brought in over thousands of miles by air transport at a cost of $5 per gallon, solar radiation might be particularly important if lightweight solar heaters could be developed.

One of the best locations in the world for solar applications is the desert of north Chile. which extends 100 miles in width from the Pacific Ocean to the Andes Mountains and for 280 miles along the coast from latitude 20° S to latitude 25° S. It has 1 mm of rainfall a year, 364 days of bright sunshine. and no dust. A thin layer of salts consolidates the surface soil. which if undisturbed prevents the dry earth from being blown about. There is no water and no life. The land is valueless now except for a few rich nitrate deposits and copper mines. In the future, when our resources of fossil fuels diminish, this area and other similar deserts could supply tremendous amounts of energy. Theoretically this waste area in north Chile alone receives annual solar heat greater than all the heat produced in the world in a year by the burning of coal, oil, gas, and wood. which in 1957 amounted to 5×10^{13} hp hr or 3.2×10^{16} kcal^{-1}. The 28,000 square miles of this desert receive about 1.3×10^{17} kcal of solar heat in a year (28,000 mile$^2 \times 1.3 \times 10^{10}$ kcal day^{-1} mile^{-2} (see Table 1) $\times$ 365 days year^{-1} = 1.3 $\times$

10^{17} kcal year^{-1}). It is clear that *theoretically* this desert could supply all the energy needs of the world. There are other sunny wastelands such as the Sahara desert in Africa, parts of the middle east, parts of the southwestern United States, parts of Australia, and calm areas of the oceans that could be used for collecting and storing solar energy. Also there are many less favorable wastelands, some of which are closer to populations where the energy is needed. The solar radiation could be used to produce hydrogen by the electrolysis of water and the hydrogen could be stored and transported through pipe lines or combined with carbon dioxide to give methanol or other transportable fuels. These and other possibilities for storing and transporting energy from the sun will be discussed in the last chapter of this book. Though not economical now, they deserve research study for possible use in the future.

In estimating the solar radiation from limited data it is necessary to consider not only several changes in weather but also differences in local conditions. For example, a station on a mountain may receive much more sunlight than a neighboring station at a lower level because it is above some of the clouds. A location near the sea will have less solar radiation than one inland if fogs are prevalent on the coast. Gräfe reports[40] variations of as much as 18 per cent in four different stations within 20 km of Hamburg, Germany, even on clear days. One station ran consistently 5 per cent higher, probably because of less air pollution than in the city. In some locations, micrometeorology is important in assessing the possibilities for using solar energy.

An excellent description is available of the radiation from the sun and sky and the reflection and emission of long infrared radiation by the earth and objects on the earth in "The Energy Environment in Which We Live," by D. M. Gates.[41]

The influence of solar radiation on man, including the factors involved in sunburn, is fully covered in "Man and Radiant Energy," by Farrington Daniels, Jr.[42]

KINDS OF SOLAR RADIATION RECORDS

In considering the practicality of using solar energy in a given location, an error of as much as 5 per cent in the solar measuring instruments can often be tolerated because the engineering performance of the solar machines cannot be predicted with precision. It is important to know (1) how reliable the records are over a period of years, (2) how many years of recording are necessary for a given accuracy of prediction, (3) the variation with the hour and the season, and (4) the sequence of low solar intensity. For example, in certain areas in New England the worst expectation might be for a succession of ten cloudy days, which would necessitate a large storage capacity if a house were to be heated entirely with the sun. If a solar refrigerator required 2 hr day^{-1} of radiation it could still operate in cloudy, rainy climates if, as is often the case in the tropics, one could be sure of having at least 2 hr of sunshine every day.

Black discusses[43] sunny-day sequences in some places where the use of solar energy might be considered, basing his calculations on 32 weather stations in the southern United States. He finds that two or more successive days with radiation of less than 100 cal cm^{-2} day^{-1} are rare but four or five periods of two or more days with less than 250 cal cm^{-2} day^{-1} may be expected each year in many climates.

If focusing devices are to be used, the distribution of solar energy between direct and diffuse radiation is significant. Such information is important to architects designing houses. Drummond[44] states that on a bright, cloudy day a north window in the northern hemisphere may receive ten times as much radiation as on a cloudless day. In much of Europe about half the total radiation is diffuse, with a higher proportion in winter and less in summer. At a station in Massachusetts 40 per cent of the total annual solar radiation is diffuse, and in South Africa in relatively sunny climates the diffuse radiation is 30 per cent of the total.

As already pointed out, solar scientists and engineers would like to know the radiation received on a tilted surface as well as on a horizontal surface. Probably the radiation received on a surface kept at right angles to the sun's rays is the most useful because it gives a record of the maximum solar energy obtainable. Only a few stations now record radiation in this way. The record of radiation on a vertical surface facing the equator is also useful, particularly in locations of large latitudes. Gräfe reports[40] at Hamburg, Germany, that such a receiver recorded for the year 90 per cent as much as a horizontal receiver. The daily radiation ratio of vertical to horizontal varied from 0.33 in summer to 2.87 in winter.

Only a few records are available of the solar radiation on a surface tilted toward the equator at an angle equal to the latitude. This usually gives the maximum radiation for a stationary collector, but when solar heating is required early in the morning this arrangement is not so satisfactory. Martin[45] has recorded the solar radiation in the morning striking a collector facing southeast and in the afternoon a second collector facing southwest. The two collectors result in appreciably better solar heating, but the cost is doubled.

Looking to a possible future development, it might be important to calculate the optimum arrangement and spacing of an area filled with many collectors, both stationary and sun-tracking, of various sizes. If the collectors are too close together they will shadow each other during part of the day; if land is cheap they can be spread out to avoid shadowing.

Great progress has been made recently in recording the solar radiation above the atmosphere and in outer space. With balloons, airplanes, rockets, and now with satellites it has been possible to determine accurately the intensity of solar radiation and the distribution among the different wavelengths. Much is now known about the absorption of part of the sun's rays as they pass through our atmosphere. Suggestions have been made for using balloons above the clouds to convert the sun's energy and bring the heat or electricity down to earth, but they do not now appear to be practical.

REFERENCES

1. Liu, B. Y., and Jordan, R. C., The interrelationship and characteristic distribution of direct, diffuse, and total solar radiation, *Solar Energy, 4* (3): 1–19. 1960; 7: 71–74. 1963.

2. Fritz, S., Some solar radiation data presentations for use in applied solar energy programs (by an international group of authors including S. Fritz, E. Barry, H. Hinzpeter, K. J. Kondratyev, M. P. Manolova, and T. H. MacDonald) *Solar Energy, 4* (1): 1–22. 1960.

3. The Available Energy, The Measurement of Radiation, in *Transactions of the Conference on the Use of Solar Energy: The Scientific Basis,* Vol. 1. Tucson, University of Arizona Press, 1958.

4. Ward, G. T., *Possibilities for the Utilization of Solar Energy in Underdeveloped Rural Areas,* Bulletin 16. Rome, Italy, Agricultural Engineering Branch, Food and Agricultural Organization of the United Nations, 1961.

5. United Nations Dept. of Economic and Social Affairs, *Solar Energy Availability and Instruments for Measurements: Radiation Data, Networks, and Instrumentation,* U.N. Conference on New

Sources of Energy, Rome, 1961. New York, United Nations, 1964. E/3577, rev. 1. Doc. ST/ECA/72.

6. Robinson, N., *Solar Radiation,* New York and Amsterdam, Elsevier, 1962.

7. Solar Energy, in *Encyclopedia of Science and Technology, 12,* New York, McGraw-Hill (1960), 467.

8. List, R. J., *Smithsonian Meteorological Tables,* Washington, D.C., Smithsonian Institution, 1951.

9. Brooks, F. A., Notes on spectral quality and measurement of solar radiation, in *Solar Energy Research,* ed. F. Daniels and J. A. Duffie. Madison, University of Wisconsin Press, 1955, pp. 19–29.

10. Fritz, S., Transmission of Solar Energy through the Earth's Clear and Cloudy Atmosphere, in *Trans. Conf. Use of Solar Energy: The Scientific Basis, 1:* 17–36. 1958.

11. Drummond, A. J., Sky Radiation, Its Importance in Solar Energy Problems, ibid., pp. 113–31.

12. Moon, P., Proposed standard solar radiation curves for engineering use, *J. Franklin Institute, 230:* 583–617, 1940.

13. Hand, I. F., Insolation on clear days at the time of solstices and equinoxes for latitude 42° N, *Heating and Ventilating, 47:* 92. 1950.

14. *Sun Angle Calculator,* Toledo, Ohio, Libby, Owens, Ford Glass Co., 1950.

15. Ward, G. T., *Possibilities for the Utilization of Solar Energy in Underdeveloped Rural Areas,* pp. 5–6.

16. Blanco, P., Solar Energy Availability and Instruments for Measurements, in *U.N. Conf. on New Sources of Energy,* E/35-GrS11, Rome, 1961.

17. Hand, I. F., in *Monthly Weather Review, 65:* 415–41. 1937. Also *U.S. Weather Report,* Nov. 1946.

18. Heywood, H., Simple Instruments for the Assessment of Daily Solar Radiation Intensity, in *U.N. Conf. on New Sources of Energy,* E 35-S9, Rome, 1961.

19. Suomi, V. E., and Kuhn, P. M., An economical net radiometer, *Tellus, 10* (1): 168. 1958. Also *Quarterly Journal, Royal Meterological Society, 84:* 134. 1958.

20. U.S. Weather Bureau, *University of Wisconsin Annual Report, 1957.* Specifications are available from the U.S. Weather Bureau Project, Department of Meteorology, University of Wisconsin, Madison, Wis.

21. Tanner, C. B., Businger, J. A., and Kuhn, P. M., The economical net radiometer, *J. Geophys. Research, 65:* 3657. 1960.

22. Schoffer, P., Kuhn, P., and Sapsford, C. M., Instrumentation for Solar Radiation Measurement, in *U.N. Conf. on New Sources of Energy,* E 35-S92, 1961.

23. Selcuk, K., and Yellott, J. I., Measurement of direct, diffuse, and total radiation with silicon photovoltaic cells, *Solar Energy, 6:* 155–63. 1962.

24. Schoffer, P., and Suomi, V. E., A direct current integrator for radiation measurements, *Solar Energy, 5* (1): 29. 1961.

25. Tonne, F., Optico-Graphic Computation of Insolation-Duration and Insolation-Energy, in *Trans. Conf. Use of Solar Energy: The Scientific Basis, 1:* 104–12. 1958.

26. Daniels, F., Williams, J. W., Bender, P., Alberty, R. A., and Cornwell, C. D., *Experimental Physical Chemistry*, New York, McGraw-Hill, 1962, p. 340.

27. Forthcoming publication.

28. *Solar Energy, 1* (1): cover. 1957.

29. Visher, S. S., *Climatic Atlas of the United States*, Cambridge, Harvard University Press, 1954.

30. Caryl, C. R., Ratio of Ultraviolet Total Radiation in Phoenix, in *Proceedings of World Symposium on Applied Solar Energy*, Phoenix, Ariz., 1955.

31. Sapsford, C. M., Solar Radiation Records in Australia and Their Presentation, in *U. N. Conf. on New Sources of Energy*, E 35-S32, Rome, 1961.

32. Truhlar, E. J., et al., Solar Radiation Measurements in Canada, ibid., E 35–S18.

33. Elnesr, M. K., and Kahlil, A. M., Solar Radiation Availability in the United Arab Republic, ibid., E 35–S62.

34. Ramdas, L. A., Solar Radiation and Its Measurement in India, ibid., E 35–S105.

35. Choudhury, N. K. D., Solar radiation at New Delhi, *Solar Energy, 7:* 44–52. 1963.

36. Sekihara, K., Solar Radiation in Japan, in *U. N. Conf. on New Sources of Energy*, E 35–S2, Rome, 1961.

37. Bleksley, A. E. H., The Intensity of Solar Radiation in Southern Africa, in *Trans. Conf. Use of Solar Energy: The Scientific Basis, 1:* 132–35. 1958.

38. Duffie, J. A., Smith, C., and Löf, G. O. G., *Analysis of World Wide Distribution of Solar Radiation*, Bulletin 21, Engineering Experiment Station, Madison, University of Wisconsin, 1964.

39. Ward, T. G., *Possibilities for the Utilization of Solar Energy in Underdeveloped Rural Areas*, World Food and Agriculture Organization, Rome, 1961, pp. 19–21.

40. Gräfe, K., Measurements of Total Radiation in Networks, in *U. N. Conf. on New Sources of Energy*, E 35–61, Rome, 1961.

41. Gates, D. M., The energy environment in which we live, *American Scientist, 5:* 327–48. 1963.

42. Daniels, F., Jr., Man and Radiant Energy: Solar Radiation, in *Handbook of Physiology*, Vol. 5, *Environment*, Washington, American Physiological Society, 1963, pp. 969–87.

43. Black, J. N., Some Aspects of the Climatology of Solar Radiation, in *U.N. Conf. on New Sources of Energy*, E 35–S13, Rome, 1961.

44. Drummond, A. J., Sky Radiation, Its Importance in Solar

Energy Problems, in *Trans. Conf. Use of Solar Energy: The Scientific Basis, 1:* 132–35. 1958.
  45. Martin, J., Private communication.

CHAPTER 4

Collectors of Solar Radiation

When an object is exposed to solar radiation its temperature rises until its heat losses become equal to its heat gains. The losses depend on the emission of radiation by the heated material, the movement of the surrounding colder air, and the thermal conductivity of the materials in contact with it. The gains depend on the intensity of solar radiation and the absorptivity of solar radiation by its surface. Solar radiation can be collected in two general ways to produce higher temperatures: by covering a receiving surface with a sunlight-transparent sheet of glass or plastic, and by focusing the solar radiation from a large area onto a receiver of small area.

Solar collectors are conveniently classified as flat-plate collectors, which do not focus, and as focusing collectors. The flat-plate collectors are usually stationary but are often moved every few days to follow the season; the focusing collectors are usually turned throughout the day to follow the sun. The flat-plate collectors are generally cheaper and they use heat from the diffuse solar radiation as well as from the direct radiation and can operate on bright cloudy days. The focusing collectors can use only the direct radiation but can produce much higher temperatures.

In both types of collectors the receiving surface should be as black as possible, to absorb over 95 per cent of the radiation and reflect only a negligible amount.

FLAT-PLATE COLLECTORS

The large flat-plate solar receivers are made of sheet metal, usually iron, copper, or aluminum, to give good heat conduction. The surfaces are blackened with dull paint which often contains carbon black, or they are covered with a black coating produced chemically, as described in Chapter 12 on radiation coatings. The plate absorbing the radiation rises in temperature and transfers the heat to a fluid, usually air or water, flowing on the back side of the collector. At the same time the heated collector wastes heat to the surroundings by convection to moving air currents, by conduction to the air and to colder parts of the structure which holds the receiver, and by infrared radiation. At temperatures of 100° to 300° C the maximum emission of radiation occurs around 8 to 10 μ in the infrared, so the loss of heat is greatly decreased and the operating temperature of the collector increased by placing one or more sheets of glass or plastic over the black receiving surface in an air-tight box. Sunlight with wavelengths of less than 2.5 μ passes through these transparent coverings but the long-wavelength infrared radiation emitted by the heated receiver does not pass back through the glass or plastic cover because it is absorbed. The air-cooled covering plates with their layers of stagnant air are poor conductors of heat and so they operate at a lower temperature than the black receiving surface. The heat losses are thus reduced.

When solar radiation continues to strike a dark receiving surface the temperature rises, and the heat losses increase until a steady state is reached in which the rate of heat losses and useful recovery is equal to the rate of the heat gain. Then for the steady state

$$HA\tau\alpha = q_\circ A = q_u A + (q_r + q_a + q_\circ)A$$

where

$H =$ rate of total solar energy received by unit area. It is expressed in cal cm^{-2} min^{-1}, in BTU ft^{-2} hr^{-1}, or in kilowatts. Usually meteorological records give H_h, the radiation on a horizontal surface, which must be multiplied by the ratio of the radiation on the tilted receiver to that on a horizontal surface. This ratio can be calculated from the cosine of the angle of incidence for the direct radiation, but not for the scattered diffuse radiation. H can be determined experimentally with a calibrated radiation meter, tilted at the same angle as the flat-plate collector.

$A =$ total area of the receiver.
$\tau =$ transmissivity of the covering plates of glass or films of plastic through which the sun's rays pass. It de-

pends on the angle of incidence if the angle is markedly oblique.

$\alpha =$ absorptivity of the receiving surface. It, too, depends
somewhat on the angle of incidence if the angle is
oblique.

$q_o =$ rate of absorption of radiant energy per unit of surface
area.

$q_o A =$ the rate at which radiant heat is absorbed on the total
area of the receiver.

$q_\mu A =$ rate of useful, collected heat energy transferred from
the receiver to the heating stream of air or water.

$q_r A =$ rate of heat loss from the collector by radiation.

$q_a A =$ rate of heat loss from the collector by convection and
conduction to the surrounding air.

$q_o A =$ rate of heat loss from the collector to colder parts of
the collecting system by conduction through the insulation and materials of construction.

The useful heat collected, $q_\mu A$, is the net heat available and

$$q_\mu A = q_o A - (q_r + q_a + q_o)A$$

The formulas for calculating the rate of heat losses by
radiation, convection, and conduction are in standard engineering books and tables; a slide rule is adequate for calculating most of these quantities. The loss of heat by convection
to the air increases markedly as the wind velocity increases
and as the temperature difference between receiver and air
increases. The loss of heat by radiation increases as the
fourth power of the temperature, therefore radiation losses
become serious at high temperatures.

The paper that first evaluated the various factors involved
in the performance of flat-plate collectors for solar radiation
is by Hottel and Woertz.[1] Complete discussion with working
formulas are given by Tabor,[2] by Hottel and Whillier,[3] and
by Threlkeld and Jordan.[4] New materials for solar collectors
are discussed by Duffie.[5]

Construction. The black absorbing sheet is placed in a
frame, usually of wood, and tilted at the proper angle. For
heating water, the water pipes are attached to the back by
means that insure good thermal contact. The absorbing sheet
may be set airtight into a long rectangular box in such a way
that there is an air duct at the back and the blackened sheet
constitutes the front surface. Or the black absorber may be

at the back of the receiver with a sheet of glass or plastic as the front cover. The box holding the collector is made of thin wood, plastic, or very thin metal to minimize heat losses by thermal conduction, and covered with insulation material such as glass wool or plastic foam to reduce heat losses to the surrounding air.

The glass or plastic transparent cover reduces the heat losses from convection and radiation. Two or more covers are more effective than one, but each transparent covering reduces the incoming solar radiation by absorption in the glass or plastic by 8 per cent because of reflection at the two glass–air interfaces. The formula for the fraction of radiation reflected at right angles by an air–glass interface is given by the formula

$$\frac{I_r}{I_i} = \left(\frac{n-1}{n+1}\right)^2$$

where I_r is the intensity of reflected light, I_i is the intensity of incident light, and n is the refractive index of the glass.

The refractive index of ordinary glass gives an I_r / I_i value of about 4 per cent at each of the two solid–air interfaces and the refractive index of most plastics is not much different, though Tedlar has a significantly lower refractive index. If, instead of air, water or other liquid with a refractive index near that of glass is placed in contact with the glass, the reflection at the glass–liquid interface is negligible.

When multiple transparent plates are used they are placed about 1 inch apart to minimize the circulation of air between plates and thus reduce the loss of heat by convection. There is an optimum number of plates at a given temperature for the most heat at the lowest cost. It involves the gain caused by decrease in heat losses, the loss caused by reflection and absorption by the "transparent" covering plates, and the cost of materials and construction. For some purposes a covering of four glass plates has been found to be optimum, but usually a single or double sheet of glass or plastic is used. Complete analyses of the factors involved in multiple glass covers are available.[3,6]

The reflectivity of the covering glass plates can be markedly reduced by a special treatment in which a thin transparent coating with a thickness of ¼ of a wavelength of sunlight is deposited on each side of the plate to produce interference.

In this way it is possible to decrease the heat losses by using more covering plates without at the same time increasing the losses caused by reflection; but the cost of the treated glass plates is greater.

The transmission of glass plates and of plastic films varies greatly. A high-quality clear glass that appears water clear when examined along an edge may absorb only 3 or 4 per cent of the solar radiation passing through it. However if the glass appears greenish when viewed on edge, owing usually to absorption of the light by iron compounds in the glass, the absorption may run up to 6 per cent. The amount of absorption depends on the thickness of the glass and for both high transmission of light and low cost the glass should be as thin as is consistent with mechanical strength. The absorption of light by glass is discussed by Hottel and Whillier[3] and by Peyches.[7]

The transmission of covering sheets of plastic film depends not only on the reflection at the surfaces in air and the absorption of light by colored materials in the plastic but also on scattering at the surface. If the plastic film is cast to give rough microimperfections, much of the light is deflected sideways, as it is in ground glass, and the transmission is seriously reduced. Edlin gives transmission curves for several different plastics which can be used in solar energy applications.[8]

Orientation. The collectors may be horizontal, vertical, or tilted, and the collection of solar heat varies as described in the preceding chapter. The orientation depends on the size and weight of the collector units, the cost, the latitude and season, and the architectural requirements. Horizontal collectors are the easiest to construct and mount and the most unobtrusive in appearance, but collectors tilted toward the equator collect a greater fraction of the solar heat. In the northern hemisphere they are faced south and tilted at an angle with the horizontal equal to the latitude. In winter it is recommended that the flat-plate collectors be tilted at the angle of latitude plus 15° and in summer at the angle of latitude minus 15°. The steeper angles give less trouble from snow, rain, and dust. The construction of tilted collectors is expensive for large and heavy units, particularly when they are large enough to constitute a wind hazard. The advantage to be gained by moving the flat-plate collectors continuously during the day to follow the sun is not large enough to justify the installation of a moving mechanism. At large latitudes, vertical collectors facing the equator are better in winter than horizontal collectors but not so good as collectors tilted at the appropriate angle.

Usually the flat-plate collectors are mounted in a fixed position, but if the units are not too large it is sometimes practical to move them a little every few days to get greater intensity as the seasons change. For example, instead of tilting the collector south at a permanent angle equal to the latitude, somewhat better results are obtained by facing the collector south and tilting it each week so that it is at right angles to the sun's rays at noon.

In good sunny weather, tilted flat-plate collectors with transparent covers can achieve temperatures of boiling water, but it is difficult to produce temperatures higher than this and not easy to obtain temperatures above 70° to 90° C.

FOCUSING COLLECTORS

With focusing collectors it is easy to obtain much higher temperatures, but they usually cost more, they need to be moved to track the sun, and they can only use the radiation that comes unscattered by clouds or haze directly from the sun. Solar radiation focused with circular parabolic mirrors can give temperatures up to 3,500° C or less depending on the optical perfection of the parabolic collector. A fairly crude parabolic collector made of aluminized plastic film lining a plastic shell can produce temperatures of 500° C and higher.

The formula for the rate of heat delivery with focused solar radiation is similar to that already given for flat-plate collectors, with additional terms. Thus at thermal equilibrium, for a collector without a cover, tracking the sun,

$$H_n A_o rs\,\alpha = q_o A_t = (q_u + q_r + q_a + q_o)\,A_t$$

where

H_n = rate of *direct* radiation per unit area intercepted by the focusing mirror which is normal to the sun's rays.

A_o = projected area of the focusing mirror.

r = effective specular reflectivity of the focusing-mirror material for direct radiation.

s = shape factor of the collector, giving the fraction of the effective specular radiation that hits the target in spite of major deviations from the parabolic, spherical, or cylindrical shape.

$sr =$ fraction of the direct radiation hitting the focusing mirror, which is focused on the target.

$\alpha =$ the absorptivity of the receiving target being heated, i.e. the fraction of the focused radiation hitting the target that is converted into heat.

$q_o =$ the rate at which radiant heat is absorbed per unit area by the receiving target.

$A_t =$ the area of the receiving target being heated. It is usually made large enough to intercept a large fraction of the focused radiation.

$q_oA_t =$ rate at which radiant heat is absorbed by the target.

$q_\mu A_t =$ rate at which heat absorbed by the target is converted into useful energy in the flowing fluid behind the receiver.

$q_rA_t =$ rate at which the target loses heat due to radiation.

$q_aA_t =$ rate at which the target loses heat to the surrounding air by convection and conduction.

$q_cA_t =$ rate at which the target loses heat through conduction to the structural parts of the collector.

Most solar radiation measurements are made on a horizontal surface, giving H_h, and include both direct and scattered radiation. To convert the values of H_h to H_n as defined in this formula, it is necessary to subtract the diffuse or scattered radiation from the total radiation and divide the difference by cos Θ, where Θ is the angle of the sun's rays with the horizontal plane. The simplest way of making use of this formula is not to rely on the measurements of H_h on a horizontal surface but to use a normal-incidence, direct-radiation meter, and point the long, blackened tube directly toward the sun and move it around slightly to obtain a maximum reading of the meter. This reading when calibrated gives the direct radiation at right angles to the sun's rays under conditions that exclude the scattered radiation that is not focusable.

The ratio of the area of the mirror to the focused image of the sun is definite for a perfect focusing mirror, but usually the reflecting mirror is not optically perfect and the sun's image is not entirely circular and uniform. Parts of the image will be much hotter than others. Usually the receiving target is made large enough to collect most of the focused solar radiation, and the material of the target is a good metallic conductor, so the receiver is heated reasonably uniformly in spite of a distorted image, and the effective concentration ratio is A_*/A_t. The size of the target depends on the perfection of the shape and surface of the focusing mirror. If it is a perfect parabola the target can be small; if it deviates in shape from a smooth parabola part of the focused light will miss the small target and a larger one must be used. The area of the target is kept as small as possible in order to reduce heat losses and give higher temperatures.

The effective reflectivity r depends on the perfection of the reflecting surface, which in turn depends on the macro and micro imperfections in the surface. Polished plate glass with a good deposit of silver gives the best reflective surface and reflects nearly all the light striking the mirrorized surface if it is on the front of the glass. If it is at the back of the glass, as is usually the case in order to ensure chemical stability and resistance to weathering, there is loss by absorption in the glass and by reflection at the air–glass interface. The reflection from a glass mirror, silvered on the back, is of the order of 92 per cent. The surface of a plastic film is much less smooth, and when it is covered with a reflecting metal the irregularities and micro hills and valleys cause deviations in reflected light. Irregularities in the shape of an aluminized plastic in a parabolic shell caused by dust particles or small wrinkles also cause part of the reflected light to miss the target.

Design. The focusing may be accomplished with glass lenses or with curved mirrors of glass, metal, or plastic. For practical use of the sun's radiation it is necessary to intercept such a large area of sunlight that glass lenses are impractically expensive and heavy.

Parabolic mirrors focus the parallel rays of the sun onto a small area and give a high intensity which produces a high temperature. The reflecting surface may be silvered glass or polished metal or plastic that has been coated with aluminum by vapor-plating in a large vacuum chamber.

Cross sections of different shapes of circular focusing collectors are shown in Figure 15.

The short-focus collector (see Fig. 15 A) has the advantage of not having to be adjusted so often for following the sun, but the steep curvature makes the construction of a good reflecting surface more difficult. The target has a rounded surface to intercept the focused radiation from the

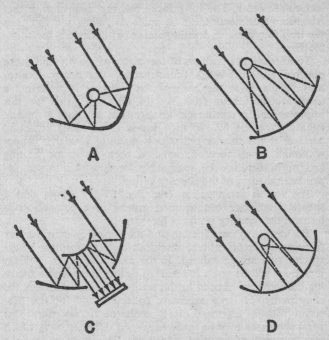

15. Cross sections of circular solar collectors.

outer rim of the mirror as well as from the bottom. Since the target is inside the collector it is partly protected from wind cooling, and for some purposes it can be further protected by stretching a transparent film of plastic across the rim of the whole mirror, which reduces the cooling but also lessens the solar radiation on the collector.

The long-focus collector with less curvature (see Fig. 15 B) is usually easier to make. A flat-bottomed receiver can be used instead of a curved bottom, and the sides and top can be insulated. The target should be at a sufficient distance so the light focused on it from the extreme outer rim of the collector does not come in at such oblique angle that part of the radiation misses the target or is not fully absorbed. A focal length equal to half the diameter of the collector gives good efficiency, though good results can be obtained with a shorter focus, up to perhaps one third of the collector's diameter. The long focus has the disadvantage that frequent adjustments must be made to follow the sun, and the long fulcrum arm creates mechanical difficulties for heavy receivers.

To improve the position of the center of gravity and make possible a lighter-weight construction, the heavy receiver may be placed at the back of the collector by inserting a small second mirror (see Fig. 15 C). The price for this improvement in mechanical arrangement is a loss in optical efficiency caused by radiation losses at a second reflecting surface. If the smaller reflector is made of plastic it cannot withstand much focused radiation because of the heating and must therefore be reasonably large, which causes appreciable shading of the primary collector.

The fourth arrangement (see Fig. 15 D) shows that a spherical collector can be used instead of a parabolic collector if the focusing need not be sharp.

The details of construction and the choice of materials for focusing collectors will be discussed in later chapters where specific uses are considered. In the section on solar cooking, directions will be given for making simple, inexpensive focusing collectors of plastic; in the section on solar furnaces the construction of large expensive collectors with optical precision will be discussed. It is sufficient to say here that parabolic shells may be made in several different ways which give a variety of focusing efficiencies. The more perfect the optical precision, the sharper the focus, the smaller the possible area of the receiver, and the less the heat losses. To get very high temperatures it is essential to have a sharp focus and a small receiver. Concentration ratios of over 1,000 to 1 are possible with high optical precision, giving equilibrium temperatures of over 3,000° C. With less perfect collectors a receiver of large area is necessary to intercept most of the radiation, but then the cooling over a large area prevents high temperatures.

A plastic collector, described on page 184, which was 6 ft in diameter with an area of 29 ft², focused the light within a target of 1/6 ft² and gave an average concentration ratio of 174 to 1. It produced an average temperature of 500° C. A 4-ft solar cooker, described on page 65, with an area of 12 ft², focused on an 8-inch kettle with a bottom area of 1/3 ft² gave an average concentration ratio of 36 to 1 and produced a temperature of about 150° C. The efficiency of heat input to the receiver depends greatly on the specular reflectivity of the collector, the perfection of its shape, and the capacity of the receiving surface for absorption and emission, as previously discussed.

To get high temperatures it is necessary to have high optical precision. Concave mirrors of glass are too expensive and heavy. The cheapest and most widely used precision mirrors for focusing sunlight are old army-surplus parabolic searchlights, described in Chapter 11.

Parabolic collectors may be made of spun sheet aluminum. Large sizes, up to 8 ft and more in diameter, have been made for focusing radar waves and are available commercially. The aluminum surface is not sufficiently polished to give satisfactory solar concentration, and they are heavy. They can be lined with good reflecting material or they can be used as forms for making plastic parabolic shells for solar collectors. Given a sufficient demand for quantity production, large parabolic collectors could be stamped out like automobile body parts from sheet aluminum, sheet iron, or plastic material, using heavy dies and power machinery. The dies would be expensive, but they could produce cheaply a large number of high-quality collectors.

Plastic collectors. An extended research program on plastic parabolic reflectors from 4 ft to 12 ft in diameter has been carried out at the University of Wisconsin for over five years.[9,10] Several different kinds will be described here, and some of them will be described more fully in later chapters.

In one method, polystyrene sheets, 4 ft square, 30 to 50 mils thick, are drape-molded over an aluminum parabolic mold. The operations are carried out by a commercial plant in a large chamber provided with radiant electric heaters and a vacuum pump. The parabolic shell has an indented outer rim into which a rigid hoop of small aluminum pipe is forced. The plastic shell is then lined with aluminized Mylar tape containing a pressure adhesive (like Scotch Tape); with practice these strips, 3 to 4 inches wide, can be overlapped smoothly without wrinkles or trapped air bubbles.

In another method a parabolic mold is made of sand, covered with a layer of concrete. Shells of fiberglass cloth, impregnated with plastic and set into hoops of thin-walled pipes, are made from it. The concrete mold may be replaced with a more perfect one of spun aluminum, or a plastic replica of a searchlight. Another technique is to coat the parabolic mold with glycerol and lay down strips of aluminized plastic (Aclar) with the aluminized side up. Overlapping the strips is necessary. They are then covered with liquid plastic. After setting, this layer is incorporated in a fiberglass and plastic shell.

Multiple mirrors. Collectors for large solar furnaces (described in Chapter 11) are usually made of many flat mirrors, 1 ft[2] or less, mounted on parabolic frames and faced so that the light from every mirror converges on the same spot. Gardner[11] demonstrated a wooden case containing a parabolic wooden frame to which were attached many 1-in.[2] glass mirrors. Khanna[12] has used a set of tilted flat mirrors for boiling water and agricultural juices. The mirrors are mounted on the ground in such a way that each mirror reflects its light on the kettle.

A simple technique has been worked out for setting a large number of 1-in.[2] mirrors into a plastic parabolic shell to make a mosaic. (It is convenient to apply the mosaic mirrors in the form of strips 2 inches wide and 20 inches long glued to a backing of cheesecloth. These cloth-mounted mosaic mirrors of high-quality glass are commercially available from the National Products Inc., Louisville, Kentucky, for less than $1 ft[2].) The front glass surfaces of the mirrors are covered with wax to permit later removal of excess plastic. The shell is painted, small areas at a time, with liquid epoxy or polyester plastic, in which the small mirrors (1700 for a collector 4 ft in diameter) are then embedded.

The mosaic mirrors are more expensive than the aluminized plastics, but their specular reflectivity is over 90 per cent compared to the 85 per cent or less of the aluminized plastics, and they will withstand scratching, weathering, and years of exposure to the ultraviolet light of solar radiation much better than Mylar and most other plastics. The single-strength mirror glass is about 2.5 mm thick and weighs about 1.2 lb ft^{-2}. Thinner mirror glass, 1.1 mm thick, is also available, with a weight of about ½ lb ft^{-2}.

Fresnel lens. Another device for focusing solar energy is the Fresnel lens. A nest of circular grooves is cut in a sheet of transparent plastic with the sides of each successive ring set in such a way that the light passing through each groove is refracted at a slightly different angle and converges on a point. Such lenses have been pressed out in plastic sheets and they are effective in giving a sharp focus.

Fresnel reflectors are made also with narrow concentric rings of aluminized plastic or polished aluminum, each ring being set at a different angle so that all the rings focus on a central target.

Spherical collectors. It is not necessary to have a perfect parabolic mirror to get solar radiation of high intensity yielding a high temperature. Spherical mirrors can give a fairly good focus, sufficient for many purposes in solar energy use. When a sheet of aluminized plastic is attached to the back of a hoop and another sheet of plastic is attached to the front and they are inflated with compressed air, each sheet bulges to a hemispherical shape with a perfectly smooth surface of high reflectivity.[18] The focal length depends upon the air pressure applied and the thickness and elasticity of the plastic film. With a hoop 4 ft in diameter attached to aluminized Mylar 1 mil thick it is easy to obtain a sharp focus at a focal length of 30 inches or more. With greater pressure it is possible to get a focal length of 20 inches or less, but this stretches the aluminized surface of the film so much that the reflectivity is appreciably less. Plastics that are more stretchable than Mylar are available, but they are limited in the attainment of short focus because spreading the aluminum–plastic interface to cover a larger area reduces the reflectivity.

The inflated aluminized plastic may be made rigid by putting the hoop in a horizontal position and covering the top with a liquid epoxy plastic and fiberglass cloth. It is important to keep the pressure constant or increasing very slightly while the plastic is setting. If there is any decrease in pressure during the setting there will be small waves or wrinkles in the reflecting surface, and there is a tendency for irregularities to form at the threads in the cloth weave. After the plastic has set the front film is removed, leaving a spherical mirror.

Cylindrical collectors. Comparing circular and cylindrical collectors, we find that the circular collectors are necessary for producing very high temperatures because the area of the receiving target may be made very small with low attendant heat losses and the concentration ratio in focusing can be large. However, the total area of a single reflecting collector is limited by construction difficulties, by the necessity for moving the collector to track the sun, and by damage from strong winds. An advantage of cylindrical collectors is that they can be made indefinitely long, and one type can be so arranged as not to need sun tracking throughout the day, but the temperatures obtainable are much lower. If a cylindrical collector is 6 ft (180 cm) wide and the receiver target is 1 inch (2.5 cm) wide, the concentration ratio is 72 to 1. By lengthening the cylinder and the receiver strip the quantity of heat is increased but the size of the target receiver is also increased, and the concentration ratio remains constant. However, a very long cylindrical collector can receive more solar energy with a single unit than a single circular collector can receive. The cylindrical shape is much easier to make than the circular shape because aluminized plastic sheet, bright anodized sheet aluminum, or other reflecting material can be easily curved to fit the cylindrical form, since it is curved only along two axes. If the collector is lined with aluminized plastic the wrinkles formed by shaping in three dimensions are avoided.

The cross section of the cylindrical collector may be either parabolic or circular. Although the parabolic cross section in general gives sharper focus, the circular cross section has an advantage in some forms by requiring less frequent adjustments to track the sun.[14,15]

Parabolic-cylindrical collectors of plastic may be made with a framework of parabolic ribs cut from plywood (as described on p. 65) and set vertically, with the curved sides up, at 2-ft intervals along a wooden base. Stiff sheet material is placed over the ribs and waxed, and then draped with fiberglass cloth and liquid plastic. A framework of electric conduit tubing is added. A convenient size is 6 ft wide and 4 ft long with three ribs. An indefinite number of these sections can be bolted together into a single long collector. After removal from the frame, the plastic shell is lined with a sheet of anodized aluminum or aluminized plastic, or with long strips of glass mirrors 1 inch wide. A collector of this type is shown in Plate 1, and its performance is described on page 87.

MOUNTINGS FOR FOCUSING COLLECTORS

There are several ways in which a circular focusing collector can be made to follow the sun and keep the front plane of the collector always at right angles to the sun.

The azimuthal type of mounting (see Fig. 16 A) involves two motions—the rotation of a vertical central shaft and the tilting of the collector around a horizontal axis. These two motions are easily made by a human operator, even by one completely unskilled, but they are not easily made with simple mechanical controls. The front plane of the parabolic collector (see Fig. 16 A) is attached to the rod that constitutes the horizontal axis, and the receiving surface of the engine, boiler, thermoelectric converter, or other solar device is attached to the rim of the collector and moves with it.

A modification of the azimuthal mounting (see Fig. 16 B) permits the receiving surface of the solar target to be kept

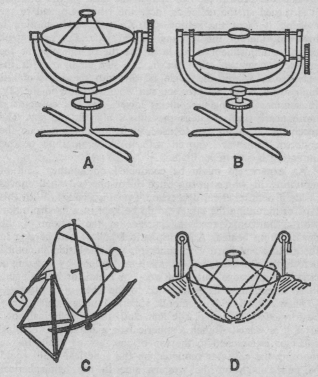

16. Mountings for tracking the sun by circular solar collectors. A. Azimuthal mounting with two motions. B. Modified azimuthal mounting with two motions which permits use of a stationary receiver. C. Equatorial mounting with one motion. D. Sliding spherical surfaces with stationary receiver.

in a fixed horizontal position. The parabolic collector is hung at a level below the axis of rotation, and the receiving target is attached at a fixed level from the ground rather than being attached rigidly to the moving mirror. A photograph of this mounting is shown in Plate 3.

In the equatorial mounting (see Fig. 16 C), the framework is set on a firm base and a strong central pipe is set into it and pointed north. It is tilted at an angle that can be changed with the season so the front plane of the collector is at right angles to the sun's rays. The collector is rotated around the central pipe to follow the sun. In the morning it is turned so the collector faces the rising sun and in the evening it faces the setting sun. Only a single motion is involved, that of the rotating central pipe. But each week or so an adjustment is made in the tilt of the pipe as the apparent height of the sun in the sky changes with the seasons. In winter the angle of tilt with the horizontal is high so the collector faces the sun when it is low in the sky. In summer the angle of tilt is lower, and the collector is more nearly horizontal as the sun is high in the sky. The receiving target for the focused sunlight is mounted on the collector frame and moved with it. A photograph of this mounting is shown in Plate 8.

An experiment might be conducted on another kind of mounting in which a suggested hemispherical shell moves inside a hemispherical depression (see Fig. 16 D). With this type of mounting the target would be kept in a fixed position with a horizontal receiving surface at the bottom of the device being heated. A hemispherical hollow can be dug in the ground and lined with concrete, and the inside smoothed before the Portland cement mixture hardens by rotating a circular knife edge, cut from wood or metal, or by swinging in all directions a large ball tied to the apex of a tripod.

Then a shell with a smooth spherical under-surface may be formed by setting plastic and cloth in the spherical bowl after it is waxed. Either a spherical or a parabolic focusing collector is attached to the top of the moving shell. In the morning the collector mounted on the spherical shell would be pulled high on the western side in the hemispherical depression to face the rising sun. Then as the sun rises the shell would be allowed to slide down toward the bottom; in the afternoon the collector would be pulled up on the eastern side of the depression to face the west. This sliding movement of the inner shell could be controlled with ropes over a windlass and pulleys and attached to heavy weights.

As the seasons change the sun rises more to the north or to the south, the line of movement of the collector shell across the hemispherical depression could be changed by moving the ropes that control the movement of the collector. The double-sphere mounting would eliminate the cost of a sturdy metal framework and provide shelter against strong winds.

Tracking the sun can be accomplished in several different ways by clockwork mechanisms, by leakage using the principle of the hourglass, by shadows and electrical circuits, or by manpower.

The clockwork mechanism is simple if alternating electrical current is available. A synchronous motor is geared down to the proper speed to rotate the collector through 15° of a circle every hour. (The earth makes one complete revolution of 360° in 24 hr, so in 1 hr it moves 360°/24 = 15°.) At this constant rate of turning the collector, if properly set, would be focused on the target all day long.

Electrical power circuits are unfortunately not available in most of the areas where there is now a demand for solar energy. It is possible to build a clockwork mechanism operated by a heavy weight and controlled by a pendulum as in the old grandfather clocks. It would be a good project to build and operate a mechanism to rotate a solar collector, using a structure with several gear wheels, controlled by a pendulum or an escapement wheel similar to those used in spring-wound clocks or watches. A 50-lb sack of sand lifted 3 ft each day could provide the power necessary to rotate a fair-sized collector.

A heavy metal counterpoise can be arranged so that it rotates the collector from facing east to facing west during the period of the day. The rate of rotation is controlled by the rate at which a piston moves in a cylinder filled with oil, which is determined by the rate of leakage of the oil through a by-pass and hand-adjustable valve. Such a mechanism is described in Chapter 15. It operated fairly well, but needed adjustment every hour or two because of air bubbles and other mechanical difficulties.

In principle it is a simple matter to have a photocell or photovoltaic cell (such as a silicon solar battery) or a thermocouple actuate the controls of an electric motor or a weight and pulley device in such a way that the shaft is allowed to turn by a small angle whenever the direct or focused sunlight hits the photocells or the thermopile. The moving edge of the sun's shadow falling on a photocell thus turns the shaft by small jerks.

Another method of automatic tracking is to use a weight on a rope wound on the rotating axle and controlled by a ratchet wheel and escape mechanism which is released by the thermal expansion of a metal heated by the focused sunlight when the light passes the target.

For some types of work, as in large solar furnaces, it is necessary to keep a heavy device in a fixed position while the sun changes its position. A reflecting mirror is moved to follow the sun.

These various mechanical and electrical devices for tracking the sun are simple and reliable, but they increase the capital cost of the solar installation and can be considered only for large units. In many places where solar energy is likely to be used first, capital is difficult to obtain, particularly if it involves foreign exchange, but labor is abundant and relatively inexpensive. Often it will be more economical to track the sun by hand operation than by automatic devices.

Of the cylindrical collectors one type of mounting (see Fig. 17 A) requires tracking of the sun similar to that described for the equatorial mounting of circular collectors. The long axis of the collector is placed at right angles to the rays from the rising sun, and the collector is faced toward the sun. As the sun moves across the sky the cylindrical collector is rotated around a central shaft so that the front plane of the collector is always at right angles to the sun. As the season changes the axis of the collector is shifted daily or weekly so that the long axis is always at right angles to the rising sun.

One of the great advantages of flat-plate collectors is that they do not have to be moved to track the sun. A cylindrical collector can also be mounted so it does not have to track the sun. The long axis of the cylindrical collector is aligned approximately east and west and adjusted each week or day so the central linear target receiver strip is always in focus (as shown in Fig. 17 B and Plate 1). The collector is then tilted so the focus of the collector coincides with the receiver throughout its length. With these adjustments the receiver will be at the focus for much of the day, except for changes in tilt in early morning and late afternoon. The angle of the collector shown in Plate 1 was occasionally changed by tightening or loosening a rope.

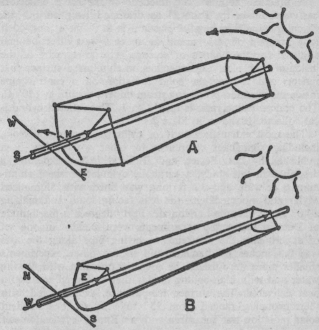

17. Mountings for cylindrical solar collectors. A. Rotating collector with north-south axis. B. Stationary collector running approximately east-west.

The difficulty with this simple arrangement is that in early morning and late afternoon the sun will be so low in the sky that the reflected light will not hit the outer ends of the receiver, especially if a long focus is used and the receiver is high above the collector. This waste of energy can be minimized by having a cylindrical collector long enough that the unilluminated end of the receiver is only a small part of the total.

The weekly alignment of the collector's position to follow the season is more difficult with a long collector. In a large unit it is easier to change the position of the receiving pipe than to move the collector.[14] The adjustment of the receiver is even easier if the collector has a circular rather than a parabolic cross section.

A practical solution for relatively inexpensive collectors has been made by Tabor,[15] as discussed later on p. 185. Circular-cylindrical bags of plastic 5 ft in diameter and 40 ft long are laid on the ground in an east–west direction and adjusted for the change of seasons. The lower part of the inside of each plastic cylinder has an aluminized surface that reflects and focuses the solar radiation on a central pipe inside the cylinder, producing steam under pressure at 150° C. The concentration ratio is only 3 to 1. This inflated cylindrical collector is shown in Plate 2.

The most exhaustive study of cylindrical solar collectors, including significant references to other works, has been published by Löf, Fester, and Duffie.[16] In the experiments described in this study, a parabolic cylinder of sheet aluminum 6 ft wide and 12 ft long was lined with aluminized Mylar and mounted with the axis facing south and making a 40° angle with the horizontal. (Forty degrees is the latitude of Denver, where the experiments were made.) In one set of experiments the blackened receiving pipe along the axis was 2.3 inches in diameter and in the other experiments smaller pipes were used. The collector operated with flowing water and with high-boiling liquids that measured the useful heat delivered. The surface temperature, as measured with thermocouples, ranged from 35° to 175° C. The incident solar radiation was measured with an Eppley pyroheliometer at normal incidence. The distribution of focused solar radiation at different positions near the central receiving pipe was measured with a silicon photovoltaic cell moved by screw adjustments. Eighty per cent of the focused radiation fell within a 1-inch strip of the focus, and very little of it fell at distances farther away than a strip 3 inches wide.

The solar radiation intensity at different positions and the efficiency of collection as a function of the receiver temperature, the wind velocity, the temperature of the air, and the diameter of the tube are illustrated by curves.[16] As is to be expected there is an optimum diameter. If the tube is too narrow some of the focused radiation misses it; if it is too wide the heat losses are excessive. The efficiencies varied from about 25 per cent at the highest receiver temperatures to nearly 70 per cent when the receiver temperature was only slightly above the temperature of the surrounding air. The many factors involved, including losses caused by reflection, imperfect shape, absorption, radiation, conduction, and convection, were studied and their effect on the efficiency of conversion into useful heat at higher temperatures is shown with the help of graphs.[16] The data check well with the values calculated from formulas similar to those given earlier in this chapter.

Considerable progress in focusing collectors has been made in the research programs for exploration of outer space.[17] Large and nearly perfect parabolic collectors 10 ft in diameter have been made with aluminized Mylar backed with polyurethane foam plastic which is forced into a mold and then set to a rigid shell. Such focusing mirrors have been made in which over 98 per cent of the surface has a tangential error of less than ½ degree.[18] Since these collectors are being considered for use in space where gravity and winds are absent, modifications will be necessary for their use on the earth. They are now very expensive, but the techniques being developed should lead to cheaper collectors that do not have to meet the rigid requirements of space exploration.

PROPERTIES OF MATERIALS

The possibilities in new materials for solar energy use are reviewed by Duffie.[5]

Glass. Glass, the oldest man-made transparent material, has been used extensively as covers for flat-plate collectors and as mirrors for focusing collectors. Single-strength window glass (3 mm thick) costs about 30¢ ft^{-2} ($3.23 m^{-2}). It is permanent and does not deteriorate with weathering, but it is heavy and breakable and requires strong structures for holding it in place. Glass is transparent to most of the sunlight except the ultraviolet, but it is opaque in the longer infrared, thus acting as an effective heat trap when used as a cover.

The reflection at each interface of glass and air amounts to about 4 per cent and the absorption of the solar radiation by the glass itself may be a few per cent, so the transmission is reduced by 10 per cent or more each time the light passes through a sheet of glass. The reflection losses at the interface are unimportant in the case of a mirror because they are merged with the light coming from the silvered surface. The losses of sunlight passing through glass plates and mirrors have been discussed by Peyches.[7] The transmission of the glass is greatly affected by its chemical composition. The presence of iron in the glass leads to absorption of light in the neighborhood of 10,000 Å. Glass with considerable iron has a greenish color when viewed edgewise. Colorless glass is better for the collection of solar energy. Picture glass 1 to 2 mm in thickness is available in the smaller sizes; its absorption is less because it is thinner, and it is lighter in weight than window glass, but no less expensive.

Plastics. The availability of thin strong sheets of plastics with particular properties is important in advancing the use of solar energy. The plastic material is transparent, and is available in thicknesses from ¼ mil (0.006 mm) to 10 mils (0.24 mm) and other thicknesses. It is strong, unbreakable, easily transported, and inexpensive, costing about 2¢ to 10¢ ft^{-2} (21¢ to \$1.07 m^{-2}) in thin sheets. The cost of constructing solar devices is much less with plastics than with glass. The deterioration in sunlight and weathering has been a serious handicap, but industrial companies have now developed several plastics with excellent characteristics. Edlin has described[8,19,20] fully the properties of these new plastics. Of particular interest are Dupont's weatherable polyester Mylar (Mylar W) and Tedlar (polyvinyl fluoride), which are now in production. Whereas Mylar will deteriorate in a year of outdoor exposure, the Mylar W, with a coating to absorb ultraviolet light, probably has a life in Florida of 3 years or more and Tedlar 5 years or more. Teflon, a fluorocarbon film, has an estimated life of 20 years. Aclar (Allied Chemical Co.) is another polyvinyl fluoride with good resistance to sunlight and weathering. Whillier[21] has studied plastic coverings for flat-plate collectors and found that Tedlar is nearly as good as glass.

Some of the common plastics such as polyethylene, cellulose, acetate, polyvinyl chloride, and polystyrene have very short life when exposed to outdoor weather. Many factors are involved including the photochemical action of ultraviolet light, moisture, temperature, continual fluttering and vibration, and strong wind stresses. Some samples that remained strong for a year on exposure to sunlight and weather failed quickly when they were constantly in contact with moisture.[22] Hydrolysis and the leaching out of certain chemicals are probably involved. When the plastic sheets were firmly attached with adhesive to a flat plate they withstood the weathering much better.

Other properties of plastics that are important in solar energy applications are ability to take on a water film, ease of removal of dust, influence of temperature on deterioration, and loss of transparency for sunlight. Some plastic films can be heat sealed and others cannot. Some plastic films are treated so they can be attached with an adhesive.

Some of the physical properties of three of the plastic films are enumerated in Table 3.[8] Other important properties include high chemical inertness, low permeability by gases, and influence of hot air and steam.[8]

The transmission of light through plastic depends on the

TABLE 3. Physical Properties of Plastic Films

	Mylar W	Tedlar 40	polyethylene
Thickness, mils	5	2	4
Density g/cc	1.39	1.38	0.91
Refractive index	1.64	1.45	1.5
Tensile strength psi, 25° C	24,000	8,000	2,000
Tensile elongation per cent, 25° C	100	250	500
Tear strength g/mil 25° C	33	180	300
Thermal coefficient linear expansion	25×10^{-6}	24×10^{-6}	300×10^{-6}

refractive index of the material and the reflections at the two air–plastic interfaces. The absorption within the material is less than within glass because the films of plastic are much thinner than the glass plates. Sunlight consists of both direct radiation and scattered radiation, and the transmission may depend in part on the ratio of the two. If the light is to be focused only the direct radiation should be measured, because the scattered radiation will not hit the focal target. Likewise when solar radiation for a focusing device is reflected from an aluminized plastic surface only the direct specular reflection is significant.

These quantities can be measured conveniently with an Eppley pyroheliometer at the end of a long, blackened tube pointed at the sun. The ratio of the reading with and without the interposed plastic film gives the percentage of transmission for a beam of focused radiation. The reflectivities are obtained in a similar manner, placing the reflecting surface firmly against an absolutely flat surface at an angle of 45° with the chimney tube. A silicon photovoltaic cell is conveniently substituted for the Eppley pyroheliometer and calibrated against it. The unobstructed tube, blackened inside, is pointed in the direction of the sun and moved around until a maximum reading is registered on the silicon cell. Then the slanting surface is put over the end of the chimney, the reflecting surface is placed against it, and the reflector is aimed toward the sun and adjusted in its direction until a maximum reading is obtained. This reading divided by the maximum reading without the reflector gives the per cent of reflection. The reading gives only the direct radiation because the scattered radiation does not enter the tube or is absorbed by the black walls.

An extended study[23] has shown that there is considerable variation in different samples of an aluminized plastic, dependent on the thickness of the aluminum deposit and the roughness of the surface. Viewed under a microscope the different plastics show large variations in the smoothness of the metallic deposit, dependent on the nature of the underlying surface.

The better samples of aluminized Mylar gave a reflection of about 70 per cent and the weatherable Mylar about 65 per cent. When the aluminized side is in front the reflectivity is about 80 per cent, but of course the exposed aluminum coating very quickly deteriorates when placed outdoors or in a moist environment.

Accelerated tests equivalent to over a year of sunlight and moisture were carried out on samples with their aluminized side attached firmly to glass plates with epoxy plastic. The aluminized Mylar gave a lowered reflectivity from about 70 to less than 60 per cent but the weatherable Mylar showed almost no loss in reflectivity.

Under similar conditions Aclar showed a reflectivity of about 80 per cent and only slightly less at the end of the exposure tests. Scotchcal showed almost no loss of reflectivity after the exposure tests.

Edlin and Willauer give[8] reflection tests for Mylar, Tedlar, and a glass mirror at angles of incidence from 0° to 60°. The reflection does not change appreciably from an angle of incidence of 0° (normal incidence) to an angle of 45°. There is a marked increase in reflection when the incident light comes in at 60°.

Data are also given[8] for the transmission of different plastic films. Tedlar showed more than 90 per cent transmission and weatherable Mylar less than 90 per cent to an angle of incidence of 45°. At greater angles of incidence the transmission dropped considerably. The effect of one to five sheets of plastic is described also.[8]

A promising plastic material, transparent Styrocel foam (Dow Chemical Co.), is available for flat-plate collectors. It is a good heat insulator and transmits over 60 per cent of the incident light. It costs 35 to 60¢ per square foot in sheets 1 inch thick. Particularly at high temperatures it reduces the heat losses more than the transmission losses, and the collectors with Styrocel at the front are better than those with glass plates or Tedlar alone. Experiments on five different collectors are reported by Selcuk.[24] Styrocel withstood temperatures of 220° F (105° C) but softened at 280° F (140° C).

Metals. Several highly polished metals have good reflectivity for sunlight. Silver is one, but it tarnishes so quickly with hydrogen sulfide in the air that it is used almost only on the back of glass mirrors. Copper and some other metals give good reflections but they quickly oxidize to a dark surface. Rhodium-plated metal surfaces were used in large searchlights. Stainless steel, nickel, and chromium are permanent and they appear to be bright, but the reflection of sunlight is low.

Aluminum is perhaps the best and cheapest metal for direct reflection of sunlight. When highly polished it has a high reflectivity and the oxide coating of Al_2O_3 forms instantly, does not penetrate deeply, and is sufficiently transparent that it does not reduce the reflection greatly. The reflectivity depends markedly on the purity of the aluminum and on the polish of the metal. Tests on sheets of several different types of aluminum gave reflections of 60 to 70 per cent. Aluminum foil used for wrapping gave about 65 per cent reflection of sunlight.

The permanence and reflectivity of an aluminum surface can be greatly improved by "anodizing" it electrochemically. The aluminum is made the anode in a phosphate or other electrolytic bath and an electric current is passed through at high amperage. Rather special conditions are needed to give optimum reflectivity.[25]

There are lacquers that preserve the shining appearance of aluminum. A commercial lacquer for this purpose reduced the reflectivity of the aluminum from 80 to 60 per cent, but it prevented deterioration of the surface, and after exposure to ultraviolet light and water, equivalent to over a year of sunlight and weathering, the reflectivity was still the same.

General Considerations

The many factors involved in collecting solar energy can now be summarized. Temperatures above 120° C need focusing collectors, but they use only direct radiation and are effective only when the sun is clear. They have to track the sun, and they are difficult to make and operate in large sizes. The higher the temperature needed the greater must be the optical precision and the structural firmness, and the greater the cost.

Both the flat-plate collectors and the focusing collectors have problems because of their large size. They should be strong enough to withstand the most severe winds in their localities and they should be fastened down in a safe position when a storm is approaching. They must be so arranged that they can be cleaned easily. Minor factors such as wind damage and the tenacity with which dust particles adhere to the surface of the collector may mean success or failure in a solar energy project.

For many projects it may be possible to build collectors for about $2 ft^{-2} ($21.50 m^{-2}), but very difficult to bring the cost down to less than $1 ft^{-2}. This lower cost is necessary for most uses. It may be in some areas where solar energy might first be used and labor is plentiful, that costs might be reduced considerably by making and cutting mirrors, assembling parts, and operating the collectors by hand. When the mass production of focusing collectors is justified, sheet metal forms, like automobile bodies, can be stamped out very cheaply with large, expensive dies. They can be aluminized, or covered with aluminized plastic or a mosaic of glass mirrors.

The requirements for focusing solar radiation for auxiliary power in space exploration has led to intensive research on the perfection of lightweight reflectors. Mathematical analysis of solar reflecting collectors has been made by Hukuo and Mii[26] and by Löf and Duffie.[27] A complete study by Schrenk and Gritton[28] is available for calculating the solar energy flux on a focal surface of any shape from any arbitrarily shaped reflector surface, and operative computer programs have been developed from the equations for evaluating solar collectors. Provisions are included for random errors of surface and orientation.

REFERENCES

1. Hottel, H. C., and Woertz, B. B., The performance of flat-plate solar heat collectors, *Trans. Am. Soc. Mech. Eng.*, *64:* 91–104. 1942.

2. Tabor, H., Solar Energy Collector Design, in *Trans. of the Conf. on Use of Solar Energy: The Scientific Basis*, *2:* 1–24. Tucson, University of Arizona Press, 1958.

3. Hottel, H. C., and Whillier, A., Evaluation of Solar Collector Performance, ibid., pp. 74–104.

4. Threlkeld, J. L., and Jordan, R. C., Solar Collector Studies at the University of Minnesota, ibid., pp. 105–14.

5. Duffie, J. A., New Materials in Solar Energy Utilization, in *United Nations Conf. on New Sources of Energy*. 35 Gr–S12. Rome, 1961.

6. Bliss, R. W., Jr., The derivations of several plate efficiency factors useful in the design of flat-plate solar heat collectors, *Solar Energy*, *3* (4): 55–64. 1958.

7. Peyches, I., Special Glasses and Mountings for the Utilization of Solar Energy, *U.N. Conf. on New Sources of Energy*. E S91. Rome, 1961.

8. Edlin, F. E., and Willauer, D. E., Plastic Films for Solar Energy Applications, ibid., E 35–S33.

9. Daniels, F., and Breihan, R., Solar Focusing Collectors of Plastics, ibid., E 35–S104.

10. Daniels, F., Construction et Essais de Reflecteurs Solaires Focalisants sans Verre, in *Applications Thermiques de l'Énergie Solaire dans le Domaine de la Recherche et de l'Industrie*, *1:* 53–67. Paris, Centre de la Recherche Scientifique, 1961.

11. Gardner, A. L., Articulated and Semi-Articulated Low-Cost Hot Focus Solar Energy Concentrators, in *New Delhi Symposium on Solar Energy and Wind Power*, pp. 209–15. Paris, UNESCO, 1956.

12. Khanna, M. L., unpublished data.

13. Daniels, F., and Breihan, R. R., Forthcoming publication.

14. Seybolt, R., *Report, Solar Energy Laboratory*, University of Wisconsin, 1957.

15. Tabor, H., and Zeimer, H., Low-Cost Focusing Collector for Solar Power Units, in *U.N. Conf. on New Sources of Energy*, Special preprint, Rome, 1961; Tabor, H., Stationary mirror systems for solar collectors, *Solar Energy*, *2:* 27–33. 1958.

16. Löf, G. O. G., Fester, D. A., and Duffie, J. A., Energy balances on a parabolic cylindrical solar collector, *Trans. Soc. Mech. Eng.*, 24–32. 1962.

17. Tanenhaus, A. M., et al., *Solar Concentrator Systems for Space Power Generator*, Ger. 9711, Akron, Ohio, Goodyear Aircraft Corp., Feb. 1960.

18. Tanenhaus, A. M., *Inflated Rigidized Paraboloidal Solar Energy Concentrator Evaluation*, Ger. 10295, Akron, Ohio, Goodyear Aircraft Corp., July 1961.

19. Edlin, F. E., Plastic glazing for solar energy absorption collectors, *Solar Energy*, 2: 3–7. 1958.

20. Edlin, F. E., Materiaux pour l'Utilization de l'Énergie Solaire, *Applications Thermiques de l'Énergie Solaire dans le Domaine de la Recherche et de l'Industrie, 1*: 539–63. 1961.

21. Whillier, A., Plastic covers for solar collectors, *Solar Energy,* 7: 148–51. 1963.

22. Bjorksten, J., and Lappala, R. P., Photodegradation of plastic films, *Plastics Technology*, Jan. 1957.

23. Daniels, F., Forthcoming publication.

24. Selcuk, M. K., Flat plate solar collector performance at high temperatures, *Solar Energy*, 8: 57–62. 1964.

25. Wernick, S., and Pinner, R., *Surface Treatment and Finishing of Aluminum and Its Alloys*, Teddington, England, Robert Draper, 1959.

26. Hukuo, N., and Mii, H., Design problems of a solar furnace, *Solar Energy, 1*: 108–14. 1957.

27. Löf, G. O. G., and Duffie, J. A., Optimization of focusing solar-collector design, *Jour. Engineering for Power*, 221–28. July 1963.

28. Schrenk, G. L., and Gritton, D. C., *Final Report, Analysis of Solar Reflectors. Mathematical Theory and Methodology for Simulation of Real Reflectors*, Allison Division, General Motors Corp., Indianapolis, EDR 3693 Contract AFO4 (695)-335, Dec. 1963.

CHAPTER 5

Cooking

Boiling and baking food with focused sunlight is one of the simplest applications of solar energy. A considerable effort has been invested in research on different types of cookers and several clever designs have been developed. A complete report on the use of solar energy for cooking has been given by Löf,[1] in which the general principles of cooking are reviewed and heat requirements given. Estimating 0.5 ft^2 (465 cm^2) surface area lb^{-1} (0.453 kg^{-1}) of food and 150-kcal (600-BTU) convection heat losses ft^{-2} hr^{-1} at the boiling temperature of water, it is found that 20 per cent of the heat is used in bringing the material to boiling, 35 per cent is consumed in vaporizing water, and 45 per cent is needed to offset the convection heat losses. The convection losses are highly dependent on the wind velocity. Löf also summarizes the characteristics and performances of six different kinds of solar cookers described at the United Nations Symposium on New Sources of Energy at Rome in August 1961.

Boiling in Kettles

In one kind of solar cooker a circular parabolic reflector is used, about 4 ft (120 cm) in diameter. It focuses the sun's rays onto the horizontal bottom of a kettle about 8 inches (20 cm) in diameter giving heat equivalent to a 500-watt electric hot plate and bringing 1 qt (1 liter) of water to boiling in about 15 min. The first cooker of this type was developed at the National Physical Laboratory of India in New Delhi.[2] It was made on a production basis with spun aluminum and a rugged iron frame and sold in India for about $15, but it was not favorably received.

A plastic solar cooker was developed at the University of Wisconsin with the help of a grant from the Rockefeller Foundation (see Plate 3).[3-5] This model, designed by Dunham and Duffie and modified by Professor W. W. Schaerff, is 4 ft (1.2 m) in diameter with a focus of 18 inches (45 cm). The plastic shell is made from 40-mil (1-mm) polystyrene sheets which are drape-molded over a parabolic aluminum mold in an electrically heated oven while air is being pumped out of holes in the mold, causing the softened plastic to take the shape of the mold. These can be produced at the rate of about one a minute. The rim of the circular shell is supported by a hoop of small aluminum tubing. The shell is lined with reflecting aluminized Mylar strips 3 inches (7 cm) wide which are firmly attached with a pressure-sensitive adhesive (Scotch Tape) on the aluminized side. Skill is needed to attach the overlapping strips without wrinkles or trapped air bubbles. Weatherable Mylar lasts much longer when exposed to sunlight and weather, but its reflectivity is less than that of Mylar. New aluminized plastic materials, Scotchcal and Aclar, mentioned in Chapter 4, appear promising for higher reflectivity and long exposures, but they are more expensive.

The reflecting shells are suspended in a U-frame as shown in Plate 3. The frame is made by bending thin-walled steel

tubing, costing about 9¢ ft⁻¹ (30 cm⁻¹), used for electric
wiring conduits. The U-frame is attached at the bottom to a
horizontal disc that rests on a circular pedestal and can be
rotated. A central horizontal rod with a circular grill is so
attached to the two ends of the U-frame that the cooking
vessel is held above the center of the shell. The frame is
rotated and the collector tilted every 15 to 20 min to keep
the shadow of the kettle in the center of the circular shell
and the focused sunlight on the bottom of the kettle. When
the proper focus is attained a screw is turned to hold the
shell tilted in position by means of a friction clutch. There
has been no difficulty in quickly teaching inexperienced
housewives to make these adjustments in order to follow
the sun. It has been estimated[5] that this type of solar cooker
could be manufactured in 10,000 lots for about $16 each
and perhaps for half as much with very large production.
At present the cost with hand labor is about $25. This solar
collector is not optically perfect and the reflectivity of the
aluminized Mylar is only about 70 per cent. Most of the
reflected sunlight is focused diffusely on the bottom of the
8-inch (20-cm) kettle, and on a bright sunny day over 1 kw
of heat is intercepted by the collector and 500 to 600 watts
of heat are delivered on the target.

A lightweight portable solar cooker developed by Löf[6]
consists of an umbrella frame with aluminized Mylar lami-
nated to the inside of the cloth and a grill for holding the
kettle or frying pan. It is a little less than 4 ft (1.2 m) in
diameter and on a bright sunny day it delivers up to 400
watts to the cooking vessel. It retails for $30 and has been
widely tested for outdoor picnic meals. The materials constitute two thirds and the labor one third of the cost.

BAKING IN OVENS

It is also possible to use insulated ovens with glass windows which admit the solar radiation but reduce the losses
of the infrared radiation emitted by the heated oven and
food. Dr. Marie Telkes[7-9] has developed an oven which is
an insulated box with a cooking vessel area 10 inches (25
cm) square, tilted toward the sun and adjusted every half
hour as the sun moves during the day. Four slanting reflectors of bright aluminum at the sides of the oven reflect
the light down through the window into the oven. The total
effective area is thus 6 ft² (0.56 m²) and temperatures of

205° C (400° F) and higher are obtained. After exposure to the sun an insulating pad is placed over the window to retain the heat. Fused salts of hydroxides in tight containers are also used to store the heat for longer periods of time. The time required for heating, the retention of heat, and the cooking behavior of various foods are described by Dr. Telkes.[8,9]

Another solar oven, somewhat smaller, with aluminum reflectors inside the cover behind the double glass window, has been described by Abou-Hussein.[10] The area of sunlight intercepted is 4 ft² (0.37 m²) and in bright sun a temperature of 256° C (494° F) was obtained.

A combination focusing collector and windowed, insulated oven, developed by Prata,[11] has cylindrical mirrors 8 ft² (0.74 m²) of nickel-plated brass that focus the sunlight onto a long narrow window of single glass in an insulated metal cylinder in which two cooking vessels are placed. Data on times required for cooking various foods are available.[11] It is estimated that the optical losses due to shape and lack of perfect reflectivity are 41 per cent, radiation heat losses are 12 per cent, and after allowing for other small losses the usable energy is 31 per cent.

The Telkes oven and the Wisconsin cooker were tested by the Nutrition Division of the Food and Agriculture Organization of the United Nations in Rome.[12] The time taken for 2 liters of water in a closed vessel to be heated from 15 to 20° to 100° C was measured under a variety of conditions. The water boiled considerably faster on the Wisconsin solar stove than in the Telkes oven. The performance of the Telkes oven was less affected by its infrequent positioning and by clouds and wind.

FIELD TESTS

The economic and social acceptance of solar cookers has been studied with the help of anthropologists in low-income rural villages in Mexico and among American Indians in Arizona. Over 200 cookers have been field tested in this way and probably more sociological information is available for the introduction of solar cookers than for the introduction of any other solar devices. Generous support from the Rockefeller Foundation has made these studies possible at the University of Wisconsin. One report by Duffie, Löf, and Beck[5] is based on a study in a village of northern Mexico where 20 cookers were observed for over a year and 6 cookers of the improved type shown in Plate 3 were observed for a few months. Additional reports will be published later. The first twenty cookers developed some mechanical difficulties which had not been noticed in the laboratory tests. Parts of the frame were not sufficiently rugged and the cookers vibrated enough in strong wind to spill food. The aluminized Mylar was not expected to withstand long continuous exposure to sunlight, but improved and more permanent reflecting surfaces are now available. In spite of these shortcomings half the cookers were still in active use after a year. The reasons for the discontinuance of the other half were varied. Petroleum was available and wood could sometimes be obtained with investment of time but no cost in money. In cloudy weather the cookers are useless and when clouds covered the sun after the solar cooking was started there were obvious frustrations. The use of solar cookers must be considered only as an alternative or as a supplement to the use of fuels. The cost must be low because the income is low in these areas where electricity is not cheap and fuel not readily available. Interest rates on borrowed capital are usually very high in these places. Technical education for use and interest in the cookers were not serious problems.

It was found in the field testing that water could be boiled in vessels of clay or earthenware nearly as well as in vessels of aluminum or steel, because the pattern of focused light was diffuse enough that the earthenware vessels were not cracked by the thermal expansion. It was necessary to blacken the bottoms of the kettles with soot, by holding them over a piece of burning cloth that had soaked up some oil.

The acceptance of solar cookers depends to a great extent on the cooking and eating habits of the people in a given area. The cooker shown in Plate 3 is best adapted to the boiling and stewing of foods in covered kettles. It can probably be used for cooking tortillas if the frying pan has a thick bottom which spreads out the heat and does not concentrate it in hot spots. This cooker is not easily used for baking. Solar cooking cannot be done very early in the morning or in the evening. The cookers are best accepted when a heavy meal at noon is customary, though the fact that the housewife must work in the hot sun and adjust the focusing every 15 min is a difficulty. The saving in the cost of fuel in a given community must be balanced against the investment cost and the inconvenience of cooking outdoors. In many cases it appears that the saving in fuel will pay for the investment in one or two years of use.

Other uses were found for the cookers besides boiling food. For example, hot water can be easily obtained for washing and irons are readily heated for ironing clothes.

CONSTRUCTION OF A SIMPLE SOLAR COOKER

The solar cookers described so far have involved electric power and machine tools. The costs of manufacture in an industrialized country and shipment to a nonindustrialized country are high. Accordingly, efforts have been made to develop simple designs and methods of manufacture which will permit local production and require the importation of a minimum of special material. Some of these designs have involved paper and aluminum foil, which will not withstand long exposure to outdoor weather.

An experiment in southern Mexico used local materials and labor, where no electricity for power tools was available. Effective cookers were made as shown in Plate 4 and their acceptance tested in a small village.[13]

The shell for this type of solar cooker is made with plastic on a hoop laid over a parabolic concrete mound. It is lined with a mosaic of 1-inch mirrors. The adjustable U-frame made of water pipe rotates around a pipe driven into the ground, and the reflecting shell is suspended from the horizontal pipe which supports the small circular grill for holding the cooking vessel. The frame is rotated, and the reflecting collector is tilted to bring the shadow of the kettle to the center of the collector by pulling a chain which can be caught over a protruding bolt in the frame.

For the parabolic mound (see Plate 5), on which an indefinite number of plastic shells can be made, a parabolic edge is sawed in a piece of plywood with a keyhole saw and rotated around a vertical pipe driven into the ground. The parabola is drawn with a square, as illustrated in Figure 18. A straight line is drawn on the plywood and below it a nail is inserted at the desired position of the focus (18 inches). The square is then rotated by small degrees around the nail sliding past it so that the corner of the square is always just touching the straight line. A pencil line is drawn along the edge of the square in each position. At first these lines nearly coincide with the original straight line but as the corner of the square is moved out the lines make increasingly sharper angles with the original straight line. This collection of many straight lines gives a figure with a true parabolic edge, as shown. A reflector diameter of 4 ft is convenient, requiring a rotating parabola a little longer than 2 ft.

It is difficult to get a perfectly smooth edge with the hand saw. Accordingly, a ⅜-inch copper tube is attached

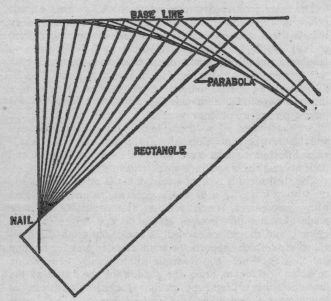

18. Method for drawing a parabola.

along the edge of the plywood with a series of nails. To the top of the plywood shaping tool are attached two protruding strips of wood, one on each side, for straddling the vertical pipe. A wooden plug is inserted between the ends of the two strips to give a square hole. The shaping tool is then mounted by slipping the hole over the pipe so that the whole plywood board can be easily rotated around the vertical pipe.

A shallow circular platform of concrete is laid on the

ground around the vertical pipe and smoothed and leveled with a hand level. This gives a flat track on which the lower end of the parabolic board rotates. A mound of wet sand is packed down on the concrete platform around the pipe and rounded off smoothly with the rotating edge to make a parabolic mound. A smooth piece of metal is nailed to a wood block attached to the bottom of the outer rim of the rotating plywood to raise the parabolic edge about ¾ inch. The center of the shaping tool is then raised until the top is exactly level, and it is kept in this position by winding a bulge of string around the pipe at the proper height.

A thorough mixture of three parts sand and one part Portland cement with water is then laid over the sand mound like frosting on a cake and the parabolic tool rotated carefully to give a smooth parabolic mound. The consistency of the cement must be just right, without too much water, so the copper tube will give a smooth surface. The cement layer on the sand mound must be high enough to be in contact everywhere with the rotating parabolic copper tube. After setting for a day the surface of the mound is still rough because of the sand, but it is smoothed with liquid plastic available from the manufacturer, from large mail-order companies, or from suppliers of motorboat building materials. A thick coat, mixed with an accelerator so it will harden in a few hours, is painted on with a brush. After setting over night the plastic surface is rubbed with steel wool to give a smooth surface. It is then rubbed vigorously with a "separation wax" so it can be used as a convex master mold to make plastic concave shells. Butcher's wax or other floor or automobile-body wax is suitable if thoroughly rubbed in to give a smooth shining surface.

Then the waxed mold is painted with liquid plastic and covered smoothly with a circular disc of cloth or preferably fiberglass cloth. A hoop of thin-walled conduit tubing, made with a pipe bender, is placed around the circumference of the mound and the plastic-coated cloth is tucked in. Reinforcement strips of cloth are added to the cloth shell. After hardening for a day the shell is pried off the parabolic mound.

The inside of the plastic shell is smoothed and covered with fresh liquid plastic, a narrow strip at a time. Several hundred square glass mirrors, rubbed with wax on the glass fronts, are quickly and carefully laid in the plastic covering to make a close-packed mosaic which sets within a few hours. Surplus plastic that oozes up in cracks between the small mirrors can be scraped off the waxed surface with a sharp knife. The mosaic mirror is then cleaned completely by rubbing it with medium steel wool and washing with a detergent.

Using another technique, strips of aluminized plastic 3 inches wide are placed over the parabolic mound with overlapping edges, like shingles. The aluminized surface is up, and the plastic surface is made to cling to the mold by painting it with glycerine. The strips are covered with a layer of plastic and later with the cloth and plastic shell.

The reflecting parabolic shell is arranged to hang about 10 inches below the central grill by means of two wooden or metal strips bolted to the hoop (see Plate 4). The crossbar holding the central circular grill is put through holes in the ends of the strips and set into vertical slots at the top of each arm of the U-frame. The grill and supporting crosspiece is made of conduit tubing with a flattened semicircular bend in the middle, which is bolted to another semicircular section to give an 8-inch ring. Round-bottomed clay or metal vessels are set into this ring at the focus of the light. A coarse wire screen is set into the ring when smaller or flatbottomed vessels are used. Suggestions for collectors and cooking vessels are given by Jenness,[14] and Stam[15] discusses certain aspects of solar cooking.

An evaluation of solar cookers has been carried out by the Volunteers for International Technical Assistance, Inc.[16] Twelve different solar cookers are described and illustrated with photographs. Appropriate weights, sizes, and costs are given when available. Of these twelve cookers four are rated very good, including the Wisconsin cooker and the Telkes oven. A solar cooker of the Fresnel type, developed by the Volunteers for International Technical Assistance, Inc., consists of a set of annular rings of Masonite, covered with aluminized plastic or aluminum, each ring slanting to focus on the bottom of a cooking vessel. Detailed directions for construction are given.[16]

HEAT STORAGE

Solar cooking might be greatly advanced if it were possible to place a heat-absorbing unit on the solar cooker for any two or three sunny hours of the day and then carry it into the kitchen and keep it in an insulated box to be used later.

The problem of developing such a heat storage device has not yet been solved. The vessel must have sufficient heat storage (Chapter 8) in a volume small enough not to shadow an appreciable part of the solar collector and a weight small enough to be supported on the grill and easily lifted and carried. Its insulation must be sufficient to prevent serious loss of heat during exposure to the focused sunlight, but after enough heat has been accumulated it can be set in a fully insulated box or corner of the floor so the heat losses after removal from the cooker will be small. Finally, it must be capable of storing heat equivalent to 1 kwhr of heat or more at a temperature high enough to permit effective cooking later. It is desirable to be able to regulate the rate of heat available for cooking with such stored heat.

These requirements are not easy to meet. A well-insulated cylinder of iron or aluminum is a possibility. A liter of iron weighing 16.7 lb (7.6 kg) has a heat capacity of 912 cal $°C^{-1}$. A liter of aluminum weighing 5.9 lb (2.7 kg) has a heat capacity of 648 cal $°C^{-1}$. A pebble bed of ceramic or glass spheres 1 liter in volume and with a void space of ⅓ weighs 3.3 lb (or 1.5 kg) and has a heat capacity of 300 cal $°C^{-1}$. If the focusing of the collector is accurate enough to permit only a small hole in the bottom of the heat collector to admit the focused solar radiation and the insulation is sufficient to keep the heat losses low it might be possible to reach temperatures of perhaps 400° C. If effective cooking continued until the temperature of the heat storage unit fell to 100° C it would be possible to store 273.0 kcal or 0.32 kwhr in the liter of iron, 194.4 kcal or 0.22 kwhr in the aluminum, and 90.0 kcal or 0.104 kwhr in the ceramic pebbles. A 2-liter volume of aluminum or a 5-liter pebble bed could store nearly ½ kwhr of heat and cook for 1 hr at a ½-kwhr rate. Allowing for heat losses and for the rise from room temperature to 100° C it would require more than 1 hr of exposure to solar heat on the solar cooker to store this ½ kwhr of heat.

The heat storage per weight of material can be increased five- to sixfold by using the heat of fusion of a high-melting chemical compound as well as the heat capacity of the material. Anhydrous sulfates and alkali hydroxides are examples of suitable materials if corrosion of the container can be avoided. Other aspects of heat storage will be discussed in Chapter 8.

REFERENCES

1. Löf, G. O. G., The Use of Solar Energy for Cooking, in *United Nations Conf. on New Sources of Energy*, 35 Gr–S16, Rome, 1961. Also *Solar Energy, 7:* 125–33. 1963.

2. Ghai, M. L., Applications of Solar Energy for Heating, Air Conditioning, and Cooking, in *Solar Energy Research,* ed. F. Daniels and J. A. Duffie, Madison, University of Wisconsin Press, 1955.

3. Duffie, J. A., Reflective Solar Cooker Designs, in *Trans. of the Conf. on Use of Solar Energy: The Scientific Basis, 3* (2): 79. Tucson, University of Arizona Press, 1958.

4. Duffie, J. A., Lappala, R. P., and Löf, G. O. G., Plastics for focussing collectors, *Solar Energy, 1* (4): 79. 1957.

5. Duffie, J. A., Löf, G. O. G., and Beck, B., Laboratory and Field Studies of Plastic Reflector Solar Cookers, in *U.N. Conf. on New Sources of Energy,* E 35–S87, Rome, 1961.

6. Löf, G. O. G., and Fester, D., Design and Performance of Folding Umbrella-Type Solar Cooker, in *U.N. Conf. on New Sources of Energy,* E 35–S100, Rome, 1961.

7. Telkes, M., Solar Stoves, in *Trans. Conf. Use of Solar Energy: The Scientific Basis, 3* (2): 87. 1958.

8. Telkes, M., Solar cooking ovens, *Solar Energy, 3:* 1–11. 1959.

9. Telkes, M., and Andrassy, S., Practical Solar Cooking Ovens, in *U.N. Conf. on New Sources of Energy,* E 35–S101, Rome, 1961.

10. Abou-Hussein, M. S. M., Temperature-Decay Curves in the Box Type Solar Cooker, in *U.N. Conf. on New Sources of Energy,* E 35–S75, Rome, 1961.

11. Prata, A. S., A Cylindro-Parabolic Cooker, in *U.N. Conf. on New Sources of Energy,* E 35–S110, Rome, 1961.

12. Nutrition Division, F.A.O., Report on Tests Conducted Using the Telkes Oven and the Wisconsin Solar Stove, in *U.N. Conf. on New Sources of Energy,* E 35–S116, Rome, 1961.

13. Forthcoming publication.

14. Jenness, J. R., Recommendations and suggested techniques for the manufacture of inexpensive solar cookers, *Solar Energy, 4:* 22–24. 1960.

15. Stam, H., cheap but practical solar kitchens, *U.N. Conf. on New Sources of Energy,* E 35–S24, Rome, 1961.

16. VITA Report 10, *Evaluation of Solar Cookers,* Publications and Technical Services Branch, U.S. Department of State 0–17, Washington, D.C. and Volunteers for International Technical Assistance, Inc., Schenectady, N.Y.

CHAPTER 6

Heating Water

The heating of water is another simple application of solar energy and up to the present time about the only commercially successful direct application. Solar water heaters have been used for several decades, and there are probably half a million in the world today. Their use is increasing rapidly in Japan and Israel and elsewhere; in California and Florida the domestic use is decreasing as natural gas and cheap petroleum are becoming more readily available, but the use for heating swimming pools is increasing.

Solar water heaters have been made for many years in many countries. A basic study of flat-plate collectors for heating water was made by Hottel and Woertz[1] in 1942. A comprehensive account of solar water heaters including over fifty figures and diagrams was published in 1953 by Petukhov.[2] Factors involved in the solar heating of water were discussed by Morse[3] and Masson[4] in 1955.

The literature on solar water heating is extensive, as shown by the 191 references to it in the bibliography published in 1959 by the Association for Applied Solar Energy.[5]

An excellent review of the present development of solar water heating was given in 1961 at the United Nations Conference on New Sources of Energy in Rome. It is well summarized by Hisada and Oshida,[6] who compare the costs of the several heaters described. Considerable progress was reported; for example, inexpensive plastic solar water heaters are being sold in Japan at the rate of 60,000 per year and in Israel a company is exporting to 25 countries a well-tested unit costing $250 to $400.

There seems to be good agreement in the estimates of many different authors. For general domestic use of hot water for bathing and washing dishes a temperature of 135° F (57° C) is considered adequate and 20 gal per person per day is a reasonable consumption. In many sunny climates these requirements can be met with an insulated storage tank and a solar radiation absorber which has an area of about 0.75 ft^2 gal^{-1} of hot water. A family of four would need

a tank of 80 gal and a solar absorber of about 60 ft². Since
the requirement of a temperature below 140° F or 60° C can
be easily met with flat stationary collectors, for domestic solar
water heating there is no need to use the more expensive
focusing collectors.

A considerable variety of solar water heaters has been
developed, varying according to relative emphasis on convenience, reliability, and low cost. Most users accept the
fact that auxiliary heaters operated by electricity or by combustion fuel are necessary for cloudy weather, and several
authors believe that for economic success the savings in electricity or fuel for standard water heaters should be sufficient
within three years to pay for the higher cost of the solar
heater. In several parts of the world this condition can apparently be met. The cost of plumbing and of a storage tank
is only slightly greater for the solar-heating units than for
the fuel-heating units, but the large solar collector is expensive. There are two other important handicaps of solar water
heaters—the architectural problem of the solar collector and
storage tank, and the danger of freezing water and damaging
pipes where frost is possible.

TYPES OF SOLAR WATER HEATERS

All solar water heaters involve a large, black, flat area
that receives the solar radiation and heats the water. There
are many different ways in which the solar heat is transferred
to the water, and several ingenious methods of construction
have been developed.

The simplest water heater is a horizontal black tray of
water or a long coil or black garden hose set in the sunshine.
As soon as the water tray heats up, however, it loses heat
by evaporation of water, by radiation in the long infrared,
by convection to the surrounding air, and by conduction to
the materials of which the collector is constructed. Solar
water heaters are accordingly provided with glass or plastic
covers to reduce re-radiation and the convection of heat to
a moving stream of air. The cover is transparent to the sunlight but opaque to the long infrared radiation emitted by
the hot water, thus trapping the heat. To reduce heat losses
by conduction and convection, the absorbing unit may be
placed in an insulated box.

To take advantage of the fact that the solar radiation
intensity is greater when the receiving surface is more nearly

perpendicular to the sun's rays, the absorber is usually faced toward the equator and tilted. It is too difficult and expensive to keep adjusting the angle of the absorber with the daily and seasonal changes of the sun. If the receiving surface is tilted at an angle corresponding to the latitude of the geographical location the absorbers are at their optimum position at noon at the equinoxes in March and September. Because more heat is needed in winter than in summer and the sun is then lower in the sky, more favorable yearly behavior is obtained by setting the angle of inclination at about 10° greater than the angle of the latitude. At latitude 30° N, for example, the receiving surface of the absorber would be faced south and tilted at an angle of 40° with the horizontal.

The large surface required for solar heating is also effective in losing heat to the surroundings, so it is customary to transfer the heated water to a large, well-insulated storage tank, particularly if overnight storage is required. The tank has a much smaller ratio of surface to volume, its whole surface can be insulated, and the heavy weight of water can be more easily supported. The circulation between solar absorber and storage tank is usually effected by thermal gradients, the hot water being less dense and rising to the tank at a higher level. Where thermal circulation is not convenient or the storage tank cannot be placed at a higher level, a pump is used to give forced circulation, if electricity is available.

The thermal efficiency of solar water heaters is usually very good even with simple construction. Although the area for losing heat is large the temperature elevation is comparatively small. It is easily possible to transfer half the sun's radiant heat into the water system and efficiencies of 70 per cent and over have been reported on a short-time basis. The efficiencies are higher, of course, with short storage times and rapid flow rates giving low exit temperatures. In order to produce temperatures above 140° F (60° C), the rate of flow must be decreased and a lower efficiency accepted.

Solar water heaters of different kinds are shown in Figures 19–28 and the construction and their performance are described in the following paragraphs.

One of the simplest types (see Fig. 19) extensively used in rural Japan,[7] is a wooden tray 3 ft (0.9 m) by 6 ft (2 m) lined with a sheet of thick black polyvinyl plastic set into

the box and overlapped at the corners. An inlet and an outlet
tube are supplied, and the box is furnished with a hinged
cover containing a glass plate. A double glass cover reduces
the condensation of moisture droplets which scatter the incoming sunlight. The tray is filled to a depth of 4 inches
(10 cm) and holds 45 gal (180 liters). The cost in Japan
is about $20, and the temperature attainable is about 55° C
in summer and 27° to 35° C in winter.

In another type an arched canopy of transparent plastic
instead of the flat glass plates is placed over the tray and
presumably the condensed droplets of moisture run down at
the side.

A shallow metal tray may be tilted to obtain a more
favorable angle of solar radiation (see Fig. 20). A black
sheet metal cover[8] is soldered to the tray and reinforced so
the tank will hold the water when tilted. The tray is packed
in insulation and set into a wooden box which has a glass
window. The box is set on three legs so it can be tilted at
different angles with the season. The heating tank holds a
little over 1 gal ft^{-2} (40.8 liters m^{-2}) of exposed area.

The least expensive solar water heater (see Fig. 21) is
made of black polyvinyl plastic sealed in the form of a
water pillow.[7] It is placed on a level wooden platform in the
yard or attached to a roof facing south. The standard size is
36 inches (90 cm) by 71 inches (180 cm) and 4.7 inches
(12 cm) thick with a capacity of 50 gal (190 liters) of water.
It sells in Japan for about $10 and has a life of about two
years. A transparent canopy cover (see Fig. 22) is necessary
in winter to furnish sufficiently hot water.

Heaters made of pipes which can be attached directly to
a water system with its hydraulic pressure and tilted to obtain
higher solar efficiency have been most widely used. A series
of parallel tubes, nearly touching, is inclined toward the
equator, and the ends of the tubes are soldered or screwed
into horizontal header pipes, the lower one for admitting
cold water and the upper one for discharging heated water
(see Fig. 23). The parallel pipes are inefficient because the
solar radiation falling between them is wasted. In a more
common arrangement the water-carrying tubes of iron or
copper are soldered to the back of a blackened sheet of
copper. The good metallic conduction of the sheet makes
less tubing necessary. This metallic sheet with the attached
tubes is placed in a tilted, fully insulated box and covered
with one or two glass plates. In a variation, the parallel tubes

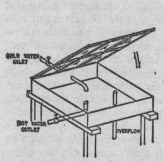

19. Water-heating tray with glass cover.

20. Tilted water-heating tray with glass cover.

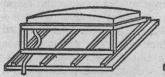

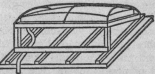

21. Plastic pillow water heater.

22. Plastic pillow water heater with plastic canopy.

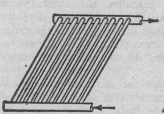

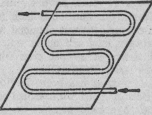

23. Parallel pipes for heating water.

24. Black metal receiver with water-heating pipe soldered to back.

are replaced with a single tube of copper bent back and forth and soldered to the copper collecting plate (see Fig. 24), simplifying the connections at the ends of the tubes.

An inexpensive construction for the parallel channels[9] (see Fig. 25) uses a sheet of standard corrugated galvanized iron roofing which is riveted to a sheet of galvanized iron and soldered at the edges. The absorber is placed in an inclined wooden box with a glass cover and 4 inches of rock wool insulation. A modification of the corrugated sheeting, in which pipes carrying the water are inserted inside the channels and connected at their ends with flexible rubber hose to the connecting pipes, has been used for large shower bath installations but the conductivity from the corrugated metal to the pipes is poor.[2]

Andrassy described[10] a clever arrangement in which thin sheet metal was corrugated with nearly closed circular channels into which an oversized plastic tube was squeezed to give tight thermal contact. The flexible tube was threaded back and forth in the parallel grooves (see Fig. 26), and the difficult problem of end connections was solved by bending the tube at the ends of the grooves to give semicircular loops. The plastic tubing was made more heat conducting by impregnating it with copper powder. The units of corrugated sheet aluminum 0.019 inch thick were 2 ft (60 cm) wide and 10 ft (300 cm) long with nine grooves containing 100 ft of plastic tubing. The labor of installation is inexpensive, and the total cost is estimated at 35¢ ft^{-2} as against $1.25 ft^{-2} estimated for a copper sheet with soldered copper tubing. This type has the advantage that the plastic tubes are not damaged by freezing. The sheets were placed on 2 inches (5 cm) of fiberglass insulation and covered with clear Mylar film 0.005 inch (0.012 cm) thick. An efficiency of 58 per cent was obtained when the temperature difference between inlet and outlet water was 60° F (33° C), and an efficiency of 37 per cent when the temperature difference was 100° F (55° C).

A process has been developed for manufacturing double sheets of metal with welded seams which are later expanded with hydraulic pressure to give "tube in sheet" for solar absorbers (see Fig. 27).[11] This material has excellent heat-transfer properties and mechanical strength and is produced with little labor, but the connections at the ends of the tubes are troublesome.

The last five solar water heaters described require an in-

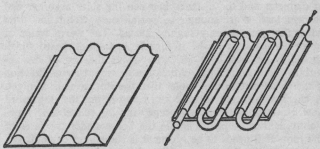

25. Water heater with corrugated iron soldered to sheet metal plate.

26. Corrugated iron soldered to metal sheet enclosing tight-fitting plastic tube.

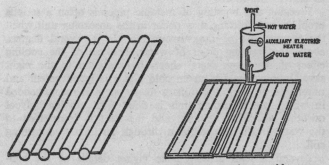

27. Tube-in-sheet water heater formed with hydraulic pressure.

28. Solar water heater with storage tank.

sulated tank for storing the heated water, and the circulation is usually accomplished thermally without a pump and electric motor (see Fig. 28). The pipes should be large enough in diameter and the distance between the solar absorber and storage tank short enough to permit easy circulation even when the water is only slightly heated. The warm water of lower density rises to the storage tank, the bottom of which should be at least 2 ft (60 cm) above the top of the absorbing unit to prevent circulation in the wrong direction if the absorber becomes cooler than the storage tank at night. A check valve may be introduced to prevent the downward flow of warm water. If a storage tank is architecturally unsightly, it may be placed inside the house under the peak of the roof. If it needs to be higher it is sometimes camouflaged with an artificial chimney. The absorber is placed to face the equator at an angle and is located on a flat roof, on a sloping roof, or on a framework protruding from a southern wall (in the northern hemisphere). It can be placed on the ground or on a framework on the ground. Economies are possible when the solar water heating is built into a new house in such a way that the absorbing unit functions also as part of the roof.

Freezing and bursting of metallic pipes is often a serious problem, and freezing may occur in the absorbing unit when the temperature of the surrounding air is several degrees above the freezing point of water, because of the cooling effect of the black metal sheets by radiation to the night sky. Draining the system on cold nights is inconvenient and unreliable. In some locations a dual system is recommended in which the absorbing unit is filled with ethylene glycol or other antifreeze solution and the heat is transferred to the water in the storage tank through an immersed heating coil.

Several articles are available giving details of the construction of solar water heaters.[12,13] Summaries of principles and practice were given at the Rome conference[14,15] in 1961, and experience with solar water heaters in multiple-story apartment houses in Morocco has been reported.[16] Manufacture and exportation of a reliable heater of the type shown in Figure 24 has been described.[17]

Using putty or calking compounds to hold the cover glass has been reported to be unsatisfactory because of deterioration after a few years of exposure to the weather. Better results are obtained by laying the glass plates on edges lined with felt or soft plastic, leaving opportunity for some movement while preventing the flow of air. New transparent plastics such as weatherable Mylar, Tedlar, and Aclar are now available, cheaper and lighter in weight than glass and easy to install, and able to withstand several years of exposure to weather and sunshine. They are as effective as glass in reducing heat losses by wind and convection, but they are much thinner than glass and are less opaque to the far infrared and therefore less effective in reducing heat losses through radiation. The use of plastic coverings instead of glass for heat traps will probably increase in the future.

In most climates auxiliary heating is necessary; the cheapest and most convenient installation is an immersion 2 kw electric heater placed in the storage tank (see Fig. 28) and arranged by a thermostat to heat the water whenever the temperature falls below a specified level such as 135° F (57° C). In another system an electrical switch is automatically operated when the sun does not shine.[18] These electrical auxiliaries may lead to heavy peak loads in bad weather and cause difficulties for the public utility services. Electrical heating of water is expensive, and a second heating unit fired with natural gas, butane, or petroleum might be connected with the hot-water storage tank. The capital cost of the dual heater system is greater.

Swimming pools are becoming more popular. In 1960 there were over 300,000 in use and they are increasing in the United States at the rate of 15,000 a year. Their requirements for heated water are so large that attention is being turned toward solar heating. Conventional solar water heaters for household use as just described are not large enough to supply the necessary heat unless several are used together, with a resulting large capital investment. The pool has a large surface and is normally heated somewhat by the sun. Another approach to increased solar heating is to pump the water to a level slightly above the pool and let it flow over outside areas of black absorbing material.

Heat losses from a pool are materially reduced by rolling a polyethylene cover over the pool when it is not in use, as done by Löf.[19] Czarnecki[20] describes a thermal cover of inflated plastic bags. A thin film of cetyl alcohol or other material which spreads over the surface in a unimolecular layer retards the rate of evaporation from the surface.[21]

La Mer[22] has carried out a comprehensive research on the suppression of evaporation by unimolecular surface layers.

Yellott[28] has planned to heat a swimming pool by pumping the water in a thin film between a black flat surface and an overlying sheet of clear plastic retained in position by the surface tension of the water. He reports effective, inexpensive solar heating with a temperature rise of about 7° F.

Andrassy has heated a swimming pool in Princeton, New Jersey, with the plastic tube in special corrugated blackened aluminum sheets, and extended the number of days on which the water temperature was above 70° F (21° C) from a normal 50 days during the summer to a total of 152 days.[10]

SIMPLE SOLAR WATER HEATER

Several of the solar water heaters already described are designed for domestic use in houses of reasonably high economic value where reliability and convenience are as important as cost. A study was made[24] in a village where there is no electricity and firewood is expensive, to ascertain whether it would be advisable to install a solar water heater at the village well and have the people carry hot water in pails to their homes for washing. The conclusion was that such a program would be acceptable only if the capital investment was extremely low. A ground-level, plastic solar water heater was designed to meet this requirement and tested on a sand beach in Wisconsin.[25]

To keep the cost of materials low, structural framework was eliminated and inexpensive plastic sheeting was laid on the ground. The length of life of the unit is short (and not yet determined), but the cost of materials and labor is so low that it could be replaced annually if necessary. Hand operation is required for filling the heater with cold water and removing the hot water, and no storage tank is included, so the schedule for use of the hot water must be adjusted to the sun through the late morning and afternoon. Other uses for a heater of this type may be developed for isolated summer cabins.

This inexpensive water heater is illustrated in Figure 29. A wooden rectangular frame of rough boards 4 inches wide and 1 inch thick is laid on level ground. The inside of the frame is 6 ft long and 4 ft wide. The earth within this frame is dug out slightly and the bottom carefully leveled. Fiberglass insulation laid on the ground increases the efficiency but costs about 7¢ ft.$^{-2}$ If labor is cheap, concrete may be economically substituted for the wooden frame.

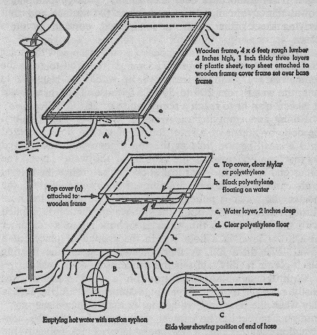

Wooden frame, 4 x 6 feet; rough lumber 4 inches high, 1 inch thick; three layers of plastic sheet, top sheet attached to wooden frame; cover frame set over base frame

Top cover (a) attached to wooden frame

a. Top cover, clear Mylar or polyethylene

b. Black polyethylene floating on water

c. Water layer, 2 inches deep

d. Clear polyethylene floor

Emptying hot water with suction syphon

Side view showing position of end of hose

29. Inexpensive solar water heater. A. Filling with cold water. B. Emptying hot water with suction syphon. C. Side view, showing position of end of hose.

Mylar or other plastic film is fitted into this rectangular wooden frame to form a tray for holding water, and a black plastic sheet is draped over it to float on a layer of water about 2 inches deep. The edges of the plastic sheets are nailed to the top of the frame by means of thin strips of wood. Black polyethylene floating on the water transmits its absorbed heat to the water effectively, whereas a transparent plastic leads to the reflection of light from a layer of air bubbles which collects under it.

A second light wooden frame slightly larger than the first frame, with a stretched film of weatherable Mylar or Tedlar, is set over it to act as a heat trap and give higher temperatures. The second, floating film is designed to keep water vapor from condensing on the upper cover and scattering the light. If some moisture does accidentally collect on the upper cover, the cover can be removed for a few minutes to permit evaporation of the water, and replaced when it becomes clear.

If the layer of water is 2 inches (5 cm) deep and the solar radiation is 1 cal cm^{-2} min^{-1}, 5 min is required to raise the temperature 1° and at least 2½ hr would be required to heat the water from 20° to 50° C. Because of the heat losses it takes 3 or 4 hr to reach a temperature of 50° C.

Filling and emptying the water heater (see Fig. 29) can be done by means of a short length of garden hose squeezed into a small square hole at the top of one wall and curved so that one end reaches the bottom of the water layer. The other end is tied to a vertical stick in the ground at a level high enough to prevent draining of the water. To fill the heater, the water is poured into the elevated end of the hose through a funnel. To drain the hot water, suction is applied with the mouth, and the water is siphoned into a container at a lower level in a hole dug in the ground or placed at a lower level on a hill. A thermometer lying on the floating black plastic readily registers the temperature of the water.

With this simple plastic tray on a sand beach it was easily possible to heat 5 gal of water to 50° C in half a day when the horizontal radiation was more than 1 cal cm^{-2} min^{-1}. The capital investment was about $5, and the construction required only a few hours' labor. Black polyethylene may become overheated and melt in spots during bright, hot weather; black butyl rubber is better. Shading the black polyethylene reduces the melting hazard.

BOILING WATER

Boiling water usually requires a focusing collector. One type of water boiler (see Plate 1), intended as a possible heater for the wool-dyeing industry in a village was designed to be made with a minimum of manufactured goods and no electric power tools.[25]

A parabolic curve was made as described on page 70 and four complete parabolas sawed out of plywood. The focal length was 24 inches and the length 4 ft. Four of these plywood parabolas were mounted vertically on a large horizontal piece of plywood and 26-gauge galvanized sheet iron was draped and nailed over the four parabolic ribs, giving an excellent parabolic-cylindrical shape 5 ft wide and 4 ft long. The sheet iron was then overlaid with waxed paper and draped tightly with two layers of fiberglass cloth or cotton cloth and soaked with polyester plastic. A framework of thin-walled steel tubing (electrical conduit tubing) was bent around the parabolic form with the help of a pipe bender, the curved and straight parts of the frame were bolted together and set firmly on the cloth and plastic, and the cloth was wrapped around the outer edge of the framework. When the plastic set (in two days) the plastic collector was removed and a second collector made of cloth and plastic.

The plastic shell was painted with small widths of polyester plastic, and long strips of glass mirror (4 ft long and 1 inch wide) were laid down lengthwise edge to edge. When the plastic set this device gave a focus sufficiently sharp to cover a 2-inch thin-walled steel tube (conduit tube or muffler pipe). Wide strips of lightweight Scotchcal or aluminized Aclar can be used instead of the strips of glass mirror, as described in Chapter 5.

The 12-ft-long tube was laid horizontally on two vertical reinforced pieces of two-by-four lumber about 3 ft above the ground. The two parabolic cylinders were suspended from the central pipe at the proper focus. The tube was painted with a flat black paint and placed in the east–west axis. The parabolic cylindrical mirrors were pulled up with small ropes to a partly vertical tilted position which focused sharply on the pipe. No adjustment was needed from 10 A.M. to 2 P.M. Early in the morning and late in the afternoon a slight adjustment of the length of rope was needed. The rope was easily pulled and wound around a couple of nails to hold the proper angle of tilt. The angle changes with the season of the year and the height of the sun in the sky. In early morning and late afternoon the sunlight focused beyond the end of the pipe, which decreased the efficiency of the heater. A rubber stopper and gooseneck of copper tubing admitted cold water at one end and allowed the exit of hot water or steam at the other.

This collector was 60 inches wide and focused onto a 2-inch pipe, giving a multiplication factor of 30 to 1. In bright sun the water boiled vigorously. Experiments were carried out at different rates of flow. At a rate of 3 gal hr^{-1} the water coming in at 25° C exited at over 95°. The rate of overflow was intermittent because of frequent boiling. The efficiency of heat transfer from solar radiation to hot water at 95° C was about 40 per cent.

There should be opportunities in sunny locations for considerable saving of fuel in chemical and industrial operations where expensive fuel is now used for heating or boiling water. Another large-scale use of solar-heated hot water might be in the removal of permafrost in the arctic and subarctic regions. A limited amount of water could be circulated into the frozen ground and reheated continuously by solar collectors.

The use of hot or boiling water or other heated liquids for solar refrigeration and air conditioning will be discussed in Chapter 13.

REFERENCES

1. Hottel, H. C., and Woertz, B. B., The performance of flat-plate collectors, *Trans. Amer. Soc. Mech. Eng., 64:* 91–104. 1942.

2. Petukhov, B. V., *Solar Water Heating Installations.* 42 pp. Moscow, U.S.S.R. Academy Sciences, 1953.

3. Morse, R. N., Solar Water Heaters, in *Proceedings, World Symposium on Applied Solar Energy,* pp. 191–200. Menlo Park, Calif., Stanford Research Institute, 1956.

4. Masson, H., Les Insolateurs à Bas Potential, in *Transactions of the Conference on the Use of Solar Energy: The Scientific Basis, 3* (2): 47–66. Tucson, University of Arizona Press, 1958.

5. *A Directory of World Activities and Bibliography of Significant Literature,* 2d ed., Phoenix, Ariz., Association for Applied Solar Energy, 1959.

6. Hisada, T., and Oshida, I., Use of Solar Energy for Water Heating, in *United Nations Conference on New Sources of Energy,* E 35 Gr–S13, Rome, 1961.

7. Tanishita, I., Recent Development of Solar Water Heaters in Japan, ibid., E 35–S68.

8. Savornin, J., Study of Solar Water Heating in Algiers, ibid., E 35–S72.

9. Mathur, K. N., and Khanna, M. L., Solar Water Heaters, ibid., E 35–S102.

10. Andrassy, S., Solar Water Heaters, ibid., E 35–S96.

11. Revere Copper and Brass Co., Bridgeport, Conn.

12. Brooks, F. A., *Use of Solar Energy for Heating Water,* Publ. 3557, Washington, D.C., Smithsonian Institution, 1939.

13. Morse, R. N., *Solar Water Heaters for Domestic and Farm Use,* Commonwealth Scientific and Industrial Research Organiza-

tion, Engineering Section Report ED 5, 1957; *Installing Solar Water Heaters*, Circular 1, 1959. Melbourne, Australia.

14. Morse, R. N., Water Heating by Solar Energy, in *U.N. Conf. on New Sources of Energy*, E 35–S38, Rome, 1961.

15. Farber, E. A., The Use of Solar Energy for Heating Water, ibid., E 35–S1.

16. Geoffroy, J., *Use of Solar Energy for Water Heating*, ibid., E 35–S58.

17. Sobotka, R., Solar Water Heaters, ibid., E 35–S26, also Mir-mit News Letters, Tel-Aviv, Israel, Mir-mit Sun Heaters.

18. Robinson, N., and Neeman, E., The Solar Switch, An Automatic Device for Economizing Auxiliary Heating of Solar Water Heaters, *U.N. Conf. on New Sources of Energy*, E 35–S31, Rome, 1961.

19. Löf, G. O. G., personal communication.

20. Czarnecki, J. T., A method of heating swimming pools by solar energy, *Solar Energy, 7:* 3–7. 1963.

21. Root, D. E., Jr., Practical aspects of solar swimming pool heating, *Solar Energy, 4* (1): 23. 1960.

22. La Mer, V. K., Ed., *Retardation of Evaporation by Monolayers*, New York, Academic Press, 1962.

23. Yellott, J. I., Thin Film Water Heater, in *Solar and Aeolian Energy*, Sounion, Greece, 1961. New York, Plenum Press, 1964, pp. 112–23.

24. Silverberg, J., and Serrie, H., Unpublished report on a village in Mexico.

25. Daniels, F., Forthcoming report.

26. Daniels, F., Forthcoming report.

CHAPTER 7

Agricultural and Industrial Drying

Solar drying of hay and other crops has been practiced since the beginning of agriculture. It is one of the largest direct uses of solar heat. The removal of moisture requires only low-temperature heating, which can be readily supplied by solar radiation. In view of the increased interest in applications of solar energy and the development of plastics and other new materials, perhaps greater use can be made of the sun to hasten agricultural drying, reduce spoilage, and improve quality of product. A beginning has been made in the scientific study of these possibilities. The latest summary of solar drying has been prepared by Löf,[1] covering the four papers on the subject presented at the United Nations Conference on New Sources of Energy in Rome in 1961.

There are many variables involved in the drying process, but the mechanisms are becoming better understood, and a few engineering and economic studies have been made for the drying of special materials. Much greater research efforts in this area appear to be justified. As a rule the products to be dried are so cheap and the labor involved in handling the bulky material is so great that an extra expense for elaborate solar equipment cannot be tolerated. Greater speed of drying in units of limited capacity, or improved quality of material, however, may often justify the extra expense of special solar drying equipment. The quality of a food product may be improved by keeping out dirt and by reducing the time of heating, which might lead, for example, to less loss of vitamin C through oxidation and to less production of materials with objectionable flavors.

Solar drying may be done directly by exposing the solid material to the sun's radiation with or without a transparent cover. It may be accomplished also indirectly by solar heating a stream of air to produce a lower relative humidity. The less humid air removes the water that evaporates from the solid material over which the air is passing. The material to be dried can therefore be placed in deep layers covering a smaller area, and the heat required to evaporate the moisture can be obtained from the heated air. Inasmuch as the heat capacity of air is low, it is necessary to use large volumes of air and to force the air through by electrically driven fans or possibly by the solar heating of tall thermal chimneys. This indirect method of heating agricultural products has an advantage in preventing overheating in local areas and can be used to save fuel in installations where artificially heated air is already being used for drying.

The mechanism of drying solids involves several steps, each of which, under certain conditions, may be rate-determining. The surface of the solid is so heated by direct radiation or a stream of hot air as to increase the vapor pressure of the water and accelerate its escape into the surrounding stream of air. More water diffuses to the surface from lower levels of the material, and heat flows to the interior from the surface of the material. The more porous the material the quicker the flow of moisture and the slower the flow of heat. The heat requirement is about 590 cal g^{-1}

of water evaporated (1,050 BTU lb^{-1} of water). A steady rate of water evaporation is reached when the heat required for evaporation and the heat losses are equal to the total heat absorbed. In direct heating the solar radiation may penetrate slightly below the surface and produce heat. In indirect heating the circulating air may penetrate pores below the top layer and accelerate the removal of moisture. The relative importance of these factors has been studied quantitatively in a few cases, and formulas are available for calculating the transfer of heat from a solar-heated plate to a stream of air. Inasmuch as the drying is carried out at a temperature not greatly above that of the surrounding air it is unnecessary to use the more elaborate solar focusing collectors. Simple flat-plate collectors of plastic or glass are adequate. An economic study of solar drying involves the capital investment for large areas of solar collectors and the cost of operating fans to blow the air through the material to be dried. The expense of electric power for the blowers depends in turn on the dimensions of the drier and the resistance offered to the passage of the heated air by the material to be dried.

Corn, wheat, and other agricultural crops from the field contain such a high moisture content (20 per cent) that they cannot be stored without serious deterioration and loss of quality. Drying in storage is necessary to produce a satisfactory grain. Fresh hay may have up to 40 per cent moisture and if placed in barns the accelerated oxidation may raise the temperature high enough to produce spontaneous combustion leading to destructive fires. Hay crops can be dried in the fields during hot summer months, but they suffer in quality if there are continued rains. The grain crops harvested in the fall and stored in barns or sheds dry out slowly in storage in the cooler weather. To ensure proper quality, and to make possible an earlier harvest, fuel-heated or solar-heated air may be blown through the stored grain or hay.

Heating the incoming air may be accomplished by solar radiation without much additional investment if an air-circulating system is already installed. It leads to a decrease in the time of drying over that required with unheated air, or a saving in fuel if the air is artificially heated. Details of such solar heating are given by Davis and Lipper[2] and by Buelow.[3] The results of the two investigations are in good agreement. Davis and Lipper give moisture contents of different grains and a chart of relative humidities at different temperatures; references to earlier work are given and the results of solar drying are summarized.[2] They blew air into a storage shed along ducts immediately below a roof of corrugated sheet metal sloping toward the south and covered with black asphalt paint. They tried drying grains in circular bins and in triangular sheds, using solar collectors of black corrugated iron and of transparent plastic. Flat-plate collectors have been reported which evaporate the moisture with an efficiency of approximately 25 per cent. A rise of 8° C (15° F) reduces the relative humidity by 20 per cent. Transparent coverings of plastic or glass over the black absorbers increase the temperature of the airstream as much as 40° F and more than double the efficiency. Flow rates of air up to 5 ft^3 min^{-1} ft^{-2} of solar absorber were studied. A table is given for the moisture content of various agricultural crops and the minimum air flow recommended.[2]

Buelow advises[8] that to avoid spoilage grain and hay crops should be stored in air with a relative humidity of about 62 per cent, in equilibrium with the crops. The humidity of the heated air blown through the storage bin must thus be less than 62 per cent, but it should not be less than 30 per cent relative humidity. The channels in the solar heater should be large enough so there is little increase in the resistance to the flow of air. A pressure drop of less than 2.5 mm (0.1 inch) of water is satisfactory. Channels with a depth of 4 cm (1.6 inch) or more are acceptable if the channel length is not greater than 3 m or 10 ft. Ten to 15 ft^3 min^{-1} ft^{-2} of absorbing area is a satisfactory rate of flow. The black roof of metal or asphalt is needed anyway, and the duct work under it is not expensive. The drying time for a crop may be reduced as much as 50 to 75 per cent by solar heating of an air duct. The agricultural use of solar heating in the United States has been discussed further by Pelletier.[4]

The solar drying of grapes in Australia has been studied by Wilson.[5] The best results were obtained by hanging the grapes in wire baskets in long tiers under metal roofs running north and south. The grapes absorb solar energy directly, and thermocouples showed that the interior of the grapes below the surface could be heated by the penetrating, short infrared radiation up to 8° C above the temperature of the surrounding air. When the grapes are shaded the interior of the grapes may be 2° to 6° C below that of the surrounding air, because of the evaporation of the moisture from the grapes. When the grapes were placed in closed containers and air that had been heated externally by solar energy was blown through the container, drying was no more rapid than in the open tiers exposed to the direct solar radiation, and the quality was inferior. The loss in weight of water was determined by hanging the grapes from a spring suspension and adding a measured quantity of water to maintain the basket at a constant level. The results showed that the chief factor in solar drying grapes is the direct absorption of solar radiation. The use of tiers of horizontal trays for drying is advocated, particularly in regions of high latitude and low sun angle.

Because of the importance of flavor, fruits and vegetables are particularly sensitive to such drying conditions as contamination by dirt, exposure to rain, overheating, extended drying time, and growth of fungus or bacteria. The quality and value of tobacco leaves depends greatly on the temperature and speed of drying. Ordinarily the leaves are hung in sheds with slotted sides, and the desired flavor depends on the temperature and humidity and the length of the cure. Circulating heated air ensures a superior grade of tobacco in spite of unfavorable weather. Successful developments have been carried out in Puerto Rico and elsewhere with solar-heated sheds in which channels for heating the air are nailed a few inches below a black roof which faces south.[6]

Solar energy might well be applied to kiln drying lumber. When lumber is dried in the open air the frequent exposure to rain and the varying degrees of humidity subject it to different rates of drying, which extends the time required between cutting and marketing and often leads to inferior lumber. Kiln drying with the circulation of fuel-heated air is a common practice. Solar heating could reduce the cost of fuel and might be extended to small units of low capital investment. Experiments on the solar drying of wood have been carried out at the United States Forest Products Laboratory and elsewhere.[7,8] A unit with a capacity of 2,500 board feet has been built, provided with a black metal absorber and two electric fans each 18 inches in diameter, and operated by 1/3-hp motors. In earlier experiments the cost of electric power was about one third of the total drying cost. Experiments are being tried with a windmill instead of electricity for circulating the air. Thermal chimneys and inexpensive coverings of plastic for small piles of stacked lumber might be studied for possible use near forests where electric power is not available.

OTHER SOLAR DRYING

For many heating operations that require high temperatures or moving equipment the use of combustion fuel is the best approach. For such low-temperature industrial operations as the heating or evaporation of aqueous solutions, however, it is possible in sunny areas to use solar radiation at a low cost and conserve the world's supply of coal, gas, and oil.

The possibilities of drying oil shale with the sun have been carefully studied.[9] An oil shale in Brazil contains 33 per cent moisture, much of which may be removed by heating with petroleum or by burning part of the shale. Spreading the shale with heavy machinery to dry in the sun can save some of this fuel cost. The increased value of the shale was found to be about three times the cost of the solar drying. The efficiency of the solar drying ranged from 45 per cent at first, when the surface was moist and black, to about 18 per cent when the moisture had been driven out of the upper layers which became less dark, and the migration of moisture to the surface had to follow a longer path. Thick beds lost less heat to the underlying ground and showed a higher efficiency of drying, but they required a longer time for evaporating a given amount of water. It was found that most of the loss of heat was by convection to the surrounding air.

Duffie and Talwalkar have carried out a comprehensive study[10] of all the factors involved in the drying of a bed of solid particles by surface radiation.

Sun drying peat has been carried on for centuries.

The evaporation of ocean water to get salt is one of the oldest chemical industries; when salt crystallizes, much of the sunlight is reflected out of the solution, and experiments have used a colored dye to increase the absorption of light.[11]

The recovery of sodium nitrate in northern Chile by the solution of Chile saltpeter and solar evaporation of the water is a large-scale industry.

GENERAL CONSIDERATIONS

In the flat-plate collectors for heating air for drying or other purposes, the transfer of heat from the black absorbing plates to the stream of air passing over them is one of the most important factors. When the flow of air is rapid this heat transfer may be the limiting factor to determine the efficiency of the operation. Shoemaker[12] has devised an effective, low-cost structure for large absorbing surface area and high heat transfer with minimum resistance to airflow. Thin sheets of aluminum, 2 mils (0.005 cm) thick, are painted black and provided with a large number of short, machine-cut slots. The sheets are then stretched laterally and the slits open to give an expanded honeycomb structure with slightly raised edges. Such a sheet absorbs about one third of the incident light. Seven layers absorb 90 per cent, and the cost of material is about 15¢ ft^{-2}. Several of these sheets are laid on top of each other and squeezed into a long inclined trough, painted black, with a glass cover. Most of the heat is generated within the blackened sheet-aluminum layers; the walls of the duct are cooler and the heat loss is reduced. A temperature rise of 20° C (37° F) was obtained in the unpacked duct and 50° C (90° F) in the packed duct when the airflow was 3 ft^3 (84 liters) ft^{-2} (0.093 m^{-2}) min^{-1} in bright sunlight. With an airflow of 4 ft^3 (112 liters) min^{-1}, the heat collected in the airstream was twice as much with the packed collector as with the unpacked collector.

These solar collectors of blackened aluminum foil with expanded slits have been studied in detail by Chiou, El-Wakil, and Duffie.[13]

The use of solar-heated air is severely handicapped when electrical power is not available for operating a blower. Falling weights and hand-operated clock mechanisms are possible but they operate for only a short time before they must be reset and the human labor involved is large. An inefficient 1/60 kw fan supplies an airstream of 30 ft^3 (850 liters) min^{-1} in open air operating without a pressure head. The generation of 1/60 kw by a falling weight would require 200 lb (90 kg) falling through 3½ ft (1.07 m) every minute, which is not a practical manual operation.

Windmills are effective in some areas if there are frequent winds with a velocity of 10 miles an hour or more. Wind funnels are also possible and a 4-mile (6.4 km) per hour wind with a velocity of 350 ft (107 m) per minute corresponds theoretically to a calculated airflow of 35 ft^3 (990 liters) min^{-1} through a duct with a cross section 1 ft (30.5 cm) by 1.2 inches (3 cm), assuming no frictional losses. A funnel with a large area facing the wind and a small area at its back could provide a higher velocity of air flow through the small duct.

Thermal chimneys are possible, but they must be tall to obtain sufficient difference in air pressure and large in cross section to prevent an undue resistance to the flow of air. The difference in density of the heated air inside and the cooler air outside creates an upward movement of the enclosed air. Research is needed before good calculations can be made on the flow of air generated in thermal chimneys of specified dimensions.

In one possible type of chimney, a tall rectangular box of transparent plastic, open at the top and bottom, is heated throughout its length by solar radiation. The chimney may be attached to a vertical wooden frame or it may be stretched over a frame laid against a steep south-facing structure or placed on a steep hill. The front of the chimney may be made of transparent Tedlar, Aclar, or Weatherable Mylar, and a black, absorbing sheet of polyethylene or metal may be run along the center of the chimney to supply the heat. Experiments with large plastic chimneys would be interesting.

Bernard[14] has measured the rate of air flow in a small thermal chimney, consisting of a sloping box with an insulated black metal back and a glass cover. The intervening space of a few centimeters contained fine black wire gauze, but honeycomb, slit-expanded absorbers (page 95) would be better. The temperature of the air becomes progressively higher at the higher levels of the chimney and at low rates of flow can reach 100° C. Mathematical analyses are given. The rates of air flow varied from about 8 to 25 liters sec^{-1} per square meter of black absorbing area.

REFERENCES

1. Löf, G. O. G., Solar energy for the drying of solids, *Solar Energy, 6:* 122–28. 1962.

2. Davis, C. P., and Lipper, R. I., Solar Energy for Crop Drying, in *United Nations Conf. on New Sources of Energy,* E 35–S53, Rome, 1961.

3. Buelow, F. H., Drying Crops with Solar Heated Air, ibid., E 35–S17.

4. Pelletier, R. J., Solar energy: Present and forseeable uses, *Agriculture Engineering, 40:* 142–44, 151. 1959.

5. Wilson, B. W., The Role of Solar Energy in the Drying of Vine Fruits, in *U.N. Conf. on New Sources of Energy,* E 35–S4, Rome, 1961.

6. Touton, R. I., Private communication.

7. Youngs, R. L., Recommendation on wood drying, *Forest Products Journal, 9* (3): 121–24. 1959.

8. Peck, E. C., Drying lumber by solar energy, *Sun at Work,* 3d quarter: 4–6. 1962.

9. Talwalker, A. T., Duffie, J. A., and Löf, G. O. G., Solar Drying of Oil Shale, in *U.N. Conf. on New Sources of Energy,* E 35–S83, Rome, 1961.

10. Talwalkar, A. T., Ph.D. Thesis, University of Wisconsin. 1964.

11. Spiegler, K. S., Solar Evaporation of Salt Brines in Open Pans, in *Solar Energy Research,* ed. F. Daniels and J. A. Duffie, Madison, University of Wisconsin Press, 1955.

12. Shoemaker, M. J., Notes on a solar collector with unique air permeable media, *Solar Energy, 5:* 138–41. 1961.

13. Chiou, J. J., El-Wakil, M. M., and Duffie, J. A., A Slit and Expanded Aluminum Foil Solar Collector, *Solar Energy Symposium,* University of Florida, April 1964; Ph.D. Thesis, J. J. Chiou, University of Wisconsin, 1964.

14. Bernard, L., Production d'Air Chaud par le Dispositif de la Cheminée Solaire, in *Applications Thermiques de l'Energie Solaire dans le Domaine de la Recherche et de l'Industrie,* Paris, Centre de la Recherche Scientifique, pp. 641–49, 1961.

CHAPTER 8

Storage of Heat

The intermittent availability of solar radiation requires the storage of the heat for many such purposes as heating houses and producing power. Storing heat is involved also in solar cooling and in the development of heat pumps; these uses will be discussed in later chapters.

Solar heat may be stored by raising the temperature of such inert substances as water or rocks or it may be stored in such reversible chemical or physicochemical reactions as the dehydration of salt hydrates or the vaporization of water.

Many possible systems are available, but the requirements of large heat storage in small volumes at low cost are difficult to meet.

STORAGE BY HEAT CAPACITY

Water has about the highest heat capacity per kilogram or per liter or per dollar of any ordinary material, but it requires containing tanks which, in sizes large enough to hold tons of water, are expensive. A liter of water raised through 20° C will return the 20 kcal which it has absorbed, when it is cooled to its original temperature. A liter of water on freezing would give 80 kcal to its surroundings at temperatures below 0° C. The heat conductance of water is rather low, but in ordinary storage tanks water is cooled by the heat losses of the tank to the surrounding air, and the colder water sinks and the warmer water rises. Thus there is rapid circulation which transfers heat in spite of the low thermal conductance. Compartmentalized water-storage tanks arranged to reduce the circulation of water could reduce the heat losses. For practical use of heat stored in water tanks, a circulating pump and electric power are necessary. The storage system occupies a comparatively small volume, and the transfer across heat exchangers is efficient. It is of course subject to the hazard of freezing in cold climates.

Pebble beds or rock piles have many advantages for storing heat that is removed from a stream of warm air. The large surface area and the tortuous path through the bed ensures very rapid heat exchange. The conduction of heat through the pebble bed itself, with one third of its volume occupied by airspaces between the pebbles, is very low because the pebbles touch each other only in limited areas at the points of contact, and the pebbles reduce the thermal circulation of the enclosed air. The loss of heat through the containing walls to the surrounding air is thus much reduced. The heat capacity of the rocks is considerably less than that of water but the density is greater and, as a result, a cubic foot (28.3 liters) of solid rock stores about 20 BTU per degree F (9.0 kcal °C^{-1}) whereas a cubic foot of water stores 62.5 BTU per degree F (28.3 kcal °C^{-1}). A blower is necessary to send the air through the pebble bed, and resistance to airflow increases as the size of the pebbles decreases. A pile of spheres closely packed leaves about one third of the volume unoccupied as void space, and this fraction is nearly independent of the size of the spheres if they are all of the same diameter. A convenient size for storing solar heat is about 2 inches in diameter (5 cm), except for high temperatures or small heat storage units. A pebble bed in a closed container may be made most cheaply of ordinary gravel, crushed rock, or brick sifted to uniform size, thus keeping the resistance of the airflow as low as possible.

For large-scale heat storage the water tanks or pebble beds are conveniently placed underground where the heat conductivity through the earth is low (particularly if it is dry) and where the heat taken up by the surrounding earth can be recovered in part when colder air or water is passed through the heat-storage unit. In small storage units, the fraction of the heat absorbed by the ground is too large. On a very large scale the storage of hot water in subterranean caverns or abandoned mines can be considered; and the storage of either heat or cold in caves is possible when air is blown through them.

For some special cases the heat capacity of metals may be used for storing heat. The heat conductance of metals is very good. The heat capacity at constant pressure in calories per degree of a gram of a chemical element is approximately equal to the atomic weight divided into a constant 6.4. Thus copper will absorb $6.4/63.6 = 0.1$ cal, iron will absorb $6.4/55.8 = 0.11$ cal, and aluminum will absorb $6.4/27 = 0.24$ cal g^{-1} when heated $1°$ C. On the basis of weight, the heat storage of these metals is only one tenth and one fourth as much as that of water. On the basis of volume, however, the difference is much less because the densities are greater. Thus 1 liter of water stores 1 kcal of heat per degree C, copper 0.89, iron 0.87, and aluminum 0.63 kcal per degree. The cost of heat storage by metals is much greater than by water or rocks.

The problems of heat storage by raising the temperature of a chemically inert material involve the volume required, the cost, the heat transfer to and from the storage unit, and the thermal insulation. At temperatures below $100°$ C a variety of excellent insulating materials is available, with small weight and low heat capacity. A large fraction of the material is occupied by small compartmentalized air pockets. At higher temperatures light, fluffy organic material cannot be used; asbestos, glass foams or fibers, and lightweight minerals must be used. Table 4 lists some of the common materials and their thermal conductivities.

TABLE 4. Heat Conductivity, k, of Materials

cal sec^{-1} cm^{-2} (°C/cm)$^{-1}$ $\times$ 10^3

Asbestos fiber	0.27
Brick	1.5
Cork	0.13
Glass (soda)	1.8
Paper	0.3
Portland cement	0.7
Sand (dry)	0.93
Sawdust (Sp. gr. 0.19)	0.14
Water	1.4

Heat losses occur by conduction to structural materials in contact with the heat-storing substance, by convection in air particularly in windy environments, and by radiation in the infrared. All these losses dictate that the heat-storage unit have as small a surface area as possible and that it be protected with adequate insulation. It has been suggested that a large iron sphere in a well-insulated box satisfies these criteria. The loss by radiation increases as the fourth power of the absolute temperature, and at high temperatures it is by far the most important factor in heat losses. Special surfaces which reduce this radiation loss will be discussed in Chapter 12.

PHYSICAL CHEMICAL STORAGE OF HEAT

Physical changes and chemical reactions involve much greater heat effects than temperature changes of inert materials. Accordingly the heat storage vessel for reacting chemicals can be smaller in size and cheaper. Moreover the temperatures may be lower, and the cost of heat insulation is reduced. Some of the chemicals are inexpensive. The chemical reaction must be easily reversible over a range of temperatures that is not too large. As in many practical chemical operations it is not sufficient to meet the thermodynamical requirements; it is also necessary to have the kinetics of the reaction favorable so that the reaction will proceed rapidly enough. In the simplest type of chemical heat storage the formation of a solid phase is involved, and the growth of the crystalline solids may be slow. Without proper nucleation agents, the crystallization may not proceed

at all, leading to a supercooled liquid phase and the failure
to produce an exothermic crystallization process.

The salt hydrates are among the simplest types of chemical
used for heat storage; the transition at 32.3° C (90° F) of
sodium sulfate between the hydrated and the unhydrated
crystals is a good example:

$$Na_2SO_4 \cdot 10\,H_2O \;\rightleftarrows\; Na_2SO_4 + 10\,H_2O$$

When the temperature is raised above 32.3° C a concentrated
solution of the anhydrous salt is formed with the absorption
of heat; when it falls below 32.3° C the anhydrous salt re-
acts with the water and evolves heat. The heat of reaction
is about 50 cal g^{-1} of hydrated salt. Particularly after many
cycles there is a tendency to give supersaturated solutions
rather than heat-evolving crystallization; also the crystals
settle to the bottom and the stratification interferes with the
reversibility. The rate of crystallization is about 0.5 inch
(1.25 cm) hr^{-1}, which sets a limit to the rate of heat evolution. The heat transfer to and from a stream of air or water
depends on the area of the heat-transfer surface, the tur-
bulence of the fluid in passing around the heat storage unit,
and the difference in temperature.

The three heat-storage media are compared in Table 5, for
which it is assumed that the water and pebble bed units
undergo a temperature rise of 20° C (36° F). The data are
for operation near room temperature. The advantage of the
large heat storage in chemical systems is often offset by other
considerations.

In comparing costs, it is evident that water is without cost
but requires tanks which are expensive for large quantities of
water. Rocks are inexpensive. Sodium sulfate is a com-

TABLE 5. Comparison of Heat-Storage Systems

	temperature	cal g^{-1} degree^{-1}	Kcal liter^{-1}	BTU lb^{-1}	BTU ft^{-3}
Water	20° C (36° F) range	1	20	36	2,247
Pebble bed (Rocks with 1/3 voids)	20° C (36° F) range		8.0		864
$Na_2SO_4 \cdot 10\,H_2O$	32.3° C (90° F)		84.5	104	9,568

paratively inexpensive chemical, though more expensive than water and rocks, and its considerably greater heat storage permits economy of container and space.[1]

The chemical storage of heat has been discussed by Telkes,[2,3] Mathur,[4] Goldstein,[5] and Speyer.[6]

Goldstein points out[5] that at reasonably low temperatures a system at equilibrium must involve a large entropy change, ΔS, if it is to give a large heat change, ΔH. At the equilibrium temperature T_e, the free energy change ΔG is zero, and the basic thermodynamic relation is

$$\Delta G = \Delta H - T\Delta S$$

becomes

$$T_e = \frac{\Delta H}{\Delta S}$$

when

$$\Delta G = 0$$

It is necessary then to find systems with large entropy changes. He considered various physical chemical processes, fusion, eutectic mixtures, crystalline transitions, vaporization, solution, change of solubility with temperature, and chemical decompositions. He examined many common inorganic substances for heats of fusion in the range 30° to 200° C. The lowest was 9 kcal per liter, 17 were below 60 kcal, 4 were in the range 60 to 80 kcal, 3 in the range 80 to 100 kcal, and 1 (Al_2Cl_6, which is abnormal) was 140 kcal per liter. An examination of organic substances showed in general lower heats of fusion, with only 8 in the range 50 to 60 kcal per liter and none above 60 kcal. Most of the heats of transition between different crystalline forms are considerably lower than the heats of fusion, and usually the transitions are very slow.

The vaporization of a liquid involves large entropy increases, and the heats of vaporization are large; for water at its boiling point it is about 530 kcal per liter whereas the heat of fusion of ice at its melting point is 73.5 kcal per liter. The storage of the large volume of a vapor is difficult. Goldstein lists some chemical systems with large heats of reaction per liter, such as the distillation of aqueous solutions and the decomposition of solid hydrates. He also suggests the use of reversible heat effects caused by solution of salts in water and by their change in solubility with temperature.

Speyer discusses[6] the requirements of heat-storage systems with reference to cost, space, the total effective storage capacity, the fraction of the heat available for use at a later time, the operating temperature range, and the rate at which heat can be put into the storage system and removed from it. If the storage capacity is large the size of the solar collector can be reduced. He states that the limiting factor in the use of solar energy in competition with fuel is the cost of the collector. If the storage cost can be reduced to one fifth its present amount, or if the cost of solar collectors can be reduced to one half or one third, or their efficiency sufficiently increased, then Speyer believes that heating may become economically competitive with fuels in some areas.

One of the difficulties of using the fusion of some materials to store heat is illustrated by experiments[7] with ammonium acetate melting at 110° C (60 cal g^{-1}), in which the samples were placed in test tubes in a liquid bath and allowed to cool after being melted. Usually the solid phase did not appear until the temperature had fallen to 20° C below the standard melting temperatures, due to supercooling.

Supercooling is a serious problem in any system of heat storage that involves a phase change with solids. Nucleating agents are often required to start crystallization, when the proper thermodynamic conditions are attained, and often they become inoperative after hundreds or thousands of cycles of fusion and recrystallization. Fundamental research on nucleation is necessary for the development of storage systems for solar energy.

Although water has about the highest heat capacity among ordinary liquids, some fluids which undergo a reversible chemical dissociation on heating may well be considered. For example gaseous nitrogen tetroxide, heated in the range 0° to 150° C, dissociates very rapidly into nitrogen dioxide with the absorption of 13 kcal $mole^{-1}$ or 141 cal g^{-1}.

The possibilities of using heavy metal cylinders or metal cylinders containing fusible salts to store heat for cooking has been discussed on page 68. Sodium hydroxide is a possibility; it has a melting point of 320° C and a heat of fusion of 40 cal g^{-1}. Another material has been proposed by Stam[8] for storing heat for cooking—$MgCl_2 \cdot 6H_2O$, which melts at 117° C with a heat of fusion of 40 cal g^{-1}.

Two-Vessel Systems

The storage systems discussed thus far have involved a single vessel holding a liquid, a pebble bed, or a substance undergoing a physical or chemical change. By using a more complicated system with two parts, one hot and one cold, it is possible to store much larger quantities of heat. For example, if a concentrated solution of sulfuric acid and water is heated sufficiently the water will be distilled out and can be condensed as liquid water in another part of the closed system, which is cooled either by circulating water or air. At a later time the residue of sulfuric acid with a small amount of remaining water may be cooled, and the liquid water then evaporates and returns to the very concentrated sulfuric acid solution which now has a lower vapor pressure. In re-entering the sulfuric acid, the water vapor gives up its heat of condensation 580 cal g^{-1} at room temperature plus the not inconsiderable heat of mixing with the sulfuric acid. A valve may be introduced between the two vessels to prevent premature mixing, thus permitting the potential chemical heat to be stored indefinitely without thermal loss. Many similar systems could be used at various temperatures: phosphoric acid and water; $Ca(OH)_2$ to give CaO and water; $CaCl_2 \cdot 6\ H_2O$; $NiCl_2 \cdot 4\ NH_3$; silica gel and water; silica gel and NO_2; and silica gel and alcohol. Two-vessel systems of this type will be discussed in Chapter 13 in connection with their use for solar refrigeration and air conditioning, where the interest is not in the heat produced when the condensed liquid is evaporated and reabsorbed but in the cooling produced by the evaporation of the pure liquid. These systems deserve greater study for the storage of heat not only at ordinary temperatures but also at high temperatures.

There are several problems connected with these separated storage compartments, but they are not insurmountable. It is necessary to exclude air or other gases because they decrease the rate of diffusion of the vapor. If the material that reabsorbs the vapor is a liquid, stirring is necessary to prevent accumulation of the condensing vapor at the surface; if it is a solid, channels must be supplied to assure access of the vapor to the interior of the solid. Trays of screens holding the absorbing solid material are effective, but then the heat transfer to the outside of the heat storage unit is slow.

One of the heat storage systems to which preliminary

study[9] has been given is that of nickel chloride and ammonia which undergoes the following reaction at 175° C and 1 atmosphere:

$$NiCl_2 \cdot 6\,NH_3 \rightarrow NiCl_2 \cdot 2\,NH_3 + 4\,NH_3$$

When the $NiCl_2 \cdot 2NH_3$ crystals are cooled, the $NiCl_2 \cdot 6\,NH_3$ is re-formed with the evolution of 250 cal g^{-1} of $NiCl_2 \cdot 6\,NH_3$.

WATER PONDS

Large shallow ponds of water with black bottoms can be used for storing heat from solar radiation for long periods of time. Small ponds are not effective because of large heat losses at the edge, but in very large ponds these losses become relatively less important, and the heat absorbed by the underlying ground is not lost because dry earth is a poor conductor of heat and the heat passing into the ground can be recovered when the temperature of the water in the pond decreases. Several days of solar heating are required to bring the pond up to temperature.

Evaporation of water at the surface of an ordinary pond prevents high temperatures. A film of oil on the surface of the water reduces the rate of evaporation and increases the temperature. Large covers of transparent plastic may also be used as barriers to vaporization and wind losses and for reducing the loss of heat through infrared radiation.

Tabor[10] has built heat-storage ponds 3.3 ft (1 m) deep in which the black bottom of the pond is filled with a concentrated brine solution obtained as a by-product from the recovery of salt from the Dead Sea. Over this brine solution is flowed a layer of ordinary water, and the great difference in density between the lower brine and the upper water prevents the brine from rising to the surface when it is heated by the sun. In this way it is possible to maintain a pond of water in which the bottom is hot and the upper surface is cooler, thus greatly reducing the vaporization of water at the surface and the consequent heat loss. After several days the solar radiation absorbed by the bottom of the pond raises the temperature of the brine toward the boiling point of water and in the absence of thermal stirring the heat is largely retained. Some heat is conducted into the earth below the pond but here much of it is also stored for later use. Coils of water pipes at the bottom of the pond become heated and give low-pressure steam for operating a turbine. Thus the solar radiation can be used for producing power day and night. One of the difficulties may be the accumulation of dust settling through the water and resting on the brine solution, decreasing the radiation that reaches the black bottom of the pond. Another difficulty is the mixing due to wave action. Weinberger[11] has published a detailed mathematical analysis of these solar heat-storage ponds.

References

1. Telkes, M., Solar Heat Storage, in *Solar Energy Research*, ed. F. Daniels, and J. A. Duffie, Madison, University of Wisconsin Press, 1955, pp. 57–62.

2. Telkes, M., Solar house heating, A problem of heat storage, *Heating and Ventilating, 44:* 68. 1947.

3. Telkes, M., Nucleation of supersaturated salt solutions, *Ind. Eng. Chem., 44:* 1308. 1952.

4. Mathur, K. N., Use of Solar Energy for Heating Purposes, Heat Storage, in *United Nations Conference on New Sources of Energy*, E 35 Gr–S17, Rome, 1961.

5. Goldstein, M., Some Physical-Chemical Aspects of Heat Storage, ibid., E 35–S7.

6. Speyer, E., Solar Buildings in Temperate and Tropical Climates, ibid., E 35–S8.

7. Seybold, R., Fusible Salts and Nitrogen Dioxide Adsorption for Utilizing Solar Energy, B.S. Thesis, University of Wisconsin, 1956.

8. Stam, H., Cheap but Practical Solar Kitchens, in *U.N. Conf. on New Sources of Energy*, E 35–S24, Rome, 1961.

9. Blytas, G. C., Unpublished investigation.

10. Tabor, H., Large Area Solar Collectors (Solar Ponds) for Power Production, in *U.N. Conf. on New Sources of Energy*, E 35–S54, Rome, 1961; *Solar Energy, 7:* 189–94, 1963.

11. Weinberger, H., The physics of the solar pond, *Solar Energy, 8:* 45–56. 1964.

CHAPTER 9

Heating Buildings

Many houses with large exposed windows or special architectural features for natural heating by the sun are called solar houses, but in this book the term "solar-heated" will be restricted to those structures in which there is storage of solar heat. Of these there are now fewer than 20 in the world, half of which were described in considerable detail at the United Nations Conference on New Sources of Energy held at Rome in August 1961. These papers have been fully summarized and critically discussed by Löf.[1]

Since about one fourth of the world's consumption of fuel is used for heating buildings, it is evident that solar energy for heating could well provide the means for conserving the world's supply of coal, oil, and gas. From a technical standpoint solar house heating is easily accomplished, but from economic and architectural standpoints there are serious difficulties. Combustion fuel in the United States and elsewhere is so cheap that it is difficult, except in special cases, to save enough fuel by using the sun to compensate the larger capital investment required for the solar heating system. In regions where most heating is needed the sunlight is usually of low intensity in the winter. An optimistic report[2] to President Truman on natural resources a decade ago suggested that by 1975 there would be a market for 13 million solar-heated houses in the United States, mostly in the southern half of the country, but practical progress toward such a situation has been almost negligible. The major cost is in the heat collector; and the expense of enough heat-storage capacity to carry a building through a week or so of cloudy weather in cold climates is excessive. Most advocates of solar heating now accept auxiliary heating by fuel as a necessity where long successions of cloudy days or extremely cold spells are likely.

All the solar-heated houses built or planned thus far require electric power for operating the system, and usually where electricity is readily available the cost of combustion fuel is not high. As in many other uses of solar energy the first economically successful applications will probably come in special cases where sunlight is abundant and fuel is expensive, but very little research has been devoted to the solar heating of one-room huts where electricity is not available. Another area where solar house heating may become important is where both solar heating and solar cooling can be accomplished with the same equipment.

Kinds of Solar Space-Heating Systems

The temperature required for heating houses is low, so it is unnecessary to use the more expensive focusing and movable solar collectors. All solar space heating is done with flat-plate collectors mounted horizontally on a flat roof, tilted toward the equator on a roof or placed vertically along the side of a building facing the equator.

The heat received from the sun is transferred from the collector to the heat-storage unit or house by a stream of circulating water or air. The water transfers heat more effectively and uses small pipes, but a watertight system is required with motors and pumps. Freezing weather can severely damage water-heating systems. Air-heating systems require larger pipes for circulation but simpler motor-driven fans.

The construction of solar water-heating systems was discussed in Chapter 6 and that of solar air-heating systems in Chapter 7. The three general ways in which solar heat can be stored—in pebble beds, in large water tanks, and in chemical systems—were discusssd in Chapter 8.

Requirements for Solar House Heating

The heating requirements for buildings are conveniently expressed in "degree days" per year. These are obtained by taking the temperature difference in Fahrenheit degrees between the heated interior (70° or 65° F) and the average outdoor temperature for each day and adding these differences for each day throughout the heating season.

In the northernmost part of the United States where the heating load is over 8,000 degree days, the heat losses from the house to the outdoor air should not exceed 40 BTU hr^{-1} ft^{-2} or 11.7 watts ft^{-2}. In the southernmost United States where it is under 3,000 degree days the heat losses should not exceed 28 BTU hr^{-1} ft^{-2} or 8.2 watts ft^{-2}. The heat losses may be kept down to these recommended values by adequate insulation of roof and walls, double windows, and reduction of air leakage around windows and doors. The extent of insulation is determined by its cost relative to the value of the fuel saved.

Considerable study has been devoted to the heating of houses and the various ways in which heat is lost. The realization of its importance for house walls has led to the development of very effective insulation of wood fiber, glass wool, or plastics, preferably with an aluminized surface which reduces heat radiation losses. The trend toward electric heating in mild climates in areas where the cost of electricity is low has accelerated these developments and prepared the way for solar heating, in which heat losses are more costly. Electric heating has been frequently used in baseboard heaters, but central electric heaters, with circulating air, are now coming in.

A scientific study[3,4] of heat losses in two one-story, insulated, untenanted houses has recently been completed in St. Paul, Minnesota. Air leakage, door openings, use of electrical appliances, body heat, and other variables were simulated with controlled machines. It was found that with one air change per hour, double windows and doors, and thick insulation the heat losses were distributed about as follows: 15 per cent through the walls, 13 per cent through the roof, 5 per cent through the floor, 27 per cent through the windows and doors, and 40 per cent through air exchanges with the colder outside. In the winter of 1959–60 the total electric heating for this house of 1,100-ft^2 (102 m^2) floor space was 11,830 kwhr (4.04 $\times$ 10^7 BTU or 1.02 $\times$ 10^7 kcal). A similar house with thinner insulation required 12,540 kwhr. Of this total heat supplied, 75 per cent came from electrical resistance baseboard heaters, 5 per cent from simulated human occupants, 11 per cent from electric lights and appliances, and 9 per cent from solar radiation.

At noon in December the sun made an angle of 22° with the horizon; in May it made an angle of 65°. The outdoor conditions are summarized in Table 6.

The cost of heating this house with electricity at 1¾ ¢ kwhr^{-1} in the winter with 7,700 degree days was $195 or 18¢ ft^{-2} of first-floor area. These controlled data for a specific house in the northern part of the United States give an indication of the requirements and costs of solar heating. Within broad limits the heat required is directly proportional

TABLE 6. Outdoor Conditions in St. Paul, Minnesota,
Winter of 1959–1960

	Nov.	Dec.	Jan.	Feb.	Mar.	Apr.	May
Average daily							
temperature °F	25	27	15	16	20	45	57
°C	−4	−3	−9.5	−9	−7	7.5	14
Degree days (°F)	1,181	1,143	1,525	1,408	1,381	589	260
Average wind veloc-ity, miles hr^{-1}		5.9	4.8	8.5	5.0	8.8	5.1
Average daily horizontal solar radiation,							
BTU ft^{-2}		345	440	870	1,185	1,150	1,320
Langleys (cal cm^{-2})		93.5	118	236	321	312	358

to the area of the house and the number of degree days
in the heating season, and it depends greatly on the insulation and airtightness of the house.

A considerable portion of the heat loss in a well-insulated
house occurs through the windows, and economies in heating
may be effected by drawing curtains over the windows at
night. Early in the studies of house heating it was found
that in some designs an increase in the number of windows
led to higher fuel consumption, the loss of heat by radiation
being greater than the gain from admittance of solar radiation into the house.

TESTS OF SOLAR HEATING

Pioneering work in solar house heating has been done at
the Massachusetts Institute of Technology under the general
direction of Professor H. C. Hottel. A significant conference
on solar space heating was held in Cambridge, Mass., in
1950.[5]

Solar house heating was discussed at a symposium at the
University of Wisconsin in 1953.[6–8]

In 1955 a panel discussion on solar house heating[9] was
held in Phoenix, Arizona, at which solar collectors, methods
of storing heat, and performance and costs of solar heating
of half a dozen houses were discussed.

A remarkably complete report of current developments
in solar house heating and an excellent critical review by

Löf[1] are available from the United Nations Conference on New Sources of Energy held in Rome in 1961. The nine solar houses described are all different in kind; their performance in general is considered technologically satisfactory. The costs are not fully avaliable but thus far they do not look favorable for the areas in which these houses are located. All the houses are between latitude 35° N and 42° N, but the winter environments vary from 1,800 to 6,100 degree days, assuming 65° F as the temperature of the houses. The average solar radiation on a horizontal surface through January varied from 125 to 300 langleys per day.

Four buildings were occupied throughout the 24-hr day; another four were laboratories occupied only in the daytime. The total winter heating of the buildings ranged from 14 million BTU (4,100 kwhr) to 52 million BTU (15,000 kwhr) of solar heat plus varying large amounts of auxiliary fuel heating. The average heating requirements in January varied a great deal but most of them were in the range of 25,000 to 35,000 BTU hr^{-1} (7.3 to 10 kw of heat). The *maximum* heating demand in January was nearly twice the average heating for the month.

All the solar collectors were of the flat-plate kind, most of them covered with glass, and tilted toward the south at angles from 7° to 60°. The area of the collecting surface varied from 300 to 1,623 ft^2 (28 to 151 m^2).

The heat storage varied from 2×10^5 to 2.5×10^6 BTU (60 to 750 kwhr of heat) and gave a range of ¼ of a normal January day's heating requirement to 1 week. The temperature of the solar collectors without glass or plastic covers was low, and the heat was used with a heat pump which also permitted cooling in the summertime. The temperature of the collectors with glass or plastic covers was 120° F (49° C) to 140° F (60° C). The auxiliary heating ranged from 5 to 74 per cent, and all solar heating systems were provided with automatic controls that turned on the auxiliary heating when the temperature fell below a predetermined minimum.

The rate of flow of the circulating fluid between collector and storage unit did not vary greatly. With air heating about 1 ft^3 of air min^{-1} was circulated ft^{-2} of solar collector, and with water heating about 1 gal hr^{-1} was pumped ft^{-2} of solar collector.

The efficiencies of winter operation in the cooler section of the temperate zone ranged from 35 to 45 per cent during operation, and from 25 to 35 per cent based on the total winter radiation.

The details of the construction and performance of each of these nine solar houses are given in the original papers which are briefly summarized below.

Bliss describes[10] a laboratory of 1,440 ft² at Tucson, Arizona, heated with a solar collector of 1,623 ft², without a glass cover. The average January radiation is 300 langleys day⁻¹ and the annual heating load is 1,800 degree days. Water is circulated through the collector and the 4,500-gal storage tank.

A Swedish solar house and laboratory[11] has been built and tested on the Isle of Capri in Italy, where the heating load is about 2,640 degree days. The collectors of 320 ft² are vertical and appear as black windows which do not detract from the appearance. The collector has one cover of plastic and one of glass, and the water storage tank contains 800 gal.

The fourth house was built and tested by M.I.T. in Lexington, Massachusetts, where there is an average of 160 langleys day⁻¹ in January, and is reported by Engebretson.[12] This residence of 1,450 ft², in a region of about 6,000 degree days of heating load per year, has a collector of 640 ft² tilted south at 60°, covered with two panes of glass. The water storage tank contains 1,500 gal. Under these conditions each square foot of collector area should give the equivalent of 1 gal of fuel oil per year. On this basis the cost of the collector and solar installation is about five times the fuel savings over a 10 year period.

A solar-heated laboratory of 1,200 ft² at Princeton, New Jersey, described by Olgyay,[13] has a double-glazed collector of 600 ft² in an area where the annual heating requirement is 5,100 degree days. Hot air is circulated through the system and heat storage of 2.5 million BTU is accomplished with a heat-of-fusion chemical in a tank of 275 ft³. An average oil-heated house in the same locality is estimated to require heating equipment costing $1,800 which would consume 1,300 gal of oil, at 14¢ gal⁻¹, costing $180 for the year. The normal annual fuel cost is about one tenth of the initial cost of the equipment. On the basis of these estimates, over a 20-year period the solar heating would be cheaper than the oil heating if the solar collector and equipment cost no more than 2.3 times as much as the installation of a conventional fuel-heating system.

Thomason reports[14] on an inexpensive solar house in

1. Cylindrical collector with parabolic cross section; 6 ft. x 10 ft. Mounted east-west.

2. Inflated plastic cylinders with reflecting bottoms for generating steam to operate a Tabor vapor engine.

3. Wisconsin solar cooker.

4. Solar cooker suitable for village manufacture without power tools.

5. Concrete parabolic mold for forming plastic solar collector shells.

6. Structures for plastic stills. Left, concrete; right, wood.

7. Plastic still in operation.

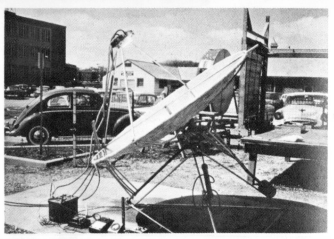

8. Solar thermoelectric generator charging storage battery.

Washington, D.C., where the average horizontal solar radiation in January is 160 langleys per day and the annual heating load is 4,300 degree days, with 1,500 ft^2 (140 m^2) of floor area. The 840-ft^2 collector, built against the back wall of the house and not visible from the front, is made of black corrugated iron sheets facing south, inclined at an angle of 60°. It is covered with one sheet of clear plastic and one layer of window glass. The total cost is $1.00 ft^{-2}. Water trickles down in each of the valleys of the corrugated sheet and is collected in a 1,600-gal (6,080-liter) water tank surrounded by 50 tons of rock pebbles. Air for heating the house is circulated through the pebble bed and around the water tank.

Two successful and attractive solar houses have been designed and tested by Yanagimachi[15,16] in Tokyo, Japan. They include solar heating and cooling with water and the use of a heat pump. The second house has a heating area of 2,460 ft^2 and a heating load of 3,800 degree days. The average January solar radiation is 228 langleys day^{-1}. The unglazed solar collector of 1,410 ft^2, including an area for domestic hot water on a nearly horizontal roof is made of expanded channels in blackened sheet aluminum; the hot-water tank of 9,600 gal holds 40 tons of water. A 3-hp motor operates the heat pump for auxiliary heating and cooling.

Fukuo and his associates report[17] on a solar-heated laboratory of 880 ft^2 at Nagoya, which has a tilted collector of 300 ft^2 made of expanded tubes in sheet aluminum and a water-storage tank of 1,480 gal.

The largest house with solar heating was reported by Löf,[18] who has had long experience with solar-heated houses. The house, of 3,200 ft^2, is in Denver, Colorado, where the average solar radiation in January is 220 langleys day^{-1} and the heating load is 6,100 degree days. The 600-ft^2 solar collector is made of overlapping glass plates inclined to the south at a 45° angle on a horizontal roof, and the heated air is stored in 12 tons of rock pieces 1½ inch in diameter contained in 250 ft^3 of vertical concrete pipes in the center of the house. The normal maximum air temperature is 140° F. The sun supplies 26.5 per cent of the heating, and natural gas supplies the rest.

ARCHITECTURAL PROBLEMS

As indicated in the preceding section, even a small house requires hundreds of square feet of solar collecting area. The collector, flat or tilted, can be hidden on a flat roof or placed at the back of a house if the back faces south; but if it is placed on a conspicuous sloping roof or vertical wall it may be as ugly as an outdoor advertising billboard. It can, however, be made flush with a sloping roof, serving as roofing.

The architectural problems were discussed at a symposium in 1955[19] and later a competition was held for designs of solar-heated houses.[20]

Houses with flat roofs are much easier to adapt to solar collectors, though in general houses with sloping roofs are more common in the areas where heating is important, because of the snow problem. A steeply-inclined solar collector involves no difficulty with snow removal because the snow slides off.

Architectural ingenuity can do much to save fuel in the winter and provide lower temperatures in the summer even without special solar devices. In the northern hemisphere, large windows facing south, or southwest and southeast, admit solar radiation directly to the inside of the house where it is stored in the heat capacity of the walls and furnishings. If this solar heat is objectionable in summer, a wide projecting roof over the windows can be arranged to admit most of the solar radiation in winter when the sun is low in the sky and to exclude much of it in summer when the sun is high. In some office buildings projections near the windows can be arranged to shadow the windows at appropriate times. Window shades that move automatically are also used. Many buildings even in rather cool climates become overheated in summer because of excessive window area facing the sun.

There are many challenging areas for research in the development of architectural and mechanical arrangements which will lead to more comfort by keeping the temperature in the neighborhood of 70° F (21° C). Special glass for windows and special paints and colors for walls and roofs are being developed which absorb or reflect radiation from the sun and emit much or little infrared radiation depending on the need for heating or cooling. Edlin[21] has found that fibrous alkali titanates reflect 92 per cent of the total solar spectrum and emit, at 140° F, 95 per cent as much thermal radiation as an ideal black body. The importance of such materials for houses in hot climates is obvious.

HEAT PUMPS

The use of heat pumps permits conservation of fuel but involves a considerable capital investment. It is technologically practical to transfer heat from a low-temperature reservoir for use at a higher temperature by doing work on the system. The system is like mechanical refrigeration in which the interest is in the hot end of the cycle rather than the cold end. If an electric-resistance heater is supplied with 1 kwhr of electricity, 1 kwhr of heat is produced. If the kwhr of electricity is used to operate an electric motor and a heat pump, however, it is possible to transfer 3 or 4 kwhr of heat under normal conditions. There has been a considerable increase in the number of heat pumps over the 6,000 operating in 1955 in the United States, but the expansion has not been rapid. The cost of the equipment and the automatic controls is high, and the requirement of a large reservoir of heat is often difficult to meet. Running water provides a good supply of heat if it is available. The heat stored in the ground can sometimes be used if there is enough available land. In congested cities there is not enough heat-storage capacity to go around, and air is usually used for heat storage. A solution to the problem of solar heat storage would also be a solution to the problem of the heat pump. A considerable amount of research effort has gone into the development of solar heat storage combined with heat pumps. The heat pump can be used equally well for cooling a house in summer and heating it in winter. The pump does not conserve as much of the world's total fuel as might be expected, because the electrical power used for operating the pump is usually made by burning fuel, with a consumption of three or four times as much heat energy as the electrical energy produced.

Several of the solar-heated houses described in the preceding section make use of heat pumps and in these houses the heat stored in the water tanks does not require as high a temperature as when the solar heat is used for the direct heating of the house. It is possible to operate the solar collectors without glass coverings, which allows the collector to be used for cooling by nocturnal radiation and convection in summer.

Heat pumps for solar house heating and cooling have been

discussed by Morgen.[22] Sporn and Ambrose describe[23] experimental studies with a conventional refrigeration cycle in which a compressor circulates a refrigerant of Freon-12 between 60° F (16° C) or lower and 110° F (43° C) or higher. In winter the refrigerant is changed from liquid to gas in an evaporator by heat from solar radiation. It is changed with an electrically driven compressor from gas to liquid in the condenser, giving up heat to the water which circulates through the house. In summer the refrigerant is vaporized by the heat of the house and condensed under pressure, using the collector (which is cooled by radiation and convection to the outdoor air) for the removal of the heat of condensation. In the experimental studies four collectors were used, each 4 ft (1.2 m) by 7 ft (2.1 m), with a compressor and a 5-hp motor. Solar-supplemented heat pumps are costly, both in mechanical equipment and solar collectors, and the solar energy does not help with the summer cooling.

Another field for research, as yet unexplored, lies in the use of solar heating and storage of heat in large community units. For example, solar collectors are difficult to arrange on a large apartment building and objectionable in a community of residences. In some locations there may be nearby a steep bank or hill with a southern exposure, which does not have much real-estate value. A large solar collector might be built on this hill and provided with a very large underground central pebble rock pile or water tank which could supply heat to many families through the circulation of hot air or hot water.

In some localities there may be cliffs or abandoned mines in which large cavities could be filled with rock pebbles or water for large-scale storage of heat or cold.

SMALL SOLAR-HEATED UNITS

Almost all the research and development of solar heating has been directed toward medium- or high-priced residences in areas where conventional fuel and electricity are plentiful and cheap. The outlook here for vigorous economic competition of solar heat with coal, oil, gas, and electricity is not yet bright. Much depends on developing a considerably cheaper, practical solar collector.

Efforts might be directed toward the development of solar heating of small houses and huts in countries that are less developed industrially. In many parts of the world small houses are heated with wood, and the demand for wood is leading to the removal of forests and an increase in soil erosion. In parts of northern Greece where the winters are cool in spite of bright sunshine, it has been reported that families often burn wood at a cost of $100 a winter.

There is a demand also for solar heating of vacation cabins in the industrialized countries, particularly in areas where wood is not plentiful.

Research should be directed toward a very inexpensive solar collector made from plastic sheets which are cheaper than glass, more easily transported, and more easily fabricated on the site. Solar-heated air is cheaper than solar-heated water and does not have the hazard of freezing. The moderate transparency of the thin plastics in the far infrared is a handicap. The limited life on exposure to weathering is the chief difficulty. Collectors of black and transparent plastic sheets, or plastic collectors filled with charcoal, are possibilities. The heat of the solar-heated air can be stored in piles of rock in underground chambers. A hill below the house with a southern exposure would be advantageous for locating a solar collector. In some places the storage unit would have to be placed under the roof.

The great handicap in the development of these small units in isolated areas is the absence of electric power. All the solar-heated units described thus far use some electricity for circulating either air or water. Thermal chimneys are the most likely substitute. Windmills and solar-power-driven fans and pumps are also possible. In some cases frequent operation of fans and pumps by hand may be the only economically feasible substitute for electric power. Lifting weights or pumping water to a higher reservoir for hydraulic power are conceivable but they require a very considerable human effort.

Some simple expedients for comfort heating and cooling with the sun are possible. Tabor has reported[24] that in Israel and similar areas of moderate climates the roofs are whitewashed in the spring to reflect the sun's rays and keep the house cool in summer. In the fall the rains wash off the whitewash, leaving a darker surface on the roof which by absorbing the sunlight contributes to heating the house in winter. In colder climates where all the solar heat is needed, the roofs and walls of the house should be highly absorptive of sunlight. A solar contribution to temperature comfort in parts of Pakistan are tall thermal chimneys which become heated during the hot day and circulate moving outdoor air through the house before it rises in the chimney.

REFERENCES

1. Löf, G. O. G., The Use of Solar Energy for Space Heating, General Report, in *United Nations Conference on New Sources of Energy,* E 35 Gr–S14, Rome, 1961.

2. The President's Materials Policy Commission Resources for Freedom, Vol. 4, *The Promise of Technology,* U.S. Government Printing Office, Washington, 1952.

3. Anderson, D. B., Erickson, G. A., Jordan, R. C., and Leonard, R. R., Field laboratory for heating studies, *American Society of Heating, Refrigerating, and Air-conditioning Engineers,* Nov. 1960.

4. *The Invisible Family Test House,* St. Paul, Minn., Wood Conversion Co., 1961.

5. *Proceedings, Symposium on Space Heating,* Cambridge, M.I.T., 1950.

6. Löf, G. O. G., House Heating and Cooling with Solar Energy in *Solar Energy Research,* ed. F. Daniels and J. A. Duffie, Madison, University of Wisconsin Press, 1955, pp. 33–45.

7. Anderson, L. B., Hottel, H. C., and Whillier, A., Solar Design Problems, ibid., pp. 47–56.

8. Telkes, M., Solar Heat Storage, ibid., pp. 57–61.

9. Hottel, H. C., Heywood, H., Whillier, A., Löf, G. O. G., Telkes, M., and Bliss, R. W., Jr., Panel on Solar House Heating, in *Proceedings, World Symposium on Applied Solar Energy, Phoenix, Ariz., 1955,* Menlo Park, Calif., Stanford Research Institute, 1956, pp. 103–58.

10. Bliss, R., Jr., Performance of an Experimental System Using Solar Energy for Heating and Night Radiation for Cooling a Building, *U.N. Conf. on New Sources of Energy,* E 35–S30, Rome, 1961.

11. Pleijel, G. V., and Lindström, B. I., Stazione Astrofisica Svedese—A Swedish Solar-Heated House at Capri, ibid., E 35–S49.

12. Engebretson, Use of Solar Energy for Space Heating, M.I.T. House IV, ibid., E 35–S67.

13. Olgyay, Design Criteria of Solar Heated House, ibid., E 35–S93.

14. Thomason, H., Solar Space Heating, Water Heating, Cooling in the Thomason Home, in *U.N. Conf. on New Sources of Energy,* E 35–S3, Rome, 1961. Also *Solar Energy, 4:* 11–19. 1960.

15. Yanagimachi, M., How to Combine Solar Energy, Nocturnal

Radiation Cooling, Radiant Panel System of Heating and Cooling, and Heat Pump to Make a Complete Year Round Air-Conditioning System, *Transactions of the Conference on the Use of Solar Energy: The Scientific Basis, 3* (2): 21–31. Tucson, University of Arizona Press, 1958.

16. Yanagimachi, M., Report on Two and One-half Years Experimental Living in Yanagimachi Solar House II, *U.N. Conf. on New Sources of Energy*, E 35–S94, Rome, 1961.

17. Fukuo, N., et al., Installations for Solar Space Heating in Gerin, ibid., E 35–S112.

18. Löf, G. O. G., El-Wakil, M., and Chiou, J., Design and Performance of Domestic Heating System Employing Solar-Heated Air, The Colorado Solar House, ibid., E 35–S114.

19. Anderson, L. B., Hunter, J. M., Dietz, R. H., and Close, W. A., The Architectural Problems of Solar Collectors, A Round Table Discussion, in *Proc., World Symp. Applied Solar Energy*, Phoenix, 1955, pp. 201–14.

20. Association for Applied Solar Energy, Phoenix, Ariz.

21. Edlin, F. E., Selective Radiation Properties of the Fibrous Alkali Titanates, *Solar Energy Symposium*, University of Florida, April 1964.

22. Morgen, R. A., The Heat Pump, in *Solar Energy Research*, ed. F. Daniels and J. A. Duffie, pp. 69–70.

23. Sporn, P., and Ambrose, E. R., The Heat Pump and Solar Energy, *Proc., World Symp. Applied Solar Energy, Phoenix, 1955*, pp. 159–70.

24. Tabor, H., Personal Communication.

CHAPTER 10

Distillation of Water

Water shortages exist in many parts of the world; even in some areas where water is reasonably abundant there are worries about the future supply. Expansion of the world's population into uninhabited land may be made possible in some areas by converting ocean water or brackish water into fresh water where none now exists.

Note for reprinted edition, 1970. Some of this chapter is now obsolete. An excellent summary has been prepared by S. G. Talbert, J. A. Eibling, and G. O. G. Löf: "Manual on Solar Distillation of Saline Water," for the Office of Saline Water, U.S. Dept. of the Interior. Battelle Memorial Institute, Columbus, Ohio, 1970.

The conversion of salt water to fresh water is technically feasible and reasonably simple, but the economic difficulties are overwhelming. Fresh water is ordinarily so cheap that demineralized salt water cannot compete, except in special cases. Though the production and delivery of 4 tons or more of high-quality material at a cost of less than $1 (U.S.) is a formidable task, it is a goal toward which scientists and engineers are working in the use of ocean water. There appears to be little chance at present of using demineralized salt water for general agriculture, but there are water-short regions in which the conversion of salt water might now be economically successful for supplying a minimum of 1 gal (3.7 liter) per day per person for drinking, or 5 to 10 gallons per day per person for general use, including water for a few animals.

As in most other applications of solar energy, the time is ripe for pioneering in special areas where unique conditions of high competitive costs exist. Through the experience gained in these places it should be possible to reduce costs so that solar applications can be extended to other areas in the future.

There are several different ways in which it is technically possible to obtain fresh water from salt water, including distillation with solar energy or fuel and with single or multiple condensation stills, vapor compression, centrifugation, ion exchange, electrochemical treatment, electrodialysis, solvent extraction, freezing, and others. These have been discussed at symposia.[1] Many ships distill ocean water, and there are also large plants that distill over 1 million gal day^{-1} of seawater with fuel oil. Plans have been proposed for very large units using the heat from nuclear reactors.

The Office of Saline Water of the United States Department of the Interior is taking a leading role in sponsoring research and development in the production of fresh water.[2] The Office of Saline Water supports an active experiment station at Daytona Beach, Florida, for the solar distillation of water.

Petroleum fuel is distilling 2.7 million gal of fresh water a day in the West Indies at a cost of about 2/10¢ gal^{-1}. A 1-million-gal plant using multiple-effect stills has been built in Texas and another of equal capacity, using a multiflash boiler process, has been built in San Diego, California. A vapor compression process is being tested in New Mexico. A large unit using a freezing process is under way. The energy requirement for freezing water is only about 1/7 as much as for distilling it, and corrosion and the formation of boiler scale are reduced. Another approach is cooling by the evaporation of immiscible butane in direct contact with the water, which reduces the need for heat exchangers. Electrodialysis is promising for brackish water of comparatively low salt content; a plant for processing a quarter of a million gal day⁻¹ is located in South Dakota.

Some of these large-unit processes for producing fresh water from salt water are in many areas now cheaper than solar distillation, but they consume large quantities of fuel and will become more expensive if fuel prices rise. For small units of a few gallons per day and up to perhaps 50,000 gallons per day solar distillation is probably the most economical; it is the purpose of this chapter to review progress and possibilities in solar distillation for both small and large units.

The limits of solar distillation are set by the heat of vaporization of water and by the amount of solar radiation. To heat 1 g or 1 cc of water from 20° to 50° C and evaporate it requires over 500 calories of heat. On a bright sunny day in summer about 500 cal of solar radiation strike 1 cm² of a horizontal surface (500 langleys day⁻¹). If all this heat were used in evaporation it would be theoretically possible to distill a layer of water 1 cm or 0.4 inch thick. If the efficiency of the solar still is taken as a reasonable value of 35 per cent, the water distilled in a day would be only 3.5 mm or 0.14 inch. A large solar still could supply a plot of land of equal area with water equivalent to 0.14 inch of rain. It is clear that very large areas of land (usually flat land) would be needed for agricultural water and that the cost of any material to cover this large area would be great.

Theoretically the absorption of 580 cal g⁻¹ for distillation can be greatly reduced by using the 580 cal of heat evolved in the condensation to heat more water. Multiple stills are simple in principle and practical in many chemical industries but they require a considerable difference in temperature for a reasonable heat transfer at each distillation stage. The small difference in temperature and the requirement of low capital investment render multiple-effect solar stills less certain of success.

An efficiency of 35 per cent and production of 1 gal per 10 ft² of solar still (4.1 liters m⁻²) is achievable with several different types of solar stills in bright sunny weather and warm air temperatures. With some designs it is possible to obtain efficiencies up to 50 and 60 per cent. In cloudy or cold weather the yields are of course very much less. Improvements in the economics of solar distillation can come from increases in the efficiency of operation.

In spite of the apparent simplicity of solar distillation there are so many factors involved that there is still good opportunity for improvements to be made through basic research. The cost of operation is low because no fuel and little labor is involved, so there is not much chance for savings in operation costs. There is a good chance to reduce the capital costs both by using cheaper materials and construction and by making the stills from materials that will have very long life. As will be seen, much effort has gone into reducing capital costs.

GLASS-ROOFED STILLS

As stated in Chapter 2 solar distillation of salt water was a technical and economic success in north Chile nearly a century ago. More than an acre of glass-covered stills gave up to 6,000 gallons of water per day with an efficiency of about 35 per cent. Wooden frames were used and made watertight with asphalt, in a region of extraordinary sunshine. The water was distilled from brackish wells and was used by workers who mined and processed Chile saltpeter.

Most solar stills are similar to the early stills used in Chile. A long narrow black tray holds the salt water and is covered with an A-tent roof of glass with gently sloping sides that end over a trough at each side of the tray. The sun's rays pass through the glass roof and are absorbed by the blackened bottom of the tray which holds about 1 inch of salt water. As the water becomes heated its vapor pressure increases; the water vapor is condensed on the underside of the roof and runs down into the troughs which conduct the distilled water to a reservoir. The still acts as a heat trap, because the roof is transparent to the incoming sunlight, but it is opaque to the long infrared radiation emitted by the hot water. The roof encloses all the vapor and prevents its loss and at the same time keeps the wind from reaching the salt water and cooling it. The water wets the glass and gives a smooth transparent film of liquid.

Stills of this type built by Telkes on wooden platforms heated the water to 150° F and were efficient.[3-5]

Howe[6,7] has extended research on this type of still in northern California, and has obtained a yearly average of about 1 gal for 14 ft^2 with a still costing about $2 ft^{-2}. He got average efficiencies of 35 per cent and maximum efficiencies up to 60 per cent.

Extended studies on solar stills have been carried out in the U.S.S.R.,[8] Spain,[9] the United Arab Republic,[10] Chile,[11] India,[12] France,[13] and Italy.[14] A survey of these papers presented at the United Nations Conference on New Sources of Energy in 1961 is given by Gomella.[15] Earlier work includes reports from Algeria,[16,17] Australia,[18] and Cyprus.[19]

A large-scale research and development program on deep-basin, glass-roofed solar stills has been carried on by the Battelle Memorial Institute at Daytona Beach, Florida, under contract with the United States Office of Saline Water. It has been described fully by Bloémer and Eibling,[20] by Strobel,[21] and by Bloemer, Collins, and Eibling.[22,23]

These stills are designed for low cost, long life, and capability for expansion to large-scale operations. The deep-basin stills, designed originally by Löf, are set directly on the sandy ground without additional insulation. The dry ground is a poor conductor of heat, and the large area (3,000 ft^2) of the still permits only a relatively small loss of heat at the edges. The 12 inches of water and the underlying dry ground hold their heat during the night and continue to distill at a reasonably constant rate throughout the twenty-four hours.

To construct one of these stills, the ground is first leveled and prepared for a layer of black asphalt mat on the bottom and curved sides. Black butyl rubber mat may be used in the future. Pillars of concrete blocks rest directly on the floor lining and support pre-cast concrete beams on which are laid two plates of window glass, 34 by 48 inches, of single strength, set at an angle of 10° with the horizontal. The glass is sealed at the edges with asphalt cement. Stainless steel troughs carry off the condensed water at the sides.

When the solar radiation was 2,000 BTU ft^{-2} day^{-1} (542 langleys day^{-1}), 11 ft^2 gave 1 gal distilled water per day. The yields were practically the same as those obtained from a similar but more expensive structure with an underlying layer of insulating material. The total cost of the still, including labor, was $2.09 ft^{-2}, and the still is estimated to last for 30 years. Large organic growths and algae developed in the stills after a few months but did not interfere with effective operation.

The solar radiation was found to be used up in different parts of the still as shown in Table 7.

TABLE 7. Distribution of Solar Energy in Glass-Roofed Still

	Dec.	May
Reflection	11.8%	11.8%
Absorption by glass cover	4.1	4.4
Loss by radiation from heated water	36.0	16.9
Internal circulation of air	13.6	8.4
Ground and edge losses	2.1	3.5
Re-evaporation, shading, etc.	7.9	14.5
Distillation of water	24.5	40.5

The performance data for selected uniform days are given in Table 8.

TABLE 8. Performance of Glass-Roofed Still

	Dec.	May
Average solar radiation, BTU ft^{-2} day^{-1}	756	2,318
Average solar radiation, langleys day^{-1}	205	628
Average cover temperature	71° F 22° C	98° F 37° C
Average brine temperature	82° F 28° C	111° F 44° C
Average production gal ft^{-2} day^{-1}	0.021	0.105
$\left(\dfrac{\text{gal day}^{-1} \text{ ft}^{-2} \times \text{heat vaporization} (8{,}913 \text{ BTU gal}^{-1})}{\text{Solar radiation BTU ft}^{-2} \text{ day}^{-1}} \right) \times 100$	24%	40%

PLASTIC STILLS

Plastic stills have advantages over glass stills in that they are cheaper, less breakable, lighter in weight for transportation, and easier to set up and mount. They have the disadvantages of shorter life and condensation of the water in drops rather than as a smooth film. These droplets scatter and reflect part of the incoming sunlight and give a silvery appearance to the roof. Moreover some of the droplets fall back into the tray of salt water before they can run down to the troughs, particularly when the plastic roof is whipped by the wind. Detergents can wet the plastic and give a temporary film of water, but they are quickly rinsed off. Vacuum-coated films of silicon monoxide and hydrolyzed films of titanium dioxide offer some improvement, and sometimes the plastic roof material picks up dirt that gives areas of smooth film formation, but none of these treatments is permanent. If the plastic material is mounted loosely in rigid frames, it flaps in the wind and will eventually break where it comes into contact with any protruding surface. Inflated stills last longer because they are not stretched over protruding structural materials, but on the other hand they become deflated when any holes are formed and they require a fan operated by electrical or other power.

The greatest drawback to the use of plastic film has now been overcome with the development of plastics that will withstand years of outdoor exposure. Weatherable Mylar (DuPont) is available with an outer coating of dye that absorbs ultraviolet light and prevents the underlying Mylar from degrading. Tedlar (DuPont) is a fluorinated polyvinyl plastic which is chemically stable and transparent to the solar ultraviolet. It is estimated to last 5 or more years. Aclar (Allied Chemical) is another plastic able to withstand continued outdoor exposure.

A report in 1958[24] discusses the properties of plastics for solar stills.

Inflated plastic stills have been developed and tested by Edlin at the Daytona Beach station[20,21] and elsewhere.* Long concrete floors 3 ft wide with low walls were covered with inflated hemicylinders of Tedlar and of Weatherable Mylar kept inflated with a small motor and fan. The layer of ocean water was 1½ to 4 inches deep. The best yields of the inflated plastic solar stills of 500 and 2,300 ft² were about the same as those cited for the deep-basin glass stills.

The Battelle Memorial Institute has worked out an expedient plastic still[22] for easy transportation and quick, inexpensive setup and operation in the field. It consists of cylinders of sealed Tedlar plastic each 20 ft long and filled with sea water to give a width of about 20 inches. The cylinders are laid on a horizontal sheet of black plastic and the condensed water is collected in plastic channels sealed to the inside of the cylinders about halfway up the circular

---

* A still of 4,000 gal a day capacity has been built on a dry island in the Mediterranean.

sides. The cylinders are kept inflated with a very low air
pressure produced with a small electric motor and fan.

A simplified solar still[25] of low cost and easy construction
is shown in Figure 30. The ground is made level and a
wooden rectangular tray 12 ft long and 2½ ft or more wide
is placed on it. The long axis lies east—west, and the front

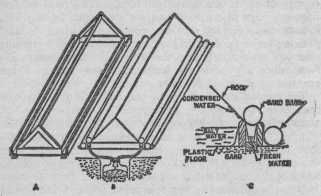

30. Plastic solar still with sandbags. A. Framework. B. Still covered
with transparent plastic roof weighted down with sandbags.
C. Enlarged cross section of trough.

and back are provided with long sloping troughs. The sides
of the tray are of rough lumber 2 inches wide and 1 inch
thick; the troughs are made by nailing three boards together
with the middle board 1 inch to 1¾ inches below the tops
of the two outer boards. The rectangular tray is then levelled,
and a floor is made by draping a large black plastic sheet
over the tray and into and over the troughs in such a way
as to hold a layer of water 1 to 2 inches deep. Black butyl
rubber, 1/32 inch thick, is the best material to use for the
water-tight floor.

A transparent plastic roof with sloping sides is placed over
the tray and supported like an A-tent with a ridgepole of 2
in. by 2 in. lumber or bamboo. The sea water, or brackish
water, is put into the tray to a depth of about 1 inch. The
bottom edges of the roof are weighted with long bags of
black polyethylene 2 or 3 inches in diameter, heat sealed and
filled with sand. The water condensing on the long sloping
roofs runs off into the troughs and down to one end where
it is collected in bottles set below the level of the floor. A

rubber tube is set into the end of the rubber trough and tied tightly with wire twisted around it. A second long sandbag is put on top of the trough in such a way that the plastic roof is held tightly against the inner walls of the trough. As the water runs down the inside of the roof, it is drawn into the trough by capillarity as soon as it strikes the edge of the trough. The sand bag gives a concave surface to the plastic roof over the trough and prevents the water from getting beyond the inner edge of the outer wall.

In a modified design, the triangular ends at the east and west are pointed to give a diamond shape and provided with grooves to collect the water from the ends as well as the front and back. Good results were obtained with a concrete platform 2 inches thick with raised concrete troughs 1 inch deep. The troughs were formed on the platform before the Portland cement had fully set. The concrete tray is cheaper than the rubber tray, but it takes longer to prepare, and its larger heat capacity lowers the temperature of distillation. The concrete and the wooden structures are shown in Plate 6 and a still in operation is shown in Plate 7.

It is important to have wettable plastic material for the roof, otherwise the water condenses in a mass of droplets which scatter the light and tend to fall back into the tray of salt water. Furthermore, a clear continuous film of water on the roof decreases the loss of heat through infrared radiation to the sky.

For the roof, cellulose acetate treated with concentrated sodium hydroxide, as recommended by Howe,[6] gives excellent results, but the material is mechanically weak and has a short life. It is wetted by the condensing water which gives a clear transparent film.

An important advance has been made by Frank Edlin of the DuPont Company in which a nonwettable plastic film is made wettable by mechanical scratching of the film by a special technique. The water condensing on this treated surface spreads uniformly as a film and the effect is permanent. Sun-resistant and mechanically strong plastics such as Tedlar are used.* Because the formation of the water film prevents the loss of water by drops falling from the roof into the tray, it is possible to use a gently sloping roof instead of a steep roof, with a shorter distance between the salt water

---

* It is expected that these treated films will be commercially available.

tray and the roof. Further research is necessary to establish the relation between short diffusion path and high efficiency.

In bright, sunny, warm weather, an improved still of this type gave over 2 gal day^{-1} of fresh distilled water at an efficiency of 30 to 40 per cent when a water-wettable roof was used, but only 20 to 30 per cent when nonwettable Mylar, Tedlar, or polyethylene was used for the roof.

These stills have withstood heavy winds without damage. The cost of a still with an area of 25 ft^2 is around $20 when untreated Mylar or Tedlar is used, and the time for setting up the solar still is less than a day. They have been tested in Madison, Wisconsin; on the shore of Lake Michigan; in Florida; and on the island of Rangiroa in the South Pacific.

At intervals of a few days, before salts start to crystallize out, the remaining water is drained into a hole dug in the ground and new seawater is added. If desired, the concentrated seawater can be evaporated to give solid salt, using plastic sheets set in depressions in the ground.

A more permanent but less efficient solar still has been developed[25] in which the ridgepole and wooden structures are eliminated (see Fig. 31) and the tray, trough, and walls are made entirely of concrete 1 or 2 inches thick. With wettable plastic, a single gently sloping roof can be used instead of the A-type roof with the creased plastic. The plastic sheet is laid over the still and held tightly with double sandbags on the walls and trough. Inlet and outlet tubes are permanently set in the concrete tray and troughs. The concrete floor is made waterproof and black by painting with airblown asphalt of high quality which does not give a taste to the distilled water. A black paint of this kind for the inside of water tanks is available (Sherwin, Williams Co.). Black Orlon mat gives a still blacker bottom. It is helpful to have sawdust or other insulation under the floor and on the walls.

Stills of this type are now being tested,* and it is hoped

---

* Several improvements have been recently made in the solar stills in Figures 30–32 (details will be reported in *Solar Energy*). It is important to stuff openings and eliminate leaks. A single line of sandbags over the troughs, a 36-inch-wide tray, and cover-slope of 23° are satisfactory; the cover is pulled tight occasionally. The black sandbags are painted white to prevent overheating. The plastic cover is scratched with waterproof grinding paper (320). Efficiencies up to 40 per cent have been obtained on good days. Stills like Figure 31 and 32 have been unsatisfactory.

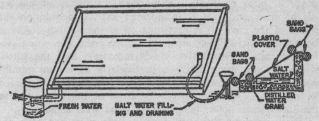

31. All concrete still with single plastic roof.

they will prove to be effective and permanent. The permanent concrete trough and tubes, like a pump installation, can be quickly put into operation by placing the flat plastic cover on the concrete walls. The life of these stills is not yet known, but when the plastic eventually deteriorates it can readily be replaced. The efficiency can be improved by insulating the walls and hanging an internal reflector at the back.

A recent study by Whillier[26] compares Tedlar and glass as covers for solar collectors. Solar stills can be used for preparing drinking water not only from salt water but also from contaminated or muddy water.

STILLS WITH WICKS

Since the vapor pressure of the water is determined by the temperature at the surface it is desirable to have the uppermost layer of water as hot as possible. If a layer of black cloth or plastic is wet by a thin film of water, this film, because of its low heat capacity, becomes hotter than a large body of water would when exposed to solar radiation, particularly if the underlying wick is a good insulator and a good barrier to reduce diffusion between this hotter film of salt water and the rest of the water. Such wicks need not be horizontal and they can be tilted to intercept more of the sunlight on a given area, as explained on page 27.

Telkes has developed an efficient solar still with a tilted wick[20,27] which has been tested at Daytona Beach. The stills, each 25 ft², are made of redwood supported by iron frames facing south at an angle of 30° with the horizontal. An insulating back is overlaid with a sheet of impermeable plastic on which rests a black cloth wick and over it is a cover of glass or plastic. Water flows in slowly at the top of the wick and part is evaporated and condensed on the inside of the cover. The rest runs off at the bottom before it becomes sufficiently concentrated to deposit the white, reflecting salts. Comparative yields indicate[20] that the tilted-wick stills are more efficient, particularly in winter months when the sun is low in the sky. Some difficulties developed in leakage, in overheating of dry areas of the wick, and in the small water inlets becoming plugged with algae.

An inexpensive tilted still with a cloth wick has been developed[25] (see Fig. 32). A wooden framework is set at a slope covered with clear plastic attached with tacks or adhesive plastic tape. The still faces south (in the Northern Hemisphere) and slopes at an angle of 20° or more. If

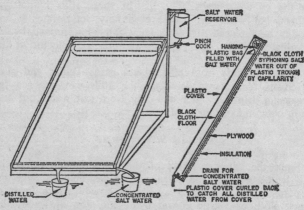

SALT WATER RESERVOIR

PINCH COCK

HANGING PLASTIC BAG FILLED WITH SALT WATER

BLACK CLOTH SYPHONING SALT WATER OUT OF PLASTIC TROUGH BY CAPILLARITY

PLASTIC COVER

BLACK CLOTH FLOOR

PLYWOOD

INSULATION

DRAIN FOR CONCENTRATED SALT WATER

PLASTIC COVER CURLED BACK TO CATCH ALL DISTILLED WATER FROM COVER

DISTILLED WATER

CONCENTRATED SALT WATER

32. Tilted plastic still of simple construction.

nonwettable plastic is used, a steeper slope is required to prevent the losses from condensed drops of water falling off the cover. The film of water on the cover runs down to the bottom of the plastic cover which is curled under the supporting strip of wood, from which it drains into a covered collecting pail. A thick black cloth covers the bottom of the sloping still and dips into a plastic trough at the top, from which the salt water is fed in slowly by capillary syphoning through the cloth. The rate of water dripping can be controlled by adjusting the height over which the syphoning water must pass, and if necessary by adding additional layers of cloth at the top. Fair efficiency has been obtained with this still when the floor is insulated. A sheet of Mylar is placed under the black cloth.

Experiments are being carried out with a concrete floor on a hill or on a mound of earth with a concrete reservoir at the top. A layer of black cloth mat is laid over the concrete surface, and black cloth dips into the reservoir and over the edge.

Bjorksten developed a vertically suspended wick still with condensing surfaces on both sides,[21] but sometimes vibrations produced by the wind brought the salt-water and fresh-water films into contact.

Floating solar stills have the advantage of simple, inexpensive structure that does not require the preparation of a level, watertight floor. Telkes[3] developed a floating plastic still with a black porous evaporator holding seawater supported below the hemispherical roof. It was heated by solar radiation to about 65° C (150° F), and the evaporated water condensed and ran down into a collecting bag at the bottom. It was used as part of a survivor's kit to accompany life rafts on the open ocean. In areas where quiet salt water is available in bays or in inland ponds the floating water still has considerable promise.

EXTERNAL CONDENSATION

If air is swept through a solar still and the moisture in it removed by passage through a water-cooled condenser a high efficiency may be obtained and the heat of condensation can be used in part to warm the incoming salt water. Air currents produced by an electric fan tend to give more rapid evaporation of the heated water. In the case of plastic roofs, the loss of incoming radiation by scattering from the droplets of water is somewhat reduced because much of the water recovered is not condensed on the roof of the still. These stills are more complicated and expensive, however, and require electric power for blowing air. Condensers of large area are required in order to obtain a reasonably rapid rate of condensation.

Experiments[28] were carried out in which a plastic tube 3 m long and 5 cm in diameter was laid out on wooden tables and filled half full of salt water, giving an elliptical cross section with an airspace above the water. The ends were fitted with circular pieces of wood provided with an inlet and outlet tube. This inner tube was surrounded by a larger slightly inflated plastic tube 10 cm in diameter which acted as a heat trap to hold back infrared radiation emitted by the hot water and to reduce heat losses from wind. Such a double layer of plastic for conserving heat is not used in the internally condensing still because the roof must be kept cool. The water was made black by adding a small amount of dye (Rit). The temperature was about 50° C. Both the enclosing outer plastic tube and the black dye were necessary for effective heating and distillation. Air was blown along the surface of salt water in the inner tube and passed through a water-cooled condenser of copper tubing. Since the air did not bubble through liquid, very little power was required for blowing the air. The optimum rate of airflow depends on the radiation intensity and other factors. A rate that is too slow fails to evaporate as much water as possible and a rate that is too fast brings in an unnecessary supply of cold air which must be heated. The efficiencies ranged from around 20 to 40 per cent on bright summer days.

An extended study of solar stills with external condensation has been carried out by Grune, Collins, and Thompson.[29] They found that the optimum rate of airflow is critical, and they obtained a minimum of 5.4 ft^2 for 1 gal day^{-1} of water at a radiation of about 2,000 BTU ft^{-2} day^{-1}. They also report on multiple-effect stills of two different kinds. In one there is a series of tanks of different depths which achieve different temperatures, the deepest tank being coldest in the morning and warmest in the evening. Air is circulated over each tank in the order of increasing temperature and is then passed under each basin in the opposite direction, so that some of the water will be condensed by the colder tanks, thus using some of the heat of condensation. A second design with forced air circulation includes three separate units—a solar collector, a packed column for evaporation, and an external condenser for removing the water vapor from the air. Both the air and the water are circulated. A serious handicap in the economics of the more complicated stills with moving parts is the fact that the still usually operates for less than half of each day but the interest and amortization charges on the capital investment go on continuously.

External condensers permit the use of steam at atmospheric pressure in solar boilers, such as a circular solar cooker (p. 69) or a hemicylindrical collector focused on a pipe as described on page 87. This distillation is efficient but requires adjustable focusing collectors, and there is considerable loss of radiant energy in the collectors. Moreover, troublesome salt deposits may be formed in the boilers.

THEORETICAL CONSIDERATIONS

Although the operation of a solar still appears to be simple in principle, it involves a great many factors which have been studied in detail by Löf,[30,31] who has long been associated with the development of solar distillation. A summary of the many energy-exchange mechanisms is given in

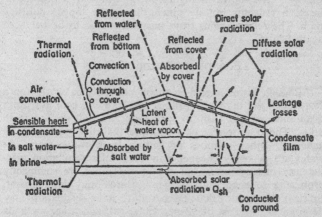

33. Energy flow diagram of basin-type solar still.
— — — — —Solar radiation, substantially below 2μ.
— — — — —Thermal radiation, substantially above 5μ.

Figure 33. Löf evaluates these several variables, making certain assumptions and using operating data from the stills at Daytona Beach. He places them in an overall energy balance equation[30] with 20 variables and obtains significant relationships by means of a computer. His graphs show the effect on solar distillation of solar radiation intensity, atmospheric temperature, cover area, cover absorptivity and reflectivity, wind velocity, and depth of water in the still.

The limiting factor in the production of solar-distilled water is the intensity of solar radiation. The rate of diffusion of water from the basin through the stagnant air films to the cover is an important factor. It is necessary to have a large difference in pressure between the salt water and the condensing water under the colder roof.

The vapor pressure–temperature curve for water rises so steeply that a 10° difference in temperature gives a much greater pressure difference at high temperatures. High-intensity solar radiation, high air temperature, low wind velocity, close approach to equilibrium at evaporating and condensing surfaces, and small condenser surface are important for a high distillation efficiency.

Further information is needed concerning the relative merits of the ridge pole type of still shown in Figure 30 and the wall type shown in Figure 31, in which it is possible to insert a reflector but in which there is a longer diffusion path. The relative gains from insulation need to be balanced against costs.

ECONOMIC CONSIDERATIONS

Although water is sold in many parts of the world for a few cents per thousand gallons, the present goal for solar distillation is less than $1 per thousand gallons for large units. The best results now indicate that this goal may be achieved. Other methods of getting fresh water from salt water are probably cheaper now than solar distillation, particularly in large units, but the opportunities are sufficiently promising to encourage further research and development. In sizes of about 1,000 gal per day, solar distillation may be possible at a cost of $2 per 1,000 gal, and other methods for obtaining fresh water are considerably more costly. In small family sizes of a few gallons per day it is not reasonable to expect very low costs by any method, and here the solar distillation is certainly the cheapest. A working unit capable of producing 1 gal of distilled water per day can be set up at a cost of materials of $5 to $10. It is probably legitimate to disregard the small labor costs for a family still.

Although seawater can be distilled effectively and cheaply with petroleum fuel in large units, solar distillation is cheaper in small units of a few thousand gallons per day and less. The capital investment for small fuel-fired stills is high, as is the cost of fuel. The cheapest ones readily available cost $200 or more and produce about 18 gal per day.

Solar distillation has the advantages of low operating cost and conserving the world's supply of fossil fuel. It has the disadvantage of requiring a large area of land for large-scale production. Flat land is usually selected, but barren hills sloping south can be adapted for use by means of terraces or tilted wicks.

The formidable economic difficulty with some solar stills lies in their high capital investment and short life. For example, if a solar still of 10 ft^2 produces an average of 1 gal day^{-1} during 333 days of a year, it will produce 1,000 gal in 3 years. If the total cost of this 1,000 gal is to be $1, the still cannot cost more than 10¢ ft^{-2}. Such a low cost does not now appear to be attainable. Longer life and higher efficiency are necessary for lower costs. Long life of up to 50 years may be expected with the deep-basin still made of concrete, glass, and asphalt. The mechanical equipment is very simple and will not wear out as boilers and compression engines do. The first large solar still (in Chile) operated for 36 years.

Strobel gives[21] details of costs for the deep-basin still of 3,000 ft^2 at Daytona Beach; a total of $2.09 ft^{-2} leads to a cost of $4.70 per 1,000 gal. He assumes 11 ft^2 gal^{-1}, an average daily production of 270 gal, and an expected life of 30 years. The assumed labor costs of construction are considerably higher than prevail in many other parts of the world. With possible improvements and extension to nearly 1 million ft^2 he estimates that the cost might be brought down to $1.22 ft^{-2}.

Bloemer and Eibling give[20] a nomograph for easy calculation which relates construction cost, efficiency of distillation, length of life, and cost of 1,000 gal of solar-distilled water. It excludes operating costs because 90 per cent of the fresh water is associated with capital costs. This chart shows that if a glass-covered still costs $2 ft^{-2} and operates for 50 years, a tilted still with a 10-year life can compete economically only if the cost is $1.30 ft^{-2} and the expedient, inflated plastic still with a 3-year life can compete only if the cost is 44¢$^{-2}$, equivalent production assumed.

Telkes considers[32] the cost of construction of tilted stills, which in high latitudes can give much higher yields than horizontal stills, and assumes a cost of $13 for a unit that will give 1 gal day^{-1} of water. The cost per 1,000 gal depends on the years of life. If it lasts 1,000 days (approximately 3 years) and produces 1,000 gal of fresh water, the cost is $13/1,000 = 1.3¢ gal^{-1}. If it lasts 10 years, the cost is 0.4¢ gal^{-1}.

While research and development continue for solar distillation in the hope of achieving a cost of less than $1 ft^{-2}, direct installations could be built as small units in special areas where water is very expensive by present methods. There are places in the world where water has to be brought by ox-cart over rough roads at a cost of many dollars per 1,000 gal. In Singapore Harbor the islands are serviced with fresh water in tank boats at a cost of $2 per 1,000 gal. On the east coast of Africa certain fisheries require fresh water which is brought a thousand miles in ships. In the interior of Australia[18] there are areas used for sheep which require up to 200 gal day^{-1}, but the water is brackish. The sheep could tolerate the water if it was diluted with an equal volume of distilled water. But transportation is difficult and fuels are very expensive. In some islands of the Pacific Ocean serious problems arise when the rains do not come. Fresh water is now transported in trucks in Spain and western Mexico and elsewhere at a cost of $2 to $6 per 1,000 gal. Solar distillation is a definite hope in situations like these.

WATER FROM THE AIR

In the discussions of this chapter it has been assumed that seawater or brackish water is available for solar distillation. Solar scientists have an opportunity to help also in areas where no salt water is available. If fresh water is not available from rivers, lakes, or from underground there is a chance of obtaining it from the air—either as liquid water in the form of mist or fog, or as dew deposited from the air during the cooler night, or as water vapor removed from humid air. Adsorption or absorption or refrigeration may be used. All of these have been tried, and further research should be encouraged for obtaining water from the air in special locations.

There is a possible historical precedent for collecting moisture from the air. In archaeological ruins at a site built in 100 B.C. near Theodosia, Crimea, large rock piles have been found with sandstone pipes leading to fountains in the city. It is thought that condensation of dew on the rocks provided a water supply. Lejeune and Savornin[33] have studied this possibility and recall the experimental work of Chaptal, who obtained up to 2.5 liters of water day^{-1} at certain times of the year from a rock pile in France of 8 m^3 in volume. They estimate on this basis that a similar pyramid of 2,500 m^3 might give 600 liters of condensed moisture on the night-cooled rocks under proper conditions of humidity and temperature. Other experiments are reported which were not successful.

Nebbia has reported[34] experiments on the condensation of moisture from the air using conventional fuel-driven refrigerating machinery. Air dehumidifiers driven by electric motors are available commercially at prices considerably lower than air-conditioning units which cool the air as well. In humid weather large amounts of water are collected from air passed through the compressor. These dehumidifying machines are ordinarily used in regions where water is abundant, and the water is discarded. In dry areas where water is valuable the condensation of moisture is difficult and too costly.

In Trombe's laboratory at Mont-Louis, France, moisture has been adsorbed from the air by passing it through an adsorbent and then heating it to drive off the water at a high vapor pressure. There is a possibility for using such a process on a large scale in some parts of the world. The humid air can be drawn through a coarse solid such as calcium chloride, anhydrous copper sulfate, or silica gel, or it may be bubbled through glycol or other water-absorbing liquid of low vapor pressure. An absorbing liquid may be added in spray towers to give large surface and low resistance to flow of air. The air might be drawn through the adsorbent by means of a thermal chimney and the water could be released later from the absorbent or adsorbent by heating with solar energy.

Nocturnal radiation offers a possibility of producing enough dew to be useful in some special areas of the world. There is an interesting opportunity for basic research here. Dew ponds were built in prehistoric Britain. On the island of Santorini in the Mediterranean tomato crops are grown without much rain and without irrigation;[35] they receive their water from the air. The soil, a white volcanic ash, apparently radiates heat at night and cools to a temperature at which moisture condenses from the air and waters the crops. If the soil was black its temperature would become so high with the daylight sun that it would not cool to the dew point at night. But the white soil reflects much of the solar radiation and does not become very much heated. Apparently the meteorological conditions are just right, with clear skies through most of the night to ensure sufficient cooling by radiation to the sky in the long infrared, followed by an influx of moist air from the sea in the early morning.

Tending to substantiate this hypothesis is a report[36] that a tobacco crop was doing well in a semiarid region until the large light-colored limestone rocks were removed, whereupon the crop withered for lack of moisture. Replacement of the rocks led to satisfactory crops again.

These situations suggest the importance of basic research on the absorption of sunlight by typical soils in semiarid regions and the emission in the far infrared when the soil is slightly heated. Field tests should be carried out in areas of marginal moisture, clear nights, and humid morning air (on the seacoast), in which black rocks are whitewashed with calcium oxide to reflect some of the sunshine and reduce the temperature of the rocks.

It is possible in many places to obtain condensed water by laying a sloping plastic cover on the ground.[37] The solar radiation heats the earth and drives out some of its moisture.

References

1. Saline Water Conversion, in *Advances in Chemistry,* Series 27, Washington, American Chemical Society, 1960.

2. O'Meara, J. W., Objectives and Status of the Federal Saline Water Conversion Program, pp. 3–6 in Reference 1.

3. Telkes, M., Fresh water from sea water by solar distillation, *Ind. Eng. Chem., 45:* 1108–14. 1953.

4. Telkes, M., Solar Stills, in *Proceedings, World Symposium on Applied Solar Energy, Phoenix, Ariz., 1955.* Menlo Park, Calif., Stanford Research Institute, 1956, pp. 73–78.

5. Telkes, M., Improved Solar Stills, in *Transactions of the Conference on the Use of Solar Energy: The Scientific Basis, 3* (2): 145–53. Tucson, University of Arizona Press, 1958.

6. Howe, E. D., Solar Distillation, ibid., pp. 159–68.

7. Howe, E. D., Solar Distillation Research at the University of California, in *United Nations Conference on New Sources of Energy,* E 35–529, Rome, 1961.

8. Baum, V. A., Solar Distillers, ibid., E 35–S119.

9. Fontan, L., and Barasoain, J. A., Some Examples of Small-Scale Solar Distillation of Water, ibid., E 35–S73.

10. Hafez, M. M., and Elnser, M. K., Demineralization of Saline Water by Solar Radiation in the United Arab Republic, ibid., E 35–S63.

11. Hirschmann, J. G., Solar Evaporation and Distilling Plant in Chile, ibid., E 35–S23.

12. Khanna, M. L., and Mathur, K. N., Experiments on Demineralization of Water in North India, ibid., E 35–S115.

13. Gomella, C., Possibilities of Increasing the Dimensions of Solar Stills, ibid., E 35–S107, Rome, 1961.

14. Nebbia, G., Present Status and Future of Solar Stills, ibid., E 35–S113.

15. Gomella, C., Use of Solar Energy for the Production of Fresh Water, ibid., E 35 Gr–S19.

16. Gomella, C., Practical Possibilities for the Use of Solar Distillation in Underdeveloped Arid Countries, in *Trans. Conf. Use of Solar Energy: The Scientific Basis, 3*: 119–33.

17. Savornin, J., Efficiency of Various Types of Solar Stills, ibid., pp. 134–37.

18. Wilson, B. W., Solar Distillation in Australia, ibid., pp. 154–58.

19. Fitzmaurice, R., and Seligman, A. C., Some Experiments on Solar Distillation of Sea Water in Cyprus, ibid., pp. 109–18.

20. Bloemer, J. W., and Eibling, J. A., A progress report on Evaluation of solar sea water stills, *Am. Soc. Mech. Eng.,* Paper 61–WA–296 1961.

21. Strobel, J. J., Developments in Solar Distillation—United States Department of Interior, in *U.N. Conf. on New Sources of Energy,* E 35–S85, Rome, 1961.

22. Bloemer, J. W., Collins, R. A., and Eibling, J. A., Field Evaluation of Solar Sea Water Stills, pp. 166–76 in Reference 1.

23. Bloemer, J. W., Collins, R. A., and Eibling, J. A., *Study and Evaluation of Solar Sea Water Stills,* PB 171,934, Washington, U.S. Department of Commerce, Office of Technical Services, 1961.

24. Lappala, R., and Bjorksten, J., Development of Plastic Solar Stills for Use in the Large-Scale, Low-Cost Demineralization of Saline Waters by Solar Evaporation, in *Trans. Conf. Use of Solar Energy: The Scientific Basis, 3* (2): 99–107.

25. Daniels, F., Forthcoming publication.

26. Whillier, A., Plastic covers for solar collectors, *Solar Energy, 7:* 148–51. 1963.

27. Telkes, M., *New and Improved Methods for Lower-Cost Solar Distillation,* PB 161,402, Washington, U.S. Department of Commerce, Office of Technical Services, 1959.

28. Salam, E., and Daniels, F., Solar distillation of salt water in plastic tubes using a flowing air stream, *Solar Energy, 3:* 19–22. 1959.

29. Grune, W. N., Collins, R. A., and Thompson, T. L., Forced Convection, Multiple-Effect Solar Still for Desalting Sea and Brackish Waters, in *U.N. Conf. on New Sources of Energy,* pp. 1–26, E 35–S14, Rome, 1961.

30. Löf, G. O. G., Fundamental problems in solar distillation, *Proc. Nat. Acad. Sci., 47:* 1279–89. 1961; *Solar Energy, 5* (special issue) 35–45. Sept. 1961.

31. Löf, G. O. G., Application of Theoretical Principles in Im-

proving the Performance of Basin-Type Solar Distillers, in *U.N. Conf. on New Sources of Energy,* E 35–S77, Rome, 1961.

32. Telkes, M., Flat Tilted Solar Stills, in *Conference on Solar and Aeolian Energy,* Sounion, Greece, 1961. New York, Plenum Press, 1964, pp. 14–18.

33. Lejeune, G. and Savornin, J., Recovering Water Vapor from the Atmosphere, in *Trans. Conf. Use of Solar Energy: The Scientific Basis, 3:* 138–40.

34. Nebbia, G., The Problem of Obtaining Water from the Air, in *Conference on Solar and Aeolian Energy,* Sounion, Greece, 1961, pp. 33–47.

35. Merlin, C., Condensation of Atmospheric Water Vapor. Discussion in *Conference on Solar and Aeolian Energy,* p. 465.

36. Private communication from C. Merlin.

37. Kobayashi, M., A method of obtaining water in arid lands, *Solar Energy, 7:* 93–99. 1963.

CHAPTER II

Solar Furnaces

Solar furnaces, which give a very high concentration of focused solar radiation, have long been used for scientific investigations and have been fully described in the literature. Lavoisier used a solar furnace in 1774, with a glass lens as tall as a man, for carrying out chemical studies at high temperatures. In the first six years after the founding of the *Journal of Solar Energy* by the Association for Applied Solar Energy, 35 of the 150 articles were concerned with solar furnaces. Arc-image furnaces with radiation from powerful electric arcs focused onto a small area have been perfected to such an extent that they are now competing with solar furnaces in scientific research. Although they are expensive, they can be used at any time and at any place, whereas the solar furnaces are restricted to outdoor use and to times when the sun is unobstructed by clouds or haze. Although for some purposes solar furnaces may become relatively less important, they will have a place in desert areas and in the future when fuel reserves begin to dwindle. The enormous effort going into space research has greatly accelerated the development of large, lightweight, focusing collectors for producing high temperatures in outer space.

Ingenious methods have been devised for opening the parabolic solar collectors after the rocket has passed beyond the regions where there is frictional resistance from air.

Since this book is concerned primarily with the possibilities of solar applications to human needs, and in view of the very extensive literature that already exists on solar furnaces, the treatment in this chapter will be brief.

The parabolic solar collectors described earlier are usually designed to hit a target a few inches in diameter and produce temperatures from one hundred to several hundred degrees centigrade for heating, cooling, and generation of power. With these rather simple demands, the collectors can be made of cheap plastic material at a cost of a dollar or a few dollars per square foot. The solar furnaces with high optical precision give temperatures of over 3,000° C and may cost over $100 ft^{-2}. One of the great limitations of solar furnaces, aside from their dependence on a clear sun, is that the area of the hot zone is often only millimeters in diameter and the heating is only on the front side. The great advantage lies in the fact that extremely high temperatures can be achieved and that the heating is carried out without contamination from fuel gas, electric heaters, or crucible material. Furthermore there is no complication from electrical or magnetic fields. The heating can be carried out in oxidizing or reducing atmospheres or in any gas atmosphere desired; and the temperature can easily be controlled by changing the position of the material in the focus. It is difficult to determine the temperature of the focal spot with precision.

Symposia dealing with solar furnaces, their construction, characteristics, and uses, have been held at the University of Wisconsin in 1953;[1-3] Phoenix, Arizona, in 1955;[4] Tucson, Arizona, in 1955;[5-9] Phoenix in 1957;[10] Mont-Louis, France, in 1958;[11] New York in 1959;[12] and Rome in 1961.[13,14]

Several articles on solar furnaces have been published in the *Solar Energy Journal*.[15-27]

DESIGN AND CONSTRUCTION

Carefully polished glass lenses can give excellent focusing and high temperatures but in sizes larger than 2 or 3 ft they are heavy and very expensive. Focusing parabolic reflectors can be made in larger sizes, using glass or spun metal or plastic materials. The very large solar furnaces are made by mounting smaller glass mirrors on a large frame and adjusting each mirror by hand to hit the central focal spot. The individual mirrors about 1 ft square, are silvered on the back so their reflecting surfaces will not deteriorate. They may be of plane glass or of glass that has been heated to the softening point and pressed against a parabolic or spherical metal mold, or they may be forced under pressure by screws to give a curved surface.

Many laboratories are using old army searchlights for solar furnaces. They are 5 ft in diameter, made of polished copper and plated with rhodium which has a reasonably high reflectivity and does not deteriorate seriously with exposure to outdoor weather. They have excellent optical properties and give focal spots about 1 cm in diameter. These army searchlights became obsolete with the development of radar for spotting airplanes and could be purchased at a very low price as surplus material. They are heavy and require a firm mounting.

In most experimental work it is inconvenient to have the hot target moving continuously. Accordingly it is customary to use for orientation a heliostat composed of a large array of flat mirrors, which follows the sun and reflects the light perpendicularly onto the stationary parabolic focusing collector. In this way the object being heated can be kept in a permanent position for ease in making measurements. Usually the heliostat and focusing collector are both set on the ground and the reflected beam is horizontal; if it is necessary to have the radiation focused downward on an object, the heliostat can be arranged to reflect the light vertically upward onto the focusing collector, which is mounted horizontally on an elevated platform with the point of focus just below it. The difficulty with the heliostat arrangement is the extra expense, the extra cleaning of the mirrors to remove dust and dirt, and particularly the loss in intensity of about 10 per cent because of added reflection and absorption. In large sizes of 20 to 100 ft, massive and expensive steel framework is required to maintain the exact positions of collector and heliostat without bending and with sufficient strength to withstand windstorms.

The heliostat, or the focusing collector if used without a heliostat, is arranged to follow the sun automatically. Several different methods have been used. The heliostat or the focusing collector may be driven by a synchronous motor to sweep out an arc angle of exactly 15 min hr^{-1} to assure that it is continuously facing the moving sun. The guidance system may be actuated by a photocell which operates a motor to turn the mirror whenever the sun moves far enough to have its beam intercepted by the mirror, causing a shadow on the photocell. In another guidance system the changing shadow of the mirror cools a bimetallic thermoregulator which switches on a motor until the mirror is turned far enough to bring sunlight back onto the thermoregulator.

General designs of solar furnaces and their accessories are fully discussed by Trombe,[13,14] Laszlo,[14] and Cotton, et al.[14] A great deal of detailed information concerning solar furnaces is available through the publication of symposia.[10,11,14]

The attainment of temperatures over 3,000° C depends on very high optical precision in the shape of the parabolic collector and in the character of its reflecting surface. The influence of focal length, rim angle, and other parameters has been throughly studied by Cobble,[24] among others. The difficulties of measuring temperatures have been studied carefully, for example by Foex.[14] Optical or radiation pyrometry offers the best approach because thermocouple material is not available at these high temperatures. A sector wheel may be used, which permits the pyrometer to register the radiation emitted from the heated spot only during very brief intervals when the focused sunlight is not striking the heated spot. The input of solar heat has been measured calorimetrically, as for example with a flowing-water calorimeter.

Liquid pools may be readily produced in a mass of ceramic powder at the focus of the solar radiation. The surrounding powder acts as a heat-insulating containing wall, and a molten cavity is formed. When the heated object is subjected to rotation and centrifugal force, the heating is not restricted to the surface alone but is applied throughout the cavity. When an atmosphere other than air is needed, the object to be heated is mounted at the center of a spherical flask of Pyrex or quartz and the gas is passed through. In the same way heating can be accomplished in a vacuum. The quartz and Pyrex absorb very little of the sunlight and do not become heated. A solid sublimate sometimes condenses on the inside of the gas-containing vessel, but there is a tendency for it to form less thickly where the radiation is focused. A moving internal wiper has been used by Laszlo[14] to keep the glass walls clear.

SOLAR FURNACE INSTALLATIONS

The laboratory at Mont-Louis, under the direction of Dr. Felix Trombe, has led in the development of solar furnaces. A survey of the 21 solar furnaces in the United States was made in 1957, and their characteristics and capacities have been summarized.[27] Large solar furnaces have also been built in the U.S.S.R., Japan, Algiers, and elsewhere, and several new ones are now available in the United States.

The first solar furnace built by Trombe at Mont-Louis in 1952 is still operating. The heliostat is 30 ft sq. The focusing collector contains 3,500 plane glass mirrors strained for focusing. At the focus it gives 200 cal cm^{-2} sec^{-1} or about 0.8 kw cm^{-2}. A much larger solar furnace, 200 ft on an edge, planned for a nearby site on a sloping hill, will deliver 1,000 kw of solar energy on a small target.

A solar furnace at Algiers is 27 ft in diameter, made of aluminum sectors stamped against rigid dies and chemically and electrochemically polished. It focuses the ultraviolet light of the sun as well as the visible and infrared, whereas most solar furnaces remove the ultraviolet light by passage through the glass mirrors.

The solar furnace at Natick, Massachusetts, described by Cotton et al.,[14,28] is composed of 180 square concave mirrors aluminized on the front surface, each 2 ft (61 cm) on a side. It has been used continuously since 1958. The focal length is 35 ft (10.7 m) and the distance between heliostat and focusing collector is 98 ft (30 m). It gives an image about 10 cm in diameter. This furnace is used for studies of the resistance of materials to intense radiation. The intensity of the radiation is measured with a radiometer and with a calorimeter and has been found to have a maximum of 100 cal cm^{-2} sec^{-1} uniform within 5 per cent over an area 2.5 cm in diameter. For a diameter of 4.2 cm the radiation is over 90 cal cm^{-2} sec^{-1}, and for a diameter of 8.2 cm it is over 50 cal cm^{-2} sec^{-1}. An overall furnace efficiency of 40 per cent and an index of geometrical perfection are calculated.

A large solar furnace at Sendai, Japan, with 181 hot-molded glass mirrors, is described by Sakurai et al.[14]

A smaller 2-m solar furnace at Mont-Louis gives a maximum of 350 cal cm^{-2} sec^{-1}. Other fluxes reported include 220 cal cm^{-2} sec^{-1} for the lens furnace of the California

Institute of Technology, 600 cal cm^{-2} sec^{-1} for the Curtiss-Wright solar furnace, and 864 cal cm^{-2} sec^{-1} for the U.S.S.R. solar furnace.

The high cost of solar furnaces is still a barrier to their wide industrial use under present economic conditions. The mirrorized glass assemblies are most widely used now. Parabolic molds described by Laszlo,[14] made by spinning and setting liquid plastics or by petal segments of sheet aluminum formed in dyes by high pressure or explosions, give some promise for lower costs if the furnaces are mass-produced.

PHYSICAL AND CHEMICAL OPERATIONS

The solar furnace is an excellent means for studying properties of ceramics at high temperatures, above the range ordinarily measured in the laboratory with flames and electric currents. Physical measurements include melting points, sublimation points, phase changes, specific heat, thermal expansion, thermal conductance, electrical conductance, magnetic susceptibility, and thermoionic emission. Clever devices have been developed for making these measurements in the solar furnaces and motion-picture studies have been made of the operations taking place in a highly heated surface.

Several metallurgical and chemical operations have been carried out at high temperatures in the solar furnaces. The melting and sintering of high-temperature ceramics such as zirconia is easily accomplished. Purification is effected by distilling more-volatile impurities from a refractory. Trombe and Foex, for example, have described[14] the purification of Al_2O_3 by subliming out Na_2O, H_2O, MgO, and other impurities at the high temperatures of the solar furnace. Sometimes an impurity with a low sublimation temperature is added so that when it is driven out it will carry along with it vapors of less volatile impurities.

Zone refining is an excellent means of purification[14] for use in the solar furnace. A rod of the material is moved slowly and continuously through the focal spot; as the impurities which concentrate in this fused area are chased along by the moving hot spot, they are forced to the end of the rod where they are cut away and discarded. The process may be repeated several times.

Chemical operations described by Trombe and Foex[14] include the direct high-temperature production of zirconia from zircon and alkali, beryllia from beryl, and tungsten oxide from wolframite. These authors show that increasing the power of a solar furnace to the large sizes such as the 1,000-kw furnace rapidly increases the yields of products which can be fused in these furnaces.

Nitric oxide has been made by passing air through the refractories at the focus of a solar furnace. A temperature over 2,000° C is required, together with a device for quickly chilling the air containing equilibrium amounts of a few per cent of nitric oxide. The heat absorbed in cooling can be used for preheating the incoming air. This method has been proposed for making nitric acid and fertilizer from air, but the fact that the furnace must be cooled down every night leads to ineffective use of the expensive equipment and to a shortening of the life of the refractory because of frequent repeated thermal shocks. Nitric acid is such a cheap product, costing only a few cents a pound, that the solar furnaces should probably be used for making more valuable products.

Solar furnaces can be used for photochemical reactions as well as for high-temperature products. If a black receiver is placed at the focus all the radiation is absorbed and the temperature will be raised to 3,000° C and over, if the receiver remains a solid or liquid. The temperature continues to rise until the losses of heat, because of radiation and convection, become equal to the heat supplied by the focused solar radiation. If a transparent body is placed at the focus, however, the radiation will pass through and the temperature will not rise. Even water in a quartz flask absorbs so little of the sunlight that it does not seriously overheat. The ultraviolet light and the visible light are present at very high flux, and if any photochemically-active, absorbing material is present there may be a very large amount of reaction. Solar furnaces (more properly called solar radiation concentrators) are useful for producing, photochemically, reactions of very low quantum yield, which require many photons of light in order to bring about the reaction of one molecule. Without the concentrated focused light it is sometimes difficult to obtain enough products to make accurate measurements, as for example in the case of the photolysis of water into hydrogen and oxygen in the presence of dissolved cerium salts. In one experiment, Marcus and Wohlers[14] obtained an increase of a millionfold in a photochemical reaction over the result with unconcentrated light. The focused sunlight may also find practical applications in certain photochemical reactions that give high-priced products.

Marcus and Wohlers[14,29] have made contributions to the use of solar furnaces for carrying out photochemical reactions. They found that flow techniques are desirable for maintaining the temperature and for minimizing any reverse reaction that may be taking place. The heating of the flowing liquid is less than with artificial sources of light in close contact with the photochemically-reacting system. The authors give[14] examples of photochemical synthetic reactions that might be used in a solar furnace.

Future uses of solar furnaces might include flash pyrolysis, in which reacting systems are passed quickly through the focus of the furnace and quickly chilled. Some organic substances, for example, might be broken down in the vapor state if momentarily in contact with black carbon particles or other absorbing molecules or particles momentarily heated to a very high temperature. The quick chilling may yield valuable intermediate compounds not obtained with ordinary heating. In the distant future, solar furnaces may be used for obtaining carbon dioxide from limestone for future synthetic fuels, and for getting water from rocks on the surface of the moon or planets. If solar furnaces can be made cheaply enough, with inexpensive reflecting surfaces costing less than $1 per square foot, they may compete with fuels for kilns and furnaces for ceramics and metallurgical operations in some special cases.

REFERENCES

1. Farber, J., Utilization of Solar Energy for the Attainment of High Temperatures, in *Solar Energy Research*, ed. F. Daniels and J. A. Duffie, pp. 157–61. Madison, University of Wisconsin Press, 1955.

2. Conn, W. M., Solar Furnaces for Attaining High Temperatures, ibid., pp. 163–67.

3. Trombe, F., Development of Large-Scale Solar Furnaces, ibid., pp. 169–71.

4. Trombe, F., High-Temperature Furnaces, in *Proceedings, World Symposium Applied Solar Energy, Phoenix, Ariz., 1955*, Menlo Park, Calif., Stanford Research Institute, 1956, pp. 63–72.

5. Trombe, F., and Foex, M., Traitements à Haute Temperature au Moyen de Fours Centrifuges Chauffés par l'Énergie Solaire, in

Transactions of the Conference on the Use of Solar Energy: The Scientific Basis, 2 (1 B): 146–86. Tucson, University of Arizona Press, 1958.

6. Conn, W. M., The Importance of Accurate Temperature Measurements in Work with Solar Furnaces, ibid., pp. 205–12.

7. Duwez, P., et al., Operation and Use of a Lens-Type Solar Furnace, ibid., pp. 213–21.

8. Laszlo, T. S., de Dufour, W. F., and Erdell, J. A., A Guiding System for Solar Furnaces, ibid., pp. 222–27.

9. Hisada, T., Construction of a Solar Furnace, ibid., pp. 228–37.

10. *Proceedings of the Solar Furnace Symposium, Phoenix, Ariz., Solar Energy, 1* (2, 3): 3–115. 1957.

11. *Applications Thermiques de l'Energie Solaire dans le Domaine de la Recherche et de l'Industrie, Symposium at Mont-Louis, France, 1958,* Paris, Centre National de la Recherche Scientifique, 1961. F. Trombe, 87–129; A. Le-Phat-Vink, 145–62; V. Baum, R. Aparissi, and D. Tepliakoff, 163–74; F. Trombe, M. Foex, and C. H. LaBlanchetais, 174–214; P. Glaser, 215–34; F. Trombe and M. Foex, 277–319; E. Roger, 319–26; M. Foex, 327–66; C. Rekar, 367–82; F. Trombe and M. Foex, 423–50.

12. Conference, Association for Applied Solar Energy, New York, 1959. Solar Furnaces, *Solar Energy, 3* (3): 39–48. 1959.

13. Trombe, F., Use of Solar Energy for High Temperature Processing (Solar Furnaces), General Report, *United Nations Conference on New Sources of Energy*, E 35 Gr–S20, Rome, 1961.

14. Papers presented at the *U.N. Conf. on New Sources of Energy*, E 35–S, *Rome, 1961*, nos.:

5. T. Laszlo, New Techniques and Possibilities in Solar Furnaces. 16. P. Glaser, Industrial Applications—The Challenge to Solar Furnace Research. 25. R. Marcus and H. Wohlers, Chemical Syntheses in the Solar Furnace. 35. F. Trombe, M. Foex, and C. H. LaBlanchetais, Conditions de Traitement et Mesures Physique dans les Fours Solaires. 48. A. Le-Phat-Vink, Etude sur les Concentrations Energetiques Données par les Miroirs Paraboliques de très Grand Surface. 66. M. Foex, Mesure des Temperatures au Four Solaire. 79. E. Cotton et al., Image and Use of the U.S. Army Quartermaster Solar Furnace. 81. F. Trombe, and M. Foex, Les Applications Practiques Actuelles des Fours Solaires et Leurs Possibilitiés Economiques de Development. Also papers 21 by T. Sakurai et al., 36 by G. Vuillard, 52 by F. Trombe and M. Foex, 57 by Noguchi, and 108 by J. Achard.

15. Hisada, T., et al., Concentration of the solar radiation in a solar furnace, *Solar Energy, 1* (4): 14–18. 1957.

16. Jose, P. D., Flux through the focal spot of a solar furnace, *Solar Energy, 1* (4): 19–22. 1957.

17. Löh, E., Hiester, N. K., and Tietz, T. E., Heat flux measure-

ments at the sun image of the California Institute of Technology lens-type solar furnace, *Solar Energy, 1* (4): 23–26. 1957.

18. Moore, J. G., and St. Amand, P., A guidance system for a solar furnace, *Solar Energy, 1* (4): 27–29. 1957.

19. Glaser, P. E., Engineering research with a solar furnace, *Solar Energy, 2* (2): 7–10. 1958.

20. Simon, A. W., Loss of energy by absorption and reflection in the heliostat and parabolic condenser of a solar furnace, *Solar Energy, 2* (2): 30–33. 1958.

21. Baum, W. A., and Strong, J. D., Basic optical considerations in the choice of a design for a solar furnace, *Solar Energy, 2* (3–4): 37–45. 1958.

22. Struss, R. G., Solar furnace determination of high temperature absorption coefficients, *Solar Energy, 4* (2): 21–26. 1960.

23. Gillette, R., Snyder, H. E., and Timar, T., Lightweight solar concentrator development, *Solar Energy, 5* (1): 24–28. 1961.

24. Cobble, M. H., Theoretical concentrations for solar furnaces, *Solar Energy, 5* (2): 61–72. 1961.

25. Bolin, J., Tenukest, C. J., and Milner, C. J., Plastic-replica mirror segments for a solar furnace, *Solar Energy 5* (3): 99–102. 1961.

26. Laszlo, T., Measurement and applications of high heat fluxes in a solar furnace, *Solar Energy, 6* (2): 69–73. 1962.

27. Cohen, R. K., and Hiester, N. K., A survey of solar furnaces in the United States, *Solar Energy, 1* (2–3): 115–17. 1957. Also *Solar Energy, 1* (4): 35. 1957.

28. Davies, J. M., and Cotton, E. S., Design of the quartermaster solar furnace, *Solar Energy, 1* (2–3): 16. 1957.

29. Marcus, R. J., and Wohlers, H. C., Photolysis of nitrosyl chloride, *Solar Energy, 4* (2): 1–8. 1960.

CHAPTER 12

Selective Radiation Surfaces

High temperatures are needed for efficient operation of engines or refrigerating machines and furnaces, but high temperatures require special equipment if solar energy is the source of heat. With either direct or focused solar radiation the target material rises in temperature as it absorbs the solar radiation, until the heat losses offset the heat gains from the solar radiation. Usually the largest heat losses are through radiation of the heated body in the far infrared, where the maximum radiation loss comes at about 10 μ if the heated body is somewhat above room temperature and at about 5 μ if it is about 300° C. If the surface of the hot target could be treated to absorb most of the solar energy (between 0.3 μ and 1.9 μ) and yet emit only a small fraction of the infrared radiation from a perfect radiator or ideal blackbody, it would be possible to increase the efficiency of heating with solar radiation by decreasing the major heat loss. It would also be possible to achieve higher temperatures.

Losses by radiation may be very large, increasing directly as the area and as the fourth power of the absolute temperature. At first sight a selective radiation surface which absorbs most of the sunlight but emits very little thermal radiation appears to be impossible because a black surface is necessary for high absorptivity and a black surface also has a high emissivity. But because the emitted radiation at common solar collector temperatures is in a wavelength range longer than that of the absorbed radiation, it is possible to make effective selective radiation surfaces.

Tabor[1-3] and Gier and Dunkle[4] first called attention to this possibility for increasing the efficiency of solar heating, although Harris[5] had observed earlier that special surfaces of smoked gold powder showed high transmission in the infrared and low transmission in the visible light.

The explanation of selective radiation surfaces involves at least two different mechanisms. According to one hypothesis, a bright, shining metal surface reflects light effectively and therefore, when heated, emits only a small fraction of the radiation emitted by an ideal blackbody. When this shiny, low-radiation-emitting surface is covered with a very thin layer of a black semiconductor, having a thickness around 10^{-4} to 10^{-5} cm, an effective selective radiation surface is produced. This black outer surface is about the thickness of 1 wavelength of visible light but it is only ⅕ or 1/10 that of the wavelengths emitted in the infrared. It absorbs almost completely the solar radiation from 0.3 μ to 2.5 μ, but does not absorb or emit much radiation in the far infrared. The infrared radiation is determined largely by the nature of the surface underlying the thin coating; if this is a bright metal like silver, aluminum, or nickel the infrared emissivity is low.

The selective radiation properties depend also on the character of the surface of the thin black covering. If it is irregular with many microcavities, and if the cavities are larger than the wavelength of the solar radiation, they will tend to absorb the radiation as in a hollow space or ideal blackbody; but if the cavities are considerably smaller than the wavelength of the infrared radiation they will neither absorb nor emit this radiation. Both thinness of the overlying black covering and microcavitation are probably factors in specially prepared selective radiation surfaces. The resistance to corrosion, moisture, and weathering of these selective coatings is important for a permanent coating.

EXPERIMENTAL WORK

Tabor prepared his first selective radiation surfaces[1-3] by covering a metal with a black sulfide layer. He obtained the best results by using a special electroplating operation with a solution containing a sulfide, which gave a deposit of controlled thickness containing both oxides and sulfides. Selective radiation surfaces of a mixture of zinc sulfide and nickel sulfide are being produced commercially. Many factors affect the optical properties of these electroplated films, including current density, pH, and temperature. Good results are obtained by changing the current density abruptly to give adjacent films with particles of different sizes. Tabor and his associates got excellent results of 92 per cent solar absorption and 10 per cent radiation emissivity.

Hottel and Unger[6] developed a detailed method for depositing fine particles of copper oxide on sheet aluminum. They sprayed droplets of copper nitrate solution on the aluminum and heated the sprayed material in a furnace to about 350° C to evaporate the water and chemically decompose the copper nitrate, leaving only the residue of black copper oxide. The concentration of the solution, the size of the droplets, the temperature, and the time of heating were all critical, indicating that particle size and distribution as well as thinness of coating are important. The copper oxide particles adhere firmly to the film of aluminum oxide that covers the surface of the aluminum.

Salam and Daniels[7] prepared selective radiation coatings on discs of copper, aluminum, iron, and nickel. In one set of experiments the metals were dipped in a boiling aqueous solution of a commercial solution called "Ebanol," which contains concentrated sodium hydroxide and sodium chlorite and other ingredients designed for use with different metals. The coatings were black and reasonably satisfactory, but they contained chlorides as well as oxides, and therefore might not withstand extended outdoor exposure to moisture and sunlight. Measurements of these coatings showed that a polished surface of metal below the thin black coating gave an appreciably lower emissivity than an unpolished undersurface, indicating that the underlying surface is important in determining the infrared emissivity. In another experiment a sandblasted metallic undersurface was found to give a considerably higher emissivity.

The best results were obtained by simply plating a metal surface with nickel or silver, polishing it to give a bright shining surface, and then plating it with a flash of copper about 5×10^{-5} cm thick. The thickness was determined by calculating the current and the time necessary to give the required thickness of copper. The thickness of the film was then checked by weighing the metal plates before and after electroplating.

Several different selective radiation surfaces prepared by electrolysis were developed and tested for stability, particularly at high temperatures.[8] Flat black paint or smoked camphor surfaces have high absorptivities in the solar region, but they also have high emissivities in the infrared. They are reasonably stable at comparatively low temperatures but no coatings that contain organic material can withstand continued exposure to air at 300° C or above. The higher temperatures are needed for producing power with either heat engines or thermoelectric units. It is possible to make an absorbing black surface by oxidizing sheet copper or iron, but the oxygen diffuses through the surface and makes a continuously thicker film of black oxide. When the sun goes down and the hot receiving surface cools off, the metal contracts considerably more than the copper oxide film, and the surface adhesion breaks down. The black oxide peels off in flakes. But the thin electroplated and oxidized coatings are so thin that they can contract and expand with the underlying metal and stretch to such a point that they still adhere to the metal in spite of alternate heating and cooling. This ability to withstand high temperatures and remain unchanged after successive heating and cooling makes the electroplated and oxidized black coatings particularly valuable for mechanical and chemical reasons as well as for their selective radiation properties. For some purposes they are about the only black coating suitable for the high temperatures needed for solar engines and solar thermoelectric generators.

Thin layers of copper are electroplated on polished nickel

or silver using a solution of 2.25 per cent CuCN, 3.4 per cent NaCN, and 1.5 per cent Na_2CO_3, at a current density of about 0.003 to 0.015 amp cm^{-2}. Cobalt is plated from a hot solution of $CoSO_4$ containing NaCl and H_3BO_3 at a current density of about 0.05 amp cm^{-2}. The copper or cobalt plating is then oxidized to the black oxide film in an electric oven at about 400° C or oxidized for a few minutes in the air by heating with focused sunlight. The absorptivity is measured by a disk, one side of which is covered with the black oxide film coating and the other with black smoke from burning camphor. A thermocouple attached to the rim, and shaded, records the temperature rise obtained with each black coating; the camphor smoke is assumed to be practically 100 per cent absorbing. On cloudless days a series of measurements was made under the same conditions, alternating the two sides every 150 sec.[8] The emissivity is measured by heating the coated disk on an insulated thermostated block of aluminum and measuring the radiation received by a sensitive black-surfaced radiometer.

Copper oxide on nickel does not give a good selective coating at red heat because the oxygen of the air diffuses through the copper oxide coating and slowly oxidizes the polished nickel surface, leading to a loss of the shining reflecting surface and a gradual increase in emissivity. If the copper is plated on a reflecting silver surface, the selective radiation property is retained up to above 600° C. Above 800° C the copper produced by the dissociation of the copper oxide alloys with the silver and thus is not available for reoxidation. Accordingly the black absorbing surface decreases in absorptivity. Thin copper plated on platinum gives an excellent coating but it alloys with the platinum above 800° C. The microcrystalline structure of the copper oxide layer is remarkably uniform.

A thin layer of electroplated cobalt on oxidation to Co_3O_4 gives excellent selective radiation properties. When the underlying metal is silver the emissivity increases at 800° C owing to the recrystallization of the underlying silver surface. When the cobalt oxide is formed on a shiny platinum undersurface, the selective radiation properties are excellent; no deterioration was observed even at 1,000° C over a period of many hours.[8]

These selective radiation coatings can be made of a very thin layer of a black oxide or other semiconducting compound adhering to a bright shining underlying metal. There is a direct connection between the selective radiation properties and the electrical conductivity of the semiconductor, which depends on the atomic number and the unfilled electronic shells. The oxides of the transition elements in the periodic table are suitable for selective radiation coatings. The dissolved oxygen in the films may be a factor in the optical properties.

If these selective radiation surfaces of thin metallic oxides are to be used in outer space for absorbing sunlight or for operating power units, a new factor must be taken into consideration. At high temperatures they dissociate into free oxygen and metal. In air at atmospheric pressure the oxygen lost is immediately replaced by fresh oxygen and the material stays as an oxide. In the vacuum of outer space, however, the oxygen molecule quickly moves away and there are no other oxygen molecules to take its place. Accordingly the metal oxide may change to the metal and lose its blackness and high absorptivity. Nevertheless, a thin coating of copper oxide on one of the early satellites continued to function satisfactorily for at least 2 years. Black, semiconducting oxides that are stable at still higher temperatures, such as uranium oxide, should be tested at high temperatures and

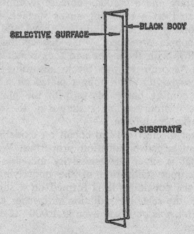

SELECTIVE SURFACE

BLACK BODY

SUBSTRATE

34. Mendenhall wedge for comparing emissivity of selective radiation surfaces.

very high vacuum. The rate of dissociation as well as the temperature of dissociation is an important factor.

An extended study of these selective radiation coatings has been carried out at high temperatures with an infrared spectrometer.[9] A Mendenhall wedge (see Fig. 34) is made of very thin platinum bent into a V-strip having an angle of about 10°. One of the outer sides is of bright polished platinum and the other has a thin coating of the cobalt oxide or other material that will give a black oxide with semiconducting properties. The wedge is mounted vertically and connected to a low-voltage transformer which gives a current of 50 amp or more. The platinum strip is heated from 800° to 1,100° C and is rotated at the proper focus in front of a slit of a large recording infrared spectrometer.

The open end of the wedge is faced toward the slit and the infrared spectrometer is turned to cover the range from 1 μ to 14 μ. A curve for the emission of an ideal blackbody is obtained, and the temperature is determined with an optical pyrometer. The vertical Mendenhall wedge is then rotated so the uncoated side of pure platinum faces the spectrometer slit while the current and temperature are kept constant and another curve is obtained in which intensity is plotted against wavelength throughout the infrared spectrum. A third curve is obtained giving intensity versus wavelength for the black-coated selective radiation surface. The temperature and other conditions are the same for each of the three curves. At short wavelengths, the face of the wedge, coated with thin NiO, gives radiation approaching that of the blackbody radiation (as given by the open wedge) (see Fig. 35). At the long wavelengths, however, its emissivity is low, like that of the bright platinum metal. These are the requirements for selective radiation coatings.

Gillette[10] has studied the properties of selective radiation surfaces of cobalt oxide on polished nickel and of a deposit of chromium, nickel, and vanadium up to 1,650° C (3,000° F). With the former he obtained 93 per cent absorptivity with solar radiation and an emissivity 0.24 as much as that of an ideal blackbody radiator, and with the latter he obtained an absorptivity of 94 per cent and an emissivity of 0.40. The studies were directed toward the use of high-precision focusing collectors in outer space for operating heat engines or other solar power units. Calculations showed that with an ideal blackbody at the focus of a collector that gives a solar radiation concentration ratio of 640 to 1 the

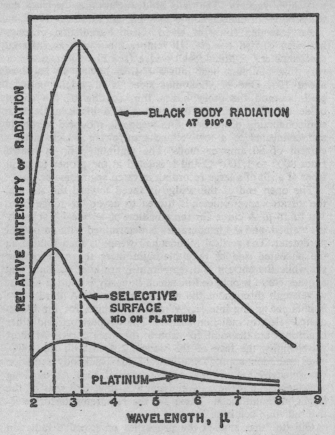

35. Relative emissivities at different wavelengths of an ideal black radiator, a bright platinum surface, and a platinum surface coated with a thin layer of nickel oxide.

temperature would rise to 1,725° C (3,130° F), at which the heat losses would equal the incoming solar radiation and there would be no heat left over to operate a machine. With an idealized selective radiation surface, however, it might be possible to retain 66 per cent of the heat at the same temperature for useful work.

Gillette tested cobalt oxide films of different thicknesses.

Above 2.5×10^{-4} cm (0.1 mil) in thickness the black coating tended to peel off, and below 5×10^{-5} cm (0.02 mil) there was considerable loss of light absorptivity. The optimum was about 1×10^{-4} cm. The coatings were quite stable in a vacuum at $621°$ C ($1,150°$ F).

Irvine et al.[11] have measured the emissivity of heated materials with an integrating radiometer and compared the relative emissivities and absorptivities of lampblack, chemically treated surfaces, and porous surfaces. The Tabor surfaces gave considerably the best selectivity, but the poroloy made from sintered wires of small size or rolled wire screens with 28 to 47 per cent porosity gave fairly good selectivity and they are probably quite stable.

THEORETICAL STUDIES

Tabor discusses the general principles and the calculations involved in the use of selective radiation surfaces[1] and reports later developments.[2,3]

Gier and Dunkle[4] give an analysis of the problem of obtaining high efficiency in heat-absorbing materials.

Shaffer[12] gives a theoretical discussion of maximum possible conversion of solar energy into useful work, assuming high solar absorptivity and low emissivity in the infrared. He gives an idealized value of 55 per cent maximum at an operating temperature of $600°$ C.

Edwards et al.[13] consider the theoretical factors involved in selective radiation coatings and give experimental data on oxidized metals such as zinc, stainless steel, and titanium and on Tabor films and Ebanol-blackened surfaces. The sunlight-absorbing semiconductor should have a band-gap energy of about 0.5 electron-volts, low absorption in the infrared, and high absorption in the visible.

Many factors are involved in the use of these selective radiation coatings. If the absorptivity is appreciably less than that of an ideal black surface, the loss of incoming heat may not be offset by the gain produced by the lower amount of infrared radiation emitted. The higher the temperature the greater is the efficiency of the Carnot engine but so also is the external loss of heat from the engine. In power applications of solar radiation in satellites and space vehicles the cooling unit as well as the heating unit is operated by radiation alone, and the convection and conductant of air are not involved. Hibbard[14] and Liebert and Hibbard[15] have analyzed the theoretical performance of selective radiation surfaces for use in outer space and conclude that these surfaces are advantageous with unfocused solar radiation but not important for highly focused radiation.

PARTICULATE COATINGS

As already explained, selective radiation properties depend not only on a thin coating of special optical properties on an underlying reflecting metal but also on the structure of particles on the surface. The surfaces described earlier in this chapter are not easy to make, particularly on flat-plate collectors of large size. The Ebanol treatment requires a hot bath, the copper nitrate spray requires a large furnace, and electroplating requires a large tank. It would be highly desirable to develop a selective radiation coating that could be easily applied like paint. It has been pointed out[16] that when the surface is covered with small particles larger than the wavelength of the incoming light, the light may be absorbed, whereas if they are smaller the layer is more transparent.

Williams, Lappin, and Duffie[17,18] have studied the selective radiation properties of black lead sulfide particles ranging in thickness from 0.01 μ to 6 μ. The spectrophotometric measurements extended throughout the visible spectrum and out to 15 μ in the infrared. Lead sulfide was chosen because it is a semiconductor with well-known optical properties and because it absorbs sunlight but is largely transparent in the longer infrared. The coating of 0.1 μ particles gave good wavelength selectivity with a reflectivity of 10 per cent for wavelengths below 2 μ and a reflectivity of 80 per cent for infrared radiation greater than 4 μ. It was possible to embed the lead sulfide particles in a silicone film and apply a selective radiation coating by spraying it on a bright surface of aluminum. The optimum size of lead sulfide particles was determined, and the best ratio of silicone to lead sulfide was found to be 0.8. Thinner coatings of silicone did not adhere tightly, and thicker ones gave excessive emissivity in the infrared at the absorption bands of silicone. Theoretical calculations and a complete bibliography are given.[17,18]

CONCLUSIONS

There are many uses for surfaces that selectively absorb and emit radiation and many different ways of accomplishing this selectivity.

Tabor has suggested[19] another way of reducing the loss of heat by radiation without materially reducing the solar radiation absorbed. The exposed surface of glass or plastic is ribbed with many long cylindrical lenses that focus the light in ribbons to the back of the transparent plate. Between these ribbons of focused sunlight, the back of the plate is silvered in long strips. The absorber is set behind this plate with an air gap to reduce heat losses by conduction. Most of the infrared radiation emitted by the heated absorber hits the strips of silvered glass and is reflected back to the absorber.

The cover glass in front of a heat absorber, which passes the sunlight but blocks the infrared radiation from the heated absorber, is widely used and has been discussed under flat-plate collectors.

There is a great need not only for surfaces that absorb much sunlight and emit little infrared radiation but also for those that absorb little sunlight and emit much infrared radiation. Such surfaces are needed for preventing overheating of houses and space vehicles. White paints that reflect sunlight but have high absorption and emission in the infrared are commonly used. In some hot areas the tree trunks are whitewashed with a suspension of calcium hydroxide in water, which turns into a thin layer of white calcium carbonate. The sunlight is largely reflected, but the heat losses due to infrared radiation are not materially reduced. Further research is needed on special paints and glasses to give increased heating or increased cooling when exposed to solar radiation.

Edlin[20] has reported that fibrous alkali titanates are excellent for keeping buildings cool. They are readily incorporated into paints for exterior walls and window shades and they reflect most of the sun's radiation without appreciably reducing the infrared radiation emitted. Yellott[21] has studied the influence of coatings on window glass to reduce the solar heating of a room.

REFERENCES

1. Tabor, H., Selective Radiation I. Wavelength Discrimination, in *Transactions of the Conference on the Use of Solar Energy: The Scientific Basis,* 2 (1 A): 24–33. Tucson, University of Arizona Press, 1958.

2. Tabor, H., Solar collectors, selective surfaces, and heat engines, *Proc. Nat. Acad. Sci.,* 47: 1271–78. 1961; *Solar Energy* (special issue) 5. Sept. 1961.

3. Tabor, H., Harris, J., Weinberger, H., and Doron, B., Further Studies on Selective Black Coatings, in *United Nations Conference on New Sources of Energy,* E 35–S46, Rome, 1961.

4. Gier, J. T., and Dunkle, R. V., Selective Spectral Characteristics as an Important Factor in the Efficiency of Solar Collectors, in *Trans. Conf. Use of Solar Energy: The Scientific Basis,* 2 (1 A): 41–56.

5. Harris, L. McGinnes, R. T., and Siegel, B. M., The preparation and optical properties of gold blacks, *J. Optic. Soc. Am.,* 38: 582–89. 1948.

6. Hottel, H. C., and Unger, T. A., The properties of a copper oxide-aluminum selective black surface absorber of solar energy, *Solar Energy* 3 (3): 10–15. 1959.

7. Salam, E., and Daniels, F., Revetement Rayonnant de Façon Selective pour le Chauffage Solaire, in *Applications Thermiques de l'Énergie Solaire dans le Domaine de la Recherche et de l'Industrie, Mont-Louis, France, 1958,* Paris, Centre National de la Recherche Scientifique, 1961, pp. 483–93.

8. Kokoropoulos, P., Salam, E., and Daniels, F., Selective radiation coatings, preparation and high temperature stability, *Solar Energy,* 3 (4): 19–23. 1959.

9. Kokoropoulos, P., and Evans, M., Infrared spectral emissivities of cobalt oxide and nickel oxide films, *Solar Energy,* 8: 69–73. 1964.

10. Gillette, R. B., Selectively emissive materials for solar heat absorbers, *Solar Energy,* 4 (4): 24–32. 1960.

11. Irvine, T. F., Jr., Hartnett, J. P., and Eckert, E. R. G., Solar collector surfaces with wavelength selective radiation characteristics, *Solar Energy,* 2 (3–4): 12–16. 1958.

12. Shaffer, L. H., Wavelength dependent (selective) processes for the utilization of solar energy, *Solar Energy,* 2 (3–4): 21–26. 1958.

13. Edwards, D. K., Gier, J. T., Nelson, K. F., and Roddick, R. D., Spectral and directional thermal radiation characteristics of selective surfaces for solar collectors, *Solar Energy,* 6 (1): 1–8. 1962.

14. Hibbard, R. R., Equilibrium temperatures of ideal spectrally selective surfaces, *Solar Energy,* 5 (4): 129–32. 1961.

15. Liebert, C. H., and Hibbard, R. R., Performance of spectrally selective collector surfaces in a solar driven carnot space-power system, *Solar Energy*, 6 (3). 84–88. 1962.

16. Kozyrev, B. P., and Vershinin, O. E., Determination of spectral coefficients of diffuse reflection of infrared radiation from blackened surfaces, *Optics and Spectroscopy*, 6: 345. 1959.

17. Williams, D. A., Lappin, T. A., and Duffie, J. A., Selective Radiation of Particulate Coatings, in *American Society of Mechanical Engineers, Symposium, New York, 1962*, Paper 62–WA–182.

18. Williams, D. A., Selective Radiation Properties of Particulate Semiconductor Coatings on Metal Substrates, Ph.D. Thesis, University of Wisconsin, 1961.

19. Tabor, H., Selective Radiation, II, Wave-Front Discrimination, in *Trans. Conf. Use of Solar Energy: The Scientific Basis*, 2 (1A): 34–40. Tucson, University of Arizona Press, 1958.

20. Edlin, F. E., Selective Radiation Reflection Properties of the Fibrous Alkali Titanates, Solar Energy Symposium, University of Florida, Gainesville, Fla., April 1946; *Trans. Am. Soc. Mech. Engineers*. 1964.

21. Yellott, J. I., Calculation of solar heat gain through single glass, *Solar Energy*, 7: 167–75. 1963.

CHAPTER 13

Cooling and Refrigeration

Of all possible direct uses of the sun's energy, the one greeted around the world with the greatest enthusiasm is solar cooling. In the United States, where fuel and electricity are abundant and cheap, solar cooling may become the most widely used application of solar energy. In tropical countries there is a special interest because everyone desires cooling devices but the ones now available are expensive, and the cost of electricity is high. Solar house cooling has the advantage that usually it is needed most when the solar radiation is most intense, and long storage of energy is not absolutely necessary. Present mechanical refrigeration and air cooling are expensive both in initial capital cost and in continued operating cost for electricity or fuel. It may cost as much to cool a house in summer in Texas as to heat a house in winter in Wisconsin. The capital cost for solar cooling will be greater than for conventional cooling with electricity but the operating cost could be much less. In isolated areas in tropical countries the cost of electricity produced by Diesel engines in small units may be more than 5¢ kwhr⁻¹, and air conditioning and refrigeration can be afforded only by the wealthy. There are no social barriers to their introduction into a tropical community, however, and it is not necessary to compete with old established customs because electrical refrigeration and air conditioning are not now widely available. However, they are increasing in the large cities.

There is an appealing challenge here. In most tropical countries, milk and meat are not traditionally used partly because they cannot be preserved. It has been stated that in some hot countries perhaps a quarter of the vegetable crop spoils because of lack of cooling facilities. Also it has been stated[1] that factories in India can never operate with as high efficiency as factories in Europe or America until they are air-conditioned. The health of a billion people could be improved by the development of solar cooling. But thus far it has been put to very little use.

Among the general references to solar cooling are a review by Löf[2] in 1955 at the World Symposium on Applied Solar Energy at Phoenix, Arizona, and a survey and critical summary by Tabor[3] in 1961 of the six papers on the subject presented at the United Nations Conference on New Sources of Energy at Rome.

Cooling can be produced by storing "cold" from the cooler night air and in some areas by radiation to the night sky. In very dry climates cooling can be effected by evaporating water from cloth wicks and in moist climates the moisture in the air can be partially removed and the dried air cooled by the evaporation of liquid water. The most widely used cooling systems depend on the vaporization of a liquid in a closed system.

The general principles of cooling with electrical energy or heat are well understood. The ordinary household refrigerator works (see Fig. 36A and B) by means of a fluid such as ammonia which is alternately vaporized under reduced pressure and condensed to a liquid under increased pressure. The vaporization extracts heat from the surroundings and cools a room or a refrigerator, or freezes water to ice. The system is regenerated by compressing the gaseous ammonia to liquid ammonia. The heat produced in the liquefaction is dissipated at a higher temperature to a stream of circulating air or water. The two operations of cooling

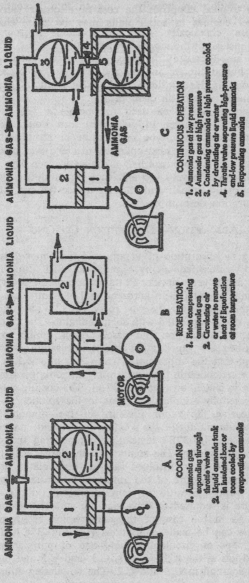

A

COOLING

1. Ammonia gas expanding through throttle valve
2. Liquid ammonia tank in insulated box or room cooled by evaporating ammonia

B

REGENERATION

1. Piston compressing ammonia gas
2. Circulating air or water to remove heat of liquefaction at room temperature

C

CONTINUOUS OPERATION

1. Ammonia gas at low pressure
2. Ammonia gas at high pressure
3. Condensing ammonia at high pressure cooled by circulating air or water
4. Throttle valve separating high-pressure and-low pressure liquid ammonia
5. Evaporating ammonia

AMMONIA GAS → AMMONIA LIQUID

AMMONIA GAS → AMMONIA LIQUID

AMMONIA GAS → AMMONIA LIQUID

AMMONIA GAS

MOTOR

36. Principle of cooling with mechanical power using the evaporation and condensation of ammonia, A. Cooling, B. Regeneration. C. Continuous operation.

and regeneration are readily combined into a continuous operation (see Fig. 36C). Commercial refrigerators ordinarily use chemically inert, fluorinated hydrocarbons (Freons) instead of the more toxic ammonia.

Kapur has discussed[4] the possibilities of air conditioning in a hot, humid climate and the requirements to be met for human comfort. He considers the relative merits of the different systems used for air cooling.

Solar energy could be used to operate a heat engine as described in Chapter 14, which in turn would operate a standard compression-type refrigerator or air conditioner (see Fig. 36). Such a solar-operated machine was operated in the U.S.S.R.[5] to produce half a ton of ice per day. Solar engines, however, have a low efficiency for producing power, and it is usually simpler and cheaper to use the sun directly in an absorption–desorption cycle.

ABSORPTION—DESORPTION COOLING

Cooling by absorption of vapors and the vaporization of the liquid was carried out by Faraday in 1824, using liquid ammonia and silver chloride. Portable absorption–desorption cooling units operated with kerosene fuel or natural gas have been on the market for the past forty years. With modifications they can be operated with solar radiation. The principle of cooling by absorption and desorption is similar to that just described for vaporization and condensation (see Fig. 36) except that the vaporization from A.2 into A.1 is produced by a reduction in the pressure of ammonia gas through absorption in a solution (see Fig. 37A). The cooling capacity is regenerated by adding solar heat to the solution in B.1, thus increasing the vapor pressure of the ammonia and distilling ammonia out of the solution in B.1 and condensing it in B.2 (see Fig. 37B) instead of compressing the vapor with a moving piston. The solution in the larger vessel (1) is so concentrated in dissolved salt (or less volatile liquid) that the vapor pressure of the ammonia is considerably less than the vapor pressure of pure ammonia, and a high temperature is required to drive out the ammonia from the solution. As in the case of the compression refrigeration, the process can be made continuous (see Fig. 37C). There are two loops of circulating fluid—one of pure ammonia liquid and gas at the right in C.1, C.3, and C.5 and one of ammonia solution in C.1 and C.2. The circulating ammonia

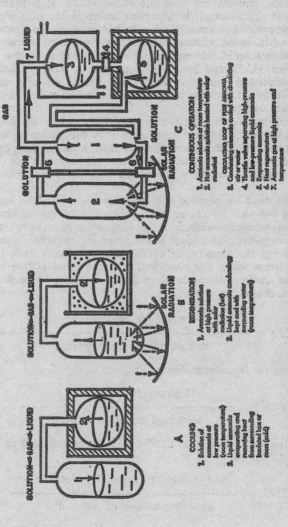

87. Principle of cooling with the absorption and desorption of ammonia dissolved in a liquid or salt solution of low volatility. A. Cooling. B. Regeneration. C. Continuous operation.

COOLING
1. Solution of ammonia at low pressure (room temperature)
2. Liquid ammonia evaporating and removing heat from surrounding insulated box or room (cold)

REGENERATION
1. Ammonia solution at high pressure with solar radiation (hot)
2. Liquid ammonia condensing kept cool with surrounding water (room temperature)

CONTINUOUS OPERATION
1. Ammonia solution at room temperature
2. Hot ammonia solution heated with solar radiation

CIRCULATING LOOP OF PURE AMMONIA
3. Condensing ammonia cooled with circulating air or water
4. Throttle valve separating high-pressure and low-pressure liquid ammonia
5. Evaporating ammonia
6. Heat regenerators
7. Ammonia gas at high pressure and temperature

solution is heated at C.2 (see Fig. 37C) to drive out ammonia gas and then cooled to room temperature in C.1 to reabsorb ammonia gas from the cooler (C.5). It is heated again at C.2 to expel the absorbed ammonia gas in a continuing cycle. The ammonia gas driven out from the heated solution is cooled to room temperature (see C.3) and condensed to a liquid, whereupon it is transferred to an insulated chamber (C.5) and evaporated to give a cooling effect. The vaporized ammonia gas is thus reabsorbed into the solution in C.1 at room temperature and reheated in C.2 to continue the cycle.

Heat exchangers (see 6–6 in Fig. 37C) reduce the heat losses between the two streams, caused by the escape of hot ammonia and the introduction of cold solution into the heated vessel (C.2). The heat of the hot ammonia gas is used in part to heat the cold solution in C.1 as it moves into C.2.

Heat must be supplied not only for vaporizing the ammonia but also for raising the temperature of the solution and its containing vessel; and cooling must be supplied at room temperature sufficient to condense the ammonia vapor and bring the temperature of the heated solution back to room temperature. The coefficient of performance (COP) of a solar cooling device involves two coefficients of performance, one for the cooler:

$$(COP)_o = \frac{\text{heat absorbed by the vaporizing coolant}}{\text{heat supplied to the generator}}$$

and one for the solar collector.

$$(COP)_H = \frac{\text{heat supplied to generator}}{\text{solar heat incident on collector}}$$

The product of these two (COP)s gives the overall coefficient of performance:

$$(COP) = \frac{\text{heat absorbed by vaporizing coolant}}{\text{solar heat incident on collector}}$$

The principle of absorption–desorption cooling has been illustrated with ammonia solutions, but many other systems may be used. Brief descriptions of some of the cooling systems reported in the literature are given in the rest of this chapter, considering first refrigeration and ice making, and second more moderate cooling for air conditioning.

REFRIGERATION

Ammonia–water system. Williams et al. described[6] a small refrigerator in which a parabolic solar reflector, 4 ft in diameter (described in Chapter 5), focused the sunlight onto a steel vessel containing ammonia and water in a closed system. The ammonia was driven out with the heat and condensed in a small vessel connected by a steel tube or a flexible rubber hose capable of withstanding high pressures. The pressure of the heated ammonia reached over 10 atmospheres (150 lb inch^{-2}) and was condensed in the external vessel which was cooled in a pail of water. After the ammonia was driven out and condensed, the two-vessel system which weighed about 25 lb, was taken into the house and the small vessel of liquid ammonia was put into an insulated box with a capacity of 2.2 ft^3. When removed from the focused sunlight the water solution cooled and reabsorbed the ammonia. The evaporation of the liquid ammonia kept the insulated box cold. An exposure of 4 hr in the bright sun kept the refrigerator below 5° C (41° F) during the 24-hr day.

The heat balances and the temperature records are given by Chung and Duffie[7] for a 4-day period of operation.

The absorptivity α of the blackened receiver holding the ammonia and water was about 0.95, and the reflectivity γ of the aluminized Mylar that lined the parabolic focusing collector was about 0.7 The fraction α of solar radiation striking the collector that was absorbed by the metal receiver was determined calorimetrically. This value was about 0.67. In an ammonia-water system with a typical solar heating of 5,300 BTU, optical losses were 33 per cent, and the heat losses into the metal containers were 3 per cent. About 40 per cent of the total solar radiation intercepted by the collector was picked up by the ammonia–water solution, and 24 per cent of this heat was lost to the surroundings by radiation and convection. The cooling ratio η (the heat absorbed by the refrigerant during refrigeration divided by the heat absorbed by the generator contents during regeneration) ranged up to 0.4; the solar heating ratio ε (heat absorbed by

ammonia and water in the generator divided by the direct
radiation striking the solar collector) was also about 0.4.
The overall performance E, equal to ηε, was 0.16. The solution contained 3.5 lb of ammonia in 4.4 lb of water, and the
maximum heating temperature was 129° C (264° F). A
special valve was developed for separating the water from
the liquefied ammonia.

This system and others are discussed further by Chung
and Duffie.[7]

Trombe and Foex have described[8,9] the production of
ice by heating ammonia and water in a central tube at the
focus of a large parabolic-cylindrical focusing collector during the day and allowing the ammonia that is driven out and
liquefied to be vaporized and reabsorbed during the night.

Chinnappa has described[10] an intermittent ammonia–water
refrigerator in which he made small quantities of ice with a
flat-plate collector containing 3 glass plates 5 ft by 3.5 ft.
The coefficient of performance was about 0.06, operating in
a hot climate. The maximum temperature of regeneration
with the flat-plate collector was 100° C (212° F) and the
temperature of the absorbing solution was 33 to 37° C (92 to
99° F).

Eisenstadt, Flanigan, and Farber[11] have also studied the
ammonia–water system for solar cooling.

Trombe and Foex have reported[12] on the economics of
solar ice-making with the ammonia–water system.

Ammonia–sodium thiocyanate system. The water–ammonia system has the disadvantage that some of the water
vaporizes along with the ammonia, and at intervals the water
must be returned to the larger vessel containing the ammonia–water solution. It is desirable to eliminate the water,
which can be done by using very concentrated solutions of
salts in liquid ammonia. The vapor pressure of liquid ammonia can thus be reduced at room temperature from 10
atmospheres to less than 1 atmosphere, and the salts have
negligible vapor pressures even at high temperatures.

Chinnappa has reported studies[13] of the efficiency of refrigeration using both the ammonia–lithium nitrate system
and the ammonia–water system. He gives detailed calculations of the operations of both systems (without solar heating) and concludes that there is not much difference in the
behavior of the two.

An extensive investigation[14,15] has been carried out to
find the salt with the best physicochemical properties for

solar cooling with ammonia. Ammonium nitrate, lithium nitrate, the alkali halides, and sodium and lithium thiocyanate were among the salts investigated theoretically and experimentally. The nitrates, dissolved in liquid ammonia, have many desirable properties, but thermodynamically there is a chance that a spontaneous reaction will produce nitrogen gas and steam with explosive violence. Preliminary tests failed to show explosion hazards, but the general use of concentrated ammonia solutions of nitrates should await official approval.

Ammonia salts are highly soluble, but in solution they are corrosive to iron containers, although they can be used in aluminum containers. Sodium thiocyanate was finally chosen as the best salt to dissolve in ammonia for use in solar cooling and refrigeration. The solutions have suitable thermodynamic properties with very high solubilities, low vapor pressures, and high heats of vaporization. They are chemically stable and inert, inexpensive, and can be used in iron vessels. They have high heat conductivities and low viscosities.

This sodium thiocyanate–ammonia system has been tested for solar refrigeration in the laboratory.[16] A 20-lb steel cylinder containing 12 lb of a solution with about equal weights of sodium thiocyanate and ammonia was placed at the focus of a 4-ft parabolic solar cooker. The cylinder was connected by a flexible pressure hose to a smaller vessel immersed in water at room temperature for the liquefaction of the ammonia. After about 4 hr much of the ammonia had been driven out and the cylinder was removed and brought to room temperature.

The vessel of liquid ammonia was placed overnight in water contained in an insulated box, and 9 lb of ice were produced. A second batch of ice could have been made with another set of vessels, using the solar collector for a second 4-hr period of the day. In case the sun is not shining, the ice can be made by ordinary fuel.

A letter published in *Solar Energy*[17] stated that a solar refrigerator capable of producing 10 lb day^{-1} of ice without electricity and costing less than $200 would find important use in a tropical country such as Burma. It is believed that these conditions have been met.

Cooling of food. Absorption–desorption cooling cycles appear to be the best means for cooling with solar energy. For the refrigeration of meat and milk and the production of ice, the temperature of regeneration of the refrigerant is usually above 100° C (212° F) at temperatures so high that flat-plate collectors are hardly practical, and movable, focusing collectors must be used. Although refrigeration is expensive with ordinary fuel or electricity and still more expensive with solar heating, solar refrigeration can be considered now where electricity and fuel are expensive or unavailable. The ammonia–sodium thiocyanate system merits further testing and development.

Large industrial refrigeration plants can achieve high coefficients of performance, up to 0.7, but small plants tend to be less efficient. Very small units are still less efficient but an argument for solar cooling is that distribution costs of electricity to small users are high. If household labor for domestic cooling is considered to be free, the small cooling units may have a place. On the other hand, the operation of a solar-cooling machine is fairly complicated, calling for some mechanical experience and skill, and solar ice production as a village industry may be more practical than individual hand-operated domestic solar refrigerators in homes. The household electrical refrigerator has been developed to give very efficient, trouble-free operation.

One of the difficulties in ice production is the slow growth of ice crystals. It may be advisable to operate several regeneration units while the sun is shining, and carry out the freezing operation at night. Trombe has used such a procedure.[8]

The economics of solar cooling has been ably discussed by Tabor,[3] Löf,[2] and Trombe and Foex.[12] Tabor concludes that the cost of operating a solar cooler would be about twice as much as operating a cooler with fuel oil delivered at a seaport. Trombe and Foex compare the cost of solar-produced ice with the cost of ice now manufactured in several countries around the world and conclude that the solar production of ice is "not very far today from being economic" and that in some areas of the world, particularly in Africa, solar-produced ice might be cheaper than the ice now being manufactured.

It is much easier to cool to 50° or 60° F and provide a decreased humidity than it is to refrigerate food to ice temperatures. As stated earlier, large savings could be effected in such vegetable crops as potatoes and tomatoes by providing this moderate cooling. The season of using these vegetables could also be greatly extended. Intensive research should be directed toward inexpensive equipment to provide such cooling in vegetable cellars that are partly underground. Stationary flat-plate collectors could be used rather than movable focusing collectors, and operation by manpower would be cheaper in some areas than automatic machines, which require larger capital investment. There is a challenging problem of operating such solar coolers in remote areas where electricity is not available.

AIR CONDITIONING

Ammonia is an excellent refrigerant because of its low boiling point ($-40°$ C) and its large heat of vaporization (327 cal g^{-1}). Water has a still larger heat of vaporization (537 cal g^{-1}) at its boiling point (100° C). The heat of vaporization of most other liquids is considerably smaller. Because of its low boiling point ammonia is particularly useful for making ice, though the toxicity of ammonia is objectionable. Water and many of the organic and inorganic vapors are satisfactory for cooling and for air conditioning but not effective for making ice. Some of the systems suitable for moderate cooling will be reviewed.

Lithium bromide–water system. The vaporization of water can be used for air cooling. The absorption of water vapor by concentrated lithium bromide solutions produces cooling in the same way as described in the preceding section for ammonia and sodium thiocyanate.

The lithium bromide solution, diluted by absorption of water vapor, is regenerated by heat to give a highly concentrated solution. It has been used in continuously operated commercial air conditioners. This type of air cooler is particularly well suited to solar operation because it can be regenerated with hot water above 77° C (170° F) but below the boiling point of water, at a temperature low enough to be obtained with a stationary flat-plate collector. With indirect heating through a heat exchanger it is possible to have extra heat storage for cloudy weather. It is not suitable for producing ice or achieving low refrigeration temperatures.

A commercial unit known as the Arkla DUC 5-2, occupying a space 4x1x6 ft, was connected both to a solar collector and to a steam supply line for a study of solar air conditioning.[18] Several rooms covering 1,200 ft^2 of area were partly cooled for several summer days with it. Operating data are given, showing the solar cooling in a continuously operating system to be technically feasible. In these experiments a flat-plate collector of 102 ft^2 transferred 30 per cent of the incident solar radiation into the circulating water during the period of operation. Optical losses amounted to 29 per cent, reradiation losses to 18 per cent, convection losses to the air from the glass cover 20 per cent, and conduction losses to the supporting structure 3 per cent. The lithium bromide and water unit had a coefficient of cooling performance of 0.6 of the heat it absorbed from the solar collector. The total COP of the whole solar-heated system was 0.18 over the time of the experiment. In the experiments a 3-ton commercial cooler (1 ton of refrigeration is equal to 12,000 BTU hr^{-1}) operated satisfactorily from solar or simulated solar heat at a rate of 1.4 or 1.3 tons of cooling.

The results indicate that a solar collector of 200 ft^2, on a bright, calm day, receiving 5.5 BTU ft^{-2} min^{-1} (1.5 langley min^{-1}), should produce 1 tone of refrigeration. Improvements in solar collection efficiency may perhaps bring the area of the solar collector down to 120 ft^2 ton^{-1} of air conditioning.

Nonvolatile solvents. The last two cooling systems described depend on the volatility of a liquid from a solution containing a nonvolatile salt. In another kind of cooling system, a volatile liquid is driven out of solution in a nonvolatile liquid. Fluorinated hydrocarbons (Freons) are largely used in commercial refrigeration because of their chemical stability and nontoxic properties. Their heats of vaporization, however, are rather small.

A mixture of Freon 21 and tetraethylene glycol dimethyl ether has been investigated for solar cooling.[6,18] The behavior of the Freon–glycol was less satisfactory in the solar cooling tests than that of the ammonia–water system. The solution was more viscous and the thermal conductivity less, leading to a higher temperature at the outer surface of the generator and greater heat losses. One of the chief difficulties was the low rate of heat exchange in the exchanger. The overall coefficient of performance COP (the ratio of the heat removed by the cooler to the incident solar radiation) was typically 0.08.

Adsorption of vapors. A liquid may be made to cool its surroundings by vaporization when its vapor is being adsorbed on an adsorbent of large surface area, such as silica gel. The operation is the same as the removal of vapors by mechanical compression or by absorption in a solution. The solid adsorbents have the advantage that the diffusion of the vapors to the surface takes place without mechanically forced circulation, and no mixing of solutions is involved. The solid adsorbents are poor conductors of heat, however, and the heat evolved on adsorption is large, which makes the removal of heat a problem. The solid adsorbents can be placed in long tubes of small diameter and surrounded with the circulating air, or water, or other liquid. Sulfur dioxide and nitrogen dioxide are liquids that can, in theory, be used for cooling by vaporizing the liquid onto the surface of the solid adsorbent at room temperature and regenerating the adsorbent by heating with solar energy—either directly or through a heat exchanger and a circulating liquid. The heat absorbed in raising the temperature of the adsorbent for regeneration is wasted, so the quantity and heat capacity of the adsorbent should be kept as small as possible.

The use of organic vapors of methyl alcohol, acetone, and diethylamine with silica gel has been explored[19] for solar cooling. The amount of the material adsorbed at equilibrium at various pressures and temperatures was conveniently determined in a system of two glass vessels, one containing a weighed quantity of silica gel and the other containing the organic liquid. The amount of liquid adsorbed was determined by measuring the decrease in volume of the liquid in a graduated vessel. The data extended from room temperature to considerably above the boiling temperature of water. The use of these data in calculating the thermodynamic performance of intermittent coolers has been described.[6]

General considerations. There is great demand for air conditioning in sunny climates, and it has been shown that air conditioning operated by solar energy is technically feasible; but there have been almost no examples of solar air conditioning. As a very rough estimate, the area of solar collectors required is about equal to the floor area to be air-conditioned. In a flat-roofed, one-story building much of the roof would have to be covered with solar collectors. It is obvious that there are difficult problems of large capital investment and architectural acceptance to be solved, but the operating cost for electrically-produced air conditioning is very high, particularly in remote tropical areas, and the cost for solar operation is very low.

Dehumidification in moist hot climates is almost as important as cooling. A person is about as comfortable at 85°

F and 10 per cent humidity as at 75° F and 80 per cent humidity. Removal of moisture from the air is much easier to achieve than cooling the air, and dehumidifiers operated by electricity are cheaper than air conditioners.

Moisture can easily be removed from the air with silica gel or other drying agent, which is then regenerated by heating. Dannies has proposed[20] a simple arrangement for dehumidifying a house with silica gel in the east and west walls.

Air can easily be cooled by evaporating water; in hot dry climates it is common practice to blow air through coarse cloth saturated with water. Even in humid climates considerable cooling can be effected by dehumidification of the air followed by evaporation of the water and restoration of part of the humidity.

Löf has proposed[21] an effective system for solar dehumidification in which the moisture of the air is absorbed by passing it through a spray tower of falling drops of ethylene–glycol. The nonvolatile glycol absorbs the water and gives drier air, and the glycol is regenerated with a stream of hot air, heated by the sun. In this way the moisture absorbed from the room air is driven out and the glycol is ready for removing more moisture.

Important cooling of houses can be achieved in hot clear climates by radiation to the sky during the night. This may amount to 10 to 35 BTU ft^{-2} hr^{-1}, and more. In the desert of north Chile it is possible to freeze water by this means when the air temperature is far above freezing.

Bliss[22] has made use of this nocturnal radiation in a house in Arizona, with a black cloth radiator 280 ft^2 in area. The "cold" amounting to 120,000 BTU was stored in a 10-ton pile of rocks buried in the ground. The cooling was equivalent to about 2 tons of refrigeration.

In many areas it is possible to use a solar collector and heat storage for both heating in winter and cooling in summer. Solar collectors for heating should be covered with glass plates or materials that transmit solar radiation and absorb radiation in the far infrared; but the collectors should be uncovered when they are to be used for cooling by nocturnal radiation.

As brought out in earlier chapters, much can be done for comfort cooling in a house by proper architectural design and selection of materials, such as the placement of more windows on the north side of the house and the use of long overhanging roofs designed to shadow the windows in summer but not in winter when the sun is low in the sky and solar heating is desired. Sunlight-reflecting light-colored paint that gives high radiation in the far infrared is useful in keeping a house from getting too hot. Selective radiation is important for cooling as well as for heating. Good house insulation is important for keeping houses cool in hot weather, as well as for keeping them warm in winter.

Excellent studies are available on the technology and economics of solar air conditioning in special areas—by Tabor for general considerations,[3] by Kapur for India,[1,4] by Ashar and Reti for India and Pakistan,[23] by Sheridan for Australia,[24] by Crausse and Gachan for the Sahara Desert,[25] and by Trombe and LaBlanchetais[26] for countries with a clear sky.

REFERENCES

1. Kapur, J. C., Socio-economic Considerations in the Utilization of Solar Energy in Under-developed Areas, in *United Nations Conference on New Sources of Energy*. Gen. 8, Rome, 1961.

2. Löf, G. O. G., Cooling with Solar Energy, in *Proceedings of the World Symposium on Applied Solar Energy, Phoenix Ariz., 1955*, Menlo Park, Calif., Stanford Research Institute, 1956, pp. 171–189.

3. Tabor, H., Use of Solar Energy for Cooling Purposes, in *U.N. Conference on New Sources of Energy*, E 35 Gr-S18, Rome, 1961.

4. Kapur, J. C., A report on the utilization of solar energy for refrigeration and air-conditioning applications, *Solar Energy, 4:* 39–47. 1960.

5. Krpichev, M. V., and Barim, V. A., Exploitation of Sun's Rays, *Privoda, 43:* 45. 1954.

6. Williams, D. A., Löf, G. O. G., Fester, D. A., and Duffie, J. A., Intermittent absorption cooling systems with solar regeneration, *Refrigeration Engineering, 66:* 33, Nov., 1958.

7. Chung, R., and Duffie, J. A., Cooling with Solar Energy, in *U.N. Conf. on New Sources of Energy*, E 35–S82.

8. Trombe, F., and Foex, M. J., Production of cold by means of solar radiation, *Solar Energy, 1* (1): 51. 1957.

9. Trombe, F., and Foex, M., Production de Glace à l'Aide de l'Énergie Solaire, in *Applications Thermiques de l'Énergie Solaire dans le Domain de la Recherche et de l'Industrie: Symposium at Mont-Louis, France, 1958*, Paris, Centre National de la Recherche Scientifique, 1961, pp. 469–481.

10. Chinnappa, J. C. V., Performance of an intermittent refrigerator operated by a flat-plate collector, *Solar Energy, 6:* 143–150. 1962.

11. Eisenstadt, M. M., Flanigan, F. M., and Farber, E. A., Solar Air Conditioning with an Ammonia–Water Absorption Refrigeration System, *Am. Soc. Mech. Eng.*, Paper 59–A–276. 1959.

12. Trombe, F., and Foex, M., Economic Balance Sheet of Ice Manufacture with an Absorption Machine Utilizing the Sun as the Source of Heat, in *U.N. Conf. on New Sources of Energy*, E 35–S109.

13. Chinnappa, J. C. V., Experimental study of the intermittent vapor absorption refrigeration cycle employing the refrigerant–absorbent systems of ammonia–water and ammonium–lithium–nitrate, *Solar Energy, 5:* 1–8. 1961.

14. Blytas, G. C., Kertesz, D. J., and Daniels, F., Concentrated solutions in liquid ammonia; vapor pressures of $LiNo_3$–NH_3 solutions, *J. Am. Chem. Soc. 84:* 1083–85. 1962.

15. Blytas, G. C., and Daniels, F., Concentrated solutions of NaSCN in liquid ammonia; Solubility, density, vapor pressure, viscosity, thermal conductance, heat of solution, and heat capacity, *J. Am. Chem. Soc., 84:* 1075–83. 1962; Ph.D. Thesis, University of Wisconsin, 1961.

16. Chung, R., in a letter to the editor, *Solar Energy, 7:* 187–88. 1963.

17. Anon. A Case for a Solar Ice Maker, *Solar Energy, 7:* 1–2. 1963.

18. Chung, R., Löf, G. O. G., and Duffie, J. A., Experimental Study of a LiBr–H_2O Absorption Air Conditioner for Solar Operation, *Amer. Soc. Mech. Eng.*, Paper 62–WA–347. 1962.

19. Salam, E. M. A., Chung, R., and Duffie, J. A., *Adsorption of Methyl Alcohol, Acetone, and Diethylamine on Silica Gel.*, Unpublished work, 1957.

20. Dannies, J. H., Solar air conditioning and solar refrigeration, *Solar Energy, 3* (1): 34–39. 1959.

21. Löf, G. O. G., in *Solar Energy Research*, ed. F. Daniels, and J. A. Duffie, University of Wisconsin Press, 1955, pp. 43–45.

22. Bliss, R. W., Jr., The Performance of an Experimental System Using Solar Energy for Heating and Night Radiation for Cooling a Building, in *U.N. Conf. on New Sources of Energy*, E 35–S30, Rome, 1961.

23. Ashar, N. G., and Reti, A. R., Engineering and Economic Study of the Use of Solar Energy Especially for Space Cooling in India and Pakistan, in *U.N. Conf. on New Sources of Energy*, E 35–S37.

24. Sheridan, N. R., Prospects for Solar Air Conditioning in Australia, ibid., E 35–S39.

25. Crausse, E., and Gachan, H., The Study of a Saharan Solar House, ibid., E 35–S76.

26. Trombe, F., and La Blanchetais, C. H., Principles of Air Conditioning in Countries with a Clear Sky, ibid., E 35–E111.

CHAPTER 14

Heat Engines

Cheap and abundant power is necessary for a high material standard of living. Only when men can multiply their mechanical work many times beyond that possible with their own muscles can enough goods and services be produced to provide a reasonably satisfactory economic standard of living. In the currently industrialized areas of the world, energy and fuel are cheap—electrical energy costing a few tenths of a cent per kilowatt hour (about 2¢ per kwhr for small domestic use), coal less than $4 per ton, petroleum less than 13 cents per gallon, and natural gas less than 35¢ per 1,000 cubic feet. These areas became industrialized because cheap fuels were available. There is no chance that solar energy can compete with power produced by conventional heat engines with fuel at such prices. But there are many parts of the world where fuel and power are expensive because of long distances from coal or oil deposits, transportation difficulties, or small-scale rather than large-scale operation. In many parts of Asia, Africa, and Latin America electricity is generated by small Diesel engines of around 25 kw capacity, and the transportation of fuel and the cost of repairs in isolated areas brings the cost of electricity to 5¢ to 15¢ per kwhr, plus $1,500 per mile for transmission power lines. At these prices, solar energy may have a chance in special circumstances of competing with conventional fuel-fired heat engines. Fortunately the regions of high fuel cost are quite often regions of abundant sunshine.

It will be remembered that if electricity is produced by solar energy with 10 per cent efficiency (an optimistic but not impossible efficiency), an area of 150 ft^2 of bright sunshine can produce 1 hp of electrical power (0.74 kw), an acre can produce 280 kw, and a square mile can produce 180,000 kw. This power is produced only while the sun is shining; expensive storage must be provided if the power is to be used continuously. If the quantity of energy produced in 8 hr of sunshine is to be used throughout a 24-hr day, the effective average power is 8/24 or 0.25 kw for 150 ft², 93 kw for an acre and 60,000 kw for a square mile.

In comparing the cost of solar power with fuel power it is clear that, although the cost of sunlight is low and the cost of fuel is high, the capital investment for the solar plant is much larger than for the fuel-operated plant. In solar devices capital costs are high and operating costs are low. Of these capital costs the dominating factor is the high cost of the solar collectors, usually at least $2 ft⁻². Although the sun's energy is cheap, one cannot afford to use an inefficient engine because the area of the collector must be increased proportionately. Large, conventional steam-driven power plants can be built for less than $150 kw⁻¹, but small solar engines will probably cost about 1,000 kw⁻¹.

Small engines of a few watts can easily be run by the sun. However, they are very inefficient because the heat losses and frictional losses are proportionately large. Very large units, of millions of watts, have not been operated by the sun. Large areas of land are required, the storage of large quantities of electricity is difficult, and the cleaning and the movement of large mirrors to follow the sun are expensive.

USES OF SOLAR HEAT ENGINES

The development of solar heat engines will most likely come first in the range of 100 to 1,000 watts or a few kw in isolated areas. It is here that fuel-fired engines and electrical power lines for small and widely distributed users are now expensive. Pumping irrigation water, which involves no storage of power, offers a good area for the early use of solar engines. In these situations the economic prospects appear to be sufficiently good to encourage immediate research and development.

Some of the primitive ways of lifting water for irrigation are illustrated in Figures 38–41, adapted in part from a report of the United Nations on water-lifting devices for irrigation.[1] Simple bucket operations by one or two men (Fig. 38) provide very simple, trouble-free irrigation with almost no capital investment, but they are ineffective and require many hours of men's time. The next step in more effective operation is the use of bullocks (Fig. 39) or camels (Fig. 40). But these animals consume food grown on the irrigated land, part of which might otherwise be used for human food.

The bucket lifted by a rope for deep wells and the paddle wheel for shallow wells are well-established devices. Pedal lifts are helpful for manpower operation (see Fig. 41). For wells not over 30 ft deep the Persian wheel (Fig. 40), in which buckets are attached to the outer rim of a rotating wheel, is quite efficient. The use of mechanical lifts or centrifugal turbines is best for large-scale pumping. The

38. Water lifting by bucket.   39. Water lifting by bullocks.

40. Water lifting by Persian wheel.   41. Water lifting by pedal wheel.

relative costs have been thoroughly studied[1] and brief summarizing comparisons are given in Table 9 and Figure 42.

In these calculations the following assumptions have been made. Annual overhead costs include capital cost and total interest at 6 per cent, divided by the number of years of life of the equipment. A 30-ft well costs $200 and has a life of 40 years; bullocks cost $150 apiece and have a life of 10 years, but only half their cost is charged to irrigation pumping and half to other operations; and food for bullocks is

TABLE 9. Annual Cost of Lifting Water

10^9 g water = 1,000 meter^3 = 10^6 liters = 10 hectare-cm = 9.7 acre-inches = 35,300 ft^3 = 264,000 gal

Method	Time (hours)	Overhead cost ($)	Operating cost ($)	Total cost ($)
			Low Lift (5 ft)	
Counterpoise pail, 2 men				
10^9 g = 10 acre-inches	143	2.20	11.70	13.90
2×10^9 g = 20 a-i	286	2.20	23.40	25.60
10×10^9 g = 100 a-i	1,430	2.20	117.00	119.20
Persian wheel				
10^9 g = 10 a-i	45	16.30	3.50	19.80
2×10^9 g = 20 a-i	90	16.30	7.00	23.30
10×10^9 g = 100 a-i	450	16.30	35.00	51.30
1-kw pump				
10^9 g = 10 a-i	4	16.00	0.30	16.30
2×10^9 g = 20 a-i	8	16.00	0.60	16.60
10×10^9 g = 100 a-i	40	16.00	3.00	19.00
1/10-kw pump				
10^9 g = 10 a-i	40	8.00	0.30	8.30
	(5 days at 8 hr day^{-1})			
2×10^9 g = 20 a-i	80	8.00	0.60	8.60
	(10 days at 8 hr day^{-1})			
10×10^9 g = 100 a-i	400	8.00	3.00	11.00
	(50 days at 8 hr day^{-1})			

TABLE 9. (Continued)

High Lift (30 ft)

Method	Time (hours)	Overhead cost ($)	Operating cost ($)	Total cost ($)
Persian wheel				
10^9 g = 10 a-i	110	40.20	8.10	48.30
2×10^9 g = 20 a-i	220	40.20	16.20	56.40
10×10^9 g = 100 a-i	1,100	40.20	81.00	121.20
Two bullocks and 1 man				
10^9 g = 10 a-i	143	26.50	14.60	41.10
2×10^9 g = 20 a-i	286	26.50	29.20	55.70
10×10^9 g = 100 a-i	1,430	26.50	146.00	172.50
1-kw pump				
10^9 g = 10 a-i	20	16.00	2.00	18.00
2×10^9 g = 20 a-i	40	16.00	4.00	20.00
10×10^9 g = 100 a-i	200	16.00	20.00	36.00
1/10-kw motor pump				
10^9 g = 10 a-i	200 (25 days at 8 hr day^{-1})	8.00	2.00	10.00
2×10^9 g = 20 a-i	400 (50 days at 8 hr day^{-1})	8.00	4.00	14.00
10×10^9 g = 100 a-i	2,000 (250 days at 8 hr day^{-1})	8.00	20.00	28.00

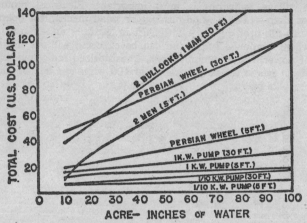

42. Costs of lifting small and large quantities of water by different methods.

estimated at 3¢ hr⁻¹ for each bullock. A Persian wheel for a well 30 ft deep costs $150 and for a well 5 ft deep $50. Each has a life of 10 years. A man's labor in 1959 was taken as only 4¢ hr⁻¹, which should be higher. A 1-kw motor and pump are estimated at $100, and a 1/10-kw motor and pump at $50, both with a life of 10 years. The small pumps are inefficient. In Table 9 the efficiency is taken as 50 per cent. Electrical power is taken as 5¢ per kwhr in some areas, and certainly for solar-produced electric power the cost would be 10¢ per kwhr or more.

The data are not given for quantities of irrigation water less than 10 inches per acre per year. For small operations where an inch of water is needed on less than an acre of land, the man-operated water-lifting devices with little or no capital investments are by far the cheapest. However, for large quantities of water where the capital investments are more fully utilized, the operating cost becomes the dominating factor in the total cost, and electrical or mechanical power is much cheaper than manpower or animal power. Whereas with manpower the cost of 10 inches of water on an acre is nearly ten times as much as for 1 inch, with electrical power the cost is nearly the same.

Next to the pumping of water, the use of electrical power

in village industries is most important. Electrical motors for cloth-weaving, wood-turning, or small mechanical operations can probably be used in certain localities and in seasons where continued bright sun can be expected without storing of power. For communications, transistorized radio and television sets in the neighborhood of 100 watts can be operated by solar heat engines. Kilowatt units for village communications can be used also. In this use for communications a storage battery is needed in the evening or in cloudy weather. For lighting houses in the evening, the load varies from 40 watts to more than 1,000 watts, and storage batteries are required. The cost of storage is a considerable addition to the cost of generating electricity with a solar focusing collector and a heat engine.

PRINCIPLES OF SOLAR ENGINES

As in all heat engines, a fluid is made to expand by absorbing heat at a high temperature and to contract by liberating heat at a lower temperature. The mechanical work produced in the expansion moves a reciprocating piston in a cylinder or rotates a turbine wheel. Frequently the mechanical work is converted into electrical work by means of a dynamo operating at a high efficiency of 90 per cent or more. The thermodynamic principles and the engineering studies were well developed many years ago. The theoretical limiting efficiency is given by the Carnot cycle,

$$\text{Efficiency} = \frac{W_{\max}}{Q_{T_2}} = \frac{T_2 - T_1}{T_2}$$

where the efficiency of converting heat into work is the maximum work $W_{\max}$ divided by the heat absorbed Q_{T_2} at the higher temperature. The efficiency is equal to the difference between the high temperature of heat delivery T_2 and the low temperature of heat rejection T_1, divided by the high temperature T_2. This limiting efficiency applies not only to heat engines but to generation of thermoelectricity and any method of producing work from heat. It is important to have the operating temperature as high as possible, and the limitations are (1) the practical attainment of the high temperature, (2) the transfer of heat, (3) the ability of the construction materials and the expanding gas to withstand the temperature, (4) the cost of the materials, and (5) the convenience of their use. Steam engines were the first to be developed, and in large installations operating at high pressures they are still the cheapest. In many applications the internal-combustion engines are the most efficient and the most widely used, largely because they operate at much higher temperatures and do not involve problems of water boilers. Hot-air engines were used many years ago; they are now the subject of renewed research and development. Special organic and inorganic vapors also offer promise of improvements in heat engines.

With solar engines, the problems involve the solar collectors as well as the engines. The solar collectors are usually more expensive than the engines. Only recently, with the demand for power in outer space, has any appreciable amount of research been devoted to them. It is comparatively easy to make an inexpensive, mirrorized plastic collector 4 to 8 ft in diameter that will focus most of the solar energy onto an 8-inch circle, but it is much more difficult and expensive to hit a 3-inch target that might be used in a heat engine operating at a high temperature. Although it is possible to achieve very high temperatures with solar collectors, as described in Chapter 11, the collectors can be very expensive. The focusing collectors must be arranged to follow the sun either with automatic mechanical trackers or with extremely cheap manual labor. If nonfocusing or stationary collectors are used, the temperature is low. Then there is the problem of effective heat transfer across a small solar-heated area. If a large area is heated by the sun there will be large heat losses because the receiver cannot be insulated with opaque insulation as in a fuel-fired boiler. Another serious handicap in solar heat engines is the fact that effective circular focusing collectors have a size limit because of wind hazard and difficulty in cleaning, as well as requiring massive structural supports for collector and engine. A practical economic limit in some areas seems to be about 8 ft in diameter with an ordinary effective delivery of not over 2 or 3 kw of heat to the target. Long cylindrical focusing collectors are capable of almost indefinite expansion in length and power, but the maximum temperature is much less with a cylindrical focusing mirror than with a circular one.

Stationary flat-plate collectors are considerably cheaper than movable focusing collectors and have been used to operate heat engines, but the practical temperatures are limited to about 100° C or less and the thermodynamic efficiency is thus comparatively low.

STEAM ENGINES

Solar steam engines have already been referred to, and a brief history of some of the early developments was given in Chapter 1. Of the dozen or more solar steam engines described in the literature, none has been much used. All seem to have been unable to compete with internal-combustion engines operating on petroleum fuel. Jordan[2,3] gives a historical review of solar engines and general principles. Tabor reviews[4] the papers on solar engines, including steam engines, presented at the United Nations Conference on New Sources of Energy and discusses present and future prospects and economics. Abbott[5] demonstrated a ⅕ hp solar steam engine in 1938 and has developed improved models with cylindrical collectors, and tubular boilers operating with high-boiling liquids in Pyrex glass.

Small solar steam engines do not appear to be very promising because in small sizes they are inefficient and expensive. In the hands of amateur users the operation of steam boilers and the treatment of impure water for the boiler are difficulties.

Small internal-combustion engines running on gasoline are widely used for motorboats, lawn mowers, snow shovelers, and water pumps. They are very efficient and inexpensive and are operated by millions of people without much technical experience. After a few hundred or a thousand hours of operation, however, they need repairs. A 2-hp engine can be purchased for about $25. Small steam engines of comparable size, if procurable at all, are much heavier, more difficult to operate, and perhaps five to ten times as expensive. An informal conference of representatives from companies in the United States that manufacture small engines was called in 1956 at Madison, Wisconsin, to inquire into the technical and economic possibilities of manufacturing small steam engines. It was generally agreed that if there were a large market for small steam engines they could be mass-produced as effectively and about as cheaply as small internal combustion engines. There are fewer parts used in the construction, and there seemed to be no basic difficulty in their manufacture.

Hsu and Leo tested several different types of small steam

engines[4] and found them very inefficient at low steam pressures of 65 lb in.$^{-2}$. Cheap solar boilers producing steam at high pressures are needed to make solar steam engines practical.

Hsu and Leo[6,7] tried to develop a very simple and inexpensive reaction engine of the Hero-engine type in which the steam is ejected from a nozzle to rotate a wheel at high velocity. Specifications are given for building such a reaction engine, which, operating at a steam pressure of 65 lb in.$^{-2}$, produced up to ⅙ hp and, at an efficiency of 1.2 per cent, nearly as high as that of the small standard reciprocating steam engines at the low steam pressures. The chief difficulty is that to be efficient the rotor must be large in diameter and rotating at a very high velocity, but then the frictional losses become very great. After trying a whirling pipe with two exit nozzles, a rotating disk of low frictional resistance with a single outlet nozzle was adopted. The steam was kept enclosed with an effective washer of Teflon attached to the steam inlet pipe. Higher efficiencies were obtained with an engine in which the exit steam from the nozzle was condensed to water in an enclosed box[7] rather than being discharged into the air.

An impractically large focusing collector is required to operate an engine of this low efficiency on solar-produced steam.

In another development of the reactor steam engine, Kurz[8] has designed an effective smooth spherical shell of steel which is rotated by the escape of steam jets. The boiler and engine are combined in one rotating unit that can be placed at the focus of a circular focusing collector. In this way there are no valves and rotating connections and no heat losses when the steam passes from the boiler to the engine. The engine operates until all the water is vaporized; the engine is then stopped for refilling. The model used operated at pressures up to 300 psi and up to 10,000 rpm with a brake thermal efficiency of 1.5 per cent and a consumption of 7.5 lb hr^{-1} of steam.

The discussion of solar steam engines thus far has been restricted to small sizes of 1 kw or less. Fifty years ago sizes larger than 10 kw were built and operated, using solar collectors up to 30 ft in diameter, as described in Chapter 2, but they have not survived competition with electric motors and petroleum-operated internal-combustion engines. A very large installation designed and reported by Baum[9] in the

U.S.S.R. has a large steam boiler on a tall tower; mirrors mounted on cars moving on surrounding circular tracks keep the sunlight focused on it. It is designed to provide power and heat for a city of 10,000 people.

Conventional low-pressure, low-temperature steam turbines of large size may find an important place in the development of solar power. It is possible under special conditions, as described in Chapter 8, to heat large shallow ponds of water with black, water-impervious bottoms to high temperatures and produce steam at less than 1 atmosphere pressure for the operation of turbines. Many days of solar heating are required, and provisions must be made to prevent cooling of the pond by the evaporation of hot water at the surface. Much of the heat that flows into the ground remains there and constitutes part of the large heat storage. If the ponds are sufficiently large (several acres), the irretrievable heat losses to the air and the ground at the edges are comparatively small. There are two important advantages of these power ponds: they are comparatively inexpensive because they do not require large areas of glass or plastics in flat-plate or focusing collectors, and there are no heavy mechanical structures. Moreover the large amounts of stored heat permit the continuous operation of the turbines, night and day and in cloudy weather.

Tabor[10] has built power ponds of this type in which the hot water, heated to 90° C, is kept at the bottom of the pond where it cannot vaporize and cool the pond. He places at the bottom of the pond a permanent concentrated salt solution of such high density that even when it is hot it is denser than the stratified layer of ordinary water which lies above it.

Consideration has been given also to power ponds in which a large area of water, held in a shallow pond of water with a black floor, is covered with layers of sheet plastic to reduce heat losses at the surface from vaporization, radiation, and heating of the air.

Interesting proposals have been made[10,11] for solar heating large, shallow basins of water to produce both power and fresh water. The water is covered with a plastic roof, the hot water vapor at 70° C and higher operates a large conventional steam turbine, and the exhaust steam is condensed to give distilled water.

HOT-AIR ENGINES

The hot-air engine is a simple type of engine in which ordinary air is expanded by heating to a high temperature and compressed at a lower temperature, with part of the difference in energy between the two operations being available as mechanical work. Air is available everywhere and there are no problems of water boilers, explosion hazards, or fuel costs. An engine of this type was invented nearly a century and a half ago (1816) by Stirling and adapted to solar operation by Erricson in 1870.[13] Stirling engines were used for pumping water in 1818 and for operating printing presses and other machines before being displaced by steam engines, electric motors, and internal-combustion engines. A model of Erricson's solar hot-air engine[13] is exhibited in a Philadelphia museum.

Hot-air engines have long been neglected, but they are efficient and noiseless and recently they have been the object of considerable activity. The principle of a hot-air engine is shown in Figure 43, which applies to a closed, constant-volume cycle. Heat from a burning flame or focused sunlight heats the air contained in the cylinder (at the left in Fig. 43 A) which then expands and forces out the piston and turns the flywheel clockwise. When the flywheel turns, it moves the second piston into the cylinder at the right and compresses

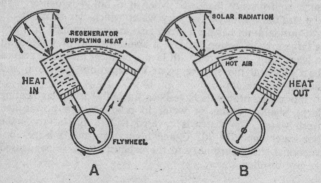

43. Principle of Stirling hot-air engine.

the air in the cylinder, forcing the air through the regenerator and into the cylinder at the left, where it is further heated and expanded. Heat is absorbed in the left cylinder and discharged in the right cylinder, either into a water-cooled jacket or an air-cooled wall with metal fins. When the left piston is at the end of its expansion stroke and the right piston is at the end of its compression stroke, the momentum of the flywheel reverses the direction of the pistons (see Fig. 43 B). The right piston now moves out in its cylinder and the left piston moves into its cylinder, forcing the heated, low-pressure air through the regenerator and into the right cylinder, where the heat is discharged to its surroundings. Much of the heat is left behind in the regenerator, which is packed with metal wool or other material of low heat capacity, large area, and good heat conductivity. This stored heat is then available on the next half cycle for preheating the incoming air. The preheated air is expanded still further by the heat applied to the cylinder at the left, and it does work by forcing out its piston. In summary, the air is expanded in the left cylinder, while hot, and compressed while cold; the net difference is thus made available for converting heat into mechanical work.

The ideal Carnot cycle applies to an operation in which all the heat is supplied isothermally at a single high temperature and dissipated isothermally at a single low temperature. Practically, engines do not operate in this way, and the heat is supplied and discharged at a series of changing temperatures, giving efficiencies considerably less than that of the limiting Carnot efficiency. In the Stirling cycle described here, however, much of the heat discharged at gradually decreasing temperatures is conserved and passed back by the regenerator into the incoming air on the next half cycle. In this way the efficiency of the hot-air engine is brought considerably closer to that of the Carnot cycle.

Regenerative thermal machines of the Stirling type can be used not only for obtaining mechanical power from heat but also for cooling and for the production of liquid air. They can be used in heat pumps for efficient heating with electrical power by transferring heat from a low temperature to a higher temperature. Intensive research by the Phillips Company in Holland and by industrial laboratories in the United States has led to the development of small hot-air engines of high efficiencies of 30 per cent and more. Finkelstein[14-16] has made comprehensive studies of hot-air engines. There are many different varieties with single and multiple cylinders and with different spatial arrangements of the cylinder and displacer.

One of the limiting factors in the operation of hot-air engines is the rate of heat transfer across the head of the cylinder. The area is small, and it is difficult to supply enough heat to the air between the cylinder head and the receding piston to produce large quantities of power. An improvement developed at the University of Wisconsin consists in having a transparent quartz window for the cylinder head to focus the solar radiation directly inside the engine. The radiation is absorbed internally and dissipated to the air contained in the cylinder without loss and without limitation of heat conductivity through a metal wall. Finkelstein describes[17] such a windowed Stirling hot-air engine (see Fig. 44). The piston (1) is forced out in its cylinder by the hot air which is heated by solar radiation focused by the parabolic mirror collector (6) and passed through the transparent quartz window (5) and onto the black, porous absorbing head (3) of the displacer and regenerator (2). The absorbing material is a screen of closely-woven fine black wires, heated by the focused sunlight. As the displacer moves up, the air is forced through the hot absorbing head and regenerator and into the working cylinder where it forces out the piston (1) and does mechanical work. When the piston is down at the end of its stroke, the flywheel (4) carries the piston upward and forces the expanded air back to the displacer–regenerator (2) where it is preheated. This low-pressure air being compressed is colder because of the work it has done in expansion and because of the cooling of the walls of the lower cylinder. In this part of the cycle the piston has moved up and the displacer down, so that most of the air is in the upper cylinder above the displacer (2), ready for heating by the radiant heat and the absorber. The expansion is done at a high temperature and the compression at a lower temperature, the net difference being available for external mechanical work (see Fig. 43). It is important to make the cylinders of thin, low-conducting metal so that heat will be transferred from the hot part of the engine to the cold part not by conduction but by compression and expansion of the enclosed air. More details of solar-operated hot-air engines are given in the references already cited.[2,3,17]

The number of hot-air engines operated by the sun is quite limited. After Erricson's attempt, Ghai and Khanna built and operated a solar Stirling hot-air engine in India in 1953.

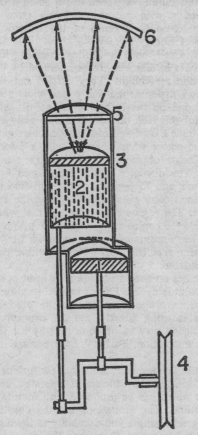

44. Stirling engine operating on solar radiation with internal
    focusing.
    1. Piston moving in cylinder.
    2. Displacer and regenerator moving in connecting parallel
       cylinder.
    3. Black, porous absorbing surface.
    4. Flywheel with shaft and cams.
    5. Transparent quartz window.
    6. Focused solar radiation.

Finkelstein and Eibling demonstrated a small Stirling hot-air engine, operating with focused radiation from an electric lamp, at the Rome Conference of the United Nations on New Sources of Energy in 1961.

Braun and Utz[18] built a Stirling engine with a quartz window 3 inches in diameter, to be operated by the sun with a 5-ft parabolic searchlight. They carried out an extensive theoretical and experimental study but were never able to make the engine do more than overcome its own friction. The reason for this lack of success is not easily explained.

Breihan[19] built a Stirling hot-air engine that gave 15 watts of mechanical power when operated with a 6-foot parabolic focusing collector of mosaic glass mirrors mounted on a plastic shell. The diameter of the engine was 4 inches, the stroke 1½ inch, and 75 per cent of the radiation was focused into a blackened cone which functioned as the heating head of the engine. The engine is so arranged that when sunshine is not available the engine can be operated with a flame from petroleum. The vibration of the engine on its 3-ft-long mounting is a present problem. Farber[20] has built and operated a solar hot-air engine.

The researches on hot-air engines have been devoted chiefly to constant-volume cycles. Efforts should be directed also to constant-pressure cycles. Cooling can be produced by the expanded air escaping directly into the atmosphere and the losses in efficiency may be offset in part by the simplicity of the engine construction. Farber[21] has reported on such an engine.

Another field for research is the hot-air turbine. Large gas turbines are simple and efficient if operated at very high temperatures which can be produced with focusing collectors of high precision. The limitations are the construction materials, with great strength and durability at the high temperatures, and the lubrication problems. The solar operation of air turbines does not lend itself easily to units of large size which give higher efficiency.

VAPOR ENGINES

Water and air are the commonest fluids for the operation of heat engines. For high thermodynamic efficiency high-boiling liquids such as mercury are available and for solar operation with nonfocusing flat-plate collectors such low-boiling liquids as sulfur dioxide can be used. Both have been tried. Mercury is expensive, heavy, and poisonous, and the sulfur dioxide engine is inefficient. A cylindrical collector can easily operate a steam engine, and a circular focusing collector, even an inexpensive plastic collector, can provide temperatures of 300 or 400° C. Among the organic liquids only those are useful which do not decompose chemically at the temperature of vaporization. A wide variety of fluorinated compounds, including Freons, is available for the lower temperature ranges.

Tabor[4,20] has carried out an excellent research program to find a liquid with improved thermodynamic properties for operating turbines with solar energy and has determined the following criteria for the operating fluid:

1. It should be chemically stable and noncorrosive.
2. It should be cheap.
3. Its boiling point should be over 100° but less than 150° C so that condensation at room temperature will not create too high a vacuum or allow too high a pressure of residual vapor which will cause undue friction on the very rapidly revolving turbine disk.
4. The molecular weight should be high, well over 100 and preferably several hundred. The velocity of steam in small turbines is excessive (1,500 ft sec^{-1}), causing difficulty in design, frictional losses, and erosion of the blades if there are any supercooled droplets of liquid. Heavy vapors can give the same kinetic energy ($\frac{1}{2} mv^2$) at lower velocities. The velocity v is inversely proportional to the square root of the molecular weight m at a given kinetic energy. Thus the ratio of the velocity of a vapor with a molecular weight of 100 to the velocity of steam with a molecular weight of 18 is 0.42. The lower heats of vaporization require a greater mass of material flowing through the turbine, which is an advantage in small turbines.
5. The entropy–temperature diagram should give a high efficiency; substances with about 5 to 10 atoms in the molecule are favorable. High molecular weight and small number of atoms in the molecule require heavy atoms such as chlorine. Liquids of this type tend not to form droplets of liquid when saturated vapor is cooled by expansion.

Tabor[21] examined 16 different liquids and decided that monochlorobenzene (C_6H_5Cl) meets these five criteria and is the best liquid to use in small turbines. He developed a 2-kw monochlorobenzene turbine operating at 150° C at 18,000 rpm, using a 6 to 1 reduction gear. The efficiency of converting heat into work was 10 to 15 per cent, whereas the efficiency of 2-kw steam engines is usually less than 5 per cent.

Tabor built a 5-hp solar-operated turbine and exhibited it pumping water near Rome in 1961 at the United Nations Conference on New Sources of Energy. The monochloroben-zene was vaporized with superheated steam produced in iron pipes at the focus of plastic cylindrical collectors 5 ft in diameter and 20 ft long. The bottom parts of the cylinders were made of aluminized plastic. The collectors remained stationary during the day but were moved with the changing seasons. They had a concentration ratio of about 3. A picture of this plastic cylindrical collector is shown in Plate 2.

Other kinds of vapor engines have been proposed. A 2½-hp engine for pumping water or generating electricity, making use of sulfur dioxide, was exhibited at the World Symposium on Applied Solar Energy at Phoenix, Arizona, in 1955. It was known as the Somor engine and was manufactured by the Societa Motori Recuperi of Lecco, Italy. The solar radiation heated three large, tilted flat-plate collectors with side wings of flat mirrors placed at an angle to increase the heating of the metal plate receiver in which the sulfur dioxide was vaporized.

An early solar device pumped water in 1885 by evaporating a volatile liquid such as ammonia in a flat-plate collector. The ammonia under pressure forced in a flat rubber diaphragm in a container and operated a system of valves.

Another solar pumping device exhibited at the Phoenix symposium was known as the Novoid solar hydraulic engine. The focused sunlight vaporized water in a tube with explosive violence and thrust. The steam condensed in the water and a series of thrusts produced mechanical power for pumping water.

If an opaque gas could be made to absorb most of the solar radiation, a windowed engine (see Fig. 44) would be interesting because the gas would expand quickly and effectively without involving heat transfer from a heated surface. Chlorine, bromine, and iodine are not sufficiently light absorbing throughout the solar spectrum, and colloidal particles of carbon floating in air would precipitate out on the window and walls. Such a gas is not now available.

ECONOMIC CONSIDERATIONS

It is important to use efficient engines for solar operation—not to economize on fuel, which is virtually free, but to reduce the cost of the focusing collector which involves much of the large capital investment needed for the solar installation. Tabor[4,22] has made a thorough study of the economic factors involved in the use of solar heat engines for power. The capital investment is considerably greater than for heat engines operating on fuel, so the operating costs and the cost of repairs must be kept very low. In Tabor's calculations,

Q = total annual solar radiation in kwhr m^{-2}
A = area of collector in m^2
E_o = efficiency of collector
E_t = efficiency of turbine
C = cost of collectors in dollars m^{-2}
T = cost of turbine and other fixed costs
J_o = annual investment costs of collector expressed as fraction of cost of collector
J_T = annual investment cost of turbine
X = utilization factor

Power produced per year = QE_oE_tA (kwhr), and the power used per year is this quantity multiplied by X.
Capital investment = $CA + T$ ($).
Annual charges on investment = $CAJ_o + TJ_T$ ($). Cost

$$\text{per kwhr} = \frac{CAJ_o + TJ_T}{XQE_oE_tA}$$

As a rough approximation it may be assumed that the cost of the turbine is negligible in comparison with the cost of the collector; therefore T is set equal to zero. It is assumed that the annual solar radiation Q is 2,000 kwhr, which is possible in a sunny area with a stationary collector. The efficiency of the collector E_o is taken as 0.4 and the efficiency of the turbine E_t as 0.15. This turbine efficiency corresponds to that of the monochlorobenzene turbine just described and is much higher than that of most small engines which have been operated by the sun. The cost of the focusing collector is taken as $20 m^{-2} or approximately $2 ft^{-2}. The fraction of the annual investment cost J_o of the collector is taken as

0.20; it includes a 6-year life for the collector and interest at 6 per cent. With these values, the collector component of the power cost is 3.4¢ kwhr⁻¹. It is clear that it will be difficult to bring the cost of solar-generated electricity produced in small heat engines below 5¢ kwhr⁻¹. Although this price is very high for American use serviced from large power stations, it is probably nearly competitive in some isolated areas where storage of power is not required and small Diesel engines are used.

With lower energy efficiencies, the cost would increase directly. The only hope for much-reduced costs lies in cheaper solar collectors—for example the power ponds previously discussed[10]—where the cost of the collector may be as low as $1 m⁻².

References

1. Molenaar, A., *Water-Lifting Devices for Irrigation*, New York, Food and Agricultural Organization, United Nations, 1956.

2. Jordan, R. C., and Ibele, W. E., Mechanical Energy from Solar Energy, in *Proceedings, World Symposium on Applied Solar Energy*, Phoenix, Ariz., 1955, Menlo Park, Calif., Stanford Research Institute, 1956, pp. 81–101.

3. Jordan, R. C., Conversion of Solar to Mechanical Energy, in *Introduction to the Utilization of Solar Energy*, ed. A. M. Zarem, and D. D. Erway, pp. 125–152. New York, McGraw-Hill, 1963.

4. Tabor, H., Use of Solar Energy for Mechanical Power and Electricity Production by Means of Piston Engines and Turbines, in *United Nations Conference on New Sources of Energy*, E 35 Gr–59, Rome, 1961.

5. Abbott, C. G., Solar Power from Collecting Mirrors, in *Solar Energy Research*, ed., F. Daniels, and J. A. Duffie, Madison, University of Wisconsin Press, 1955, pp. 91–95.

6. Hsu, S. T., and Leo, B. S., A simple reaction turbine as a solar engine, *Solar Energy, 2* (3–4): 7–11. 1958.

7. Hsu, S. T., and Leo, B. S., A simple reaction turbine as a solar engine, *Solar Energy, 4* (2): 16–20. 1960.

8. Kurz, J. L., A Combination Boiler-Reaction Turbine as a Solar Engine (special project in Mechanical Engineering 151 with Professor S. T. Hsu, University of Wisconsin, 1962).

9. Baum, V., Prospects for the Application of Solar Energy and Some Research Results in the U.S.S.R., in *Proceedings, World Symposium Applied Solar Energy*, Phoenix, Ariz., 1955, pp. 289–98.

10. Tabor, H., Large-Area Solar Collectors (Solar Ponds) for

Power Production, in *U.N. Conf. on New Sources of Energy*, E 35–S47; *Solar Energy, 7:* 189–94. 1963.

11. Hirschmann, J., A solar energy pilot plant for northern Chile, *Solar Energy, 5:* 37–43. 1961.

12. Hummel, R., Power as a By-product of Competitive Solar Distillation, in *U.N. Conf. on New Sources of Energy*, E 35–S15, Rome, 1961.

13. Erricson, J., Sun Power; The Solar Engine, *Contributions to the Centennial*, pp. 571–77, Philadelphia, 1870.

14. Finkelstein, T., Generalized Thermodynamic Analysis of Stirling Engines. *Am. Soc. of Automotive Engineers*, Paper 118 B. Annual meeting, 1960.

15. Finkelstein T., Cyclic Processes in Closed Regenerative Gas Machines, *Am. Soc. of Mech. Engineers*, Paper 61–SA–21. Annual Meeting, 1961.

16. Finkelstein, T., Conversion of Solar Radiation into Power, *Am. Soc. of Mech. Engineers*, Paper 61–WA–297. Annual Meeting, 1961.

17. Finkelstein, T., Internally Focussing Solar Power Systems, *Am. Soc. of Mech. Engineers*, Paper 61–WA–297. Annual Meeting, 1961.

18. Utz, J. A., and Braun, R. A., Design and Initial Tests of a Stirling Engine for Solar Energy Applications, M. S. Thesis, Mechanical Engineering Dept., University of Wisconsin, 1960.

19. Breihan, R. R., Madison, Wis., Forthcoming publication.

20. Farber, E. A., A Closed Cycle Solar Engine, Solar Energy Symposium, University of Florida, Gainesville, 1964.

21. Farber, E. A., An Open Cycle Solar Engine, Solar Energy Symposium, University of Florida, Gainesville, 1964.

22. Tabor, H., and Bronicki, J. L., Small Turbine for Solar Energy Power Package, in *U.N. Conf. on New Sources of Energy*, E 35–S54, Rome, 1961.

CHAPTER 15

Thermoelectric and Thermoionic Conversion

It is possible to convert solar energy directly into electrical energy by means of thermocouples with no machinery and no moving parts. A thermocouple is made by joining alternate lengths of electrical conductors or semiconductors of different kinds, and heating one junction and cooling the other. This production of a potential difference and the generation of electrical energy by a thermocouple of dissimilar metals was discovered by Seebeck in 1821. Thermocouples have long been used for measuring temperatures and for operating thermostat circuits. Such thermocouples are often made of copper and a copper–nickel alloy called constantan, or alloys of chromium and aluminum called alumel–chromel. These metal thermocouples give voltages of 42 microvolts and 65 microvolts°C^{-1}, respectively. Coblentz described[1] a thermoelectric converter for solar energy in 1922.

To be effective in the conversion of solar energy into electricity the thermocouple must meet three requirements—a high voltage per degree, a high electrical conductivity to avoid loss by internal heating, and a low thermal conductivity to prevent transfer of heat between the hot junction and the cold junction without contributing electrical energy. The requirement of low heat conductivity with high electrical conductivity is difficult to fulfill. The thermoelectric force of metals and the conversion of heat into work are too low for the efficient conversion of solar energy into electrical power. Semiconductors, however, with their higher thermoelectric forces, have a more encouraging prospect. They include such elements in the middle of the periodic table as silicon and compounds like sulfides and oxides.

Telkes summarized[2] the situation at a symposium in 1953 and reported her work on the development of thermocouples for solar energy conversion. It was felt at the time that it would be difficult to obtain conversion with an efficiency of more than about 3 per cent. The advances in solid-state physics of the decade following have been so rapid that considerably higher efficiencies are now possible.

In 1955 Telkes gave a comprehensive report[3] on materials for thermoelectric generators, and other papers[4–6] on thermoelectric conversion of solar radiation were presented at a symposium in Phoenix, Arizona.

In 1961 at the United Nations Conference on New Sources of Energy there were several contributions to thermoelectric conversion of solar energy, ably summarized by Baum.[7] Important among these was one by Katz[8] giving the theory and experimental technique for making solar thermoelectric converters, together with a detailed description of one type that was tested with the sun and found to deliver 40 watts. Katz also gives calculations for the use of thermoelectric generators to pump irrigation water and for the consideration of costs.

Many books on the theory and practice of thermoelectricity have appeared recently.[9-14] Joffe[15] covers the extensive work done in the U.S.S.R. and gives a comprehensive discussion of thermoelectricity.

Early optimism for thermoelectric generators has been somewhat tempered by the fact that some of them deteriorate with continued operation at high temperatures where the efficiencies are high.

PRINCIPLES

In a metal the electrons are free to move and to flow toward a positively-charged electrode placed in contact with the metal, thus carrying a current of electricity. When a piece of metal is heated there will be some migration of electrons from the heated end to the colder end, and the rate of accumulation at the colder end will depend on the nature of the metal. When alternate sections of wires of two different metals A and B are welded or soldered together in series giving the arrangement $A_1–B_1–A_2$, and the junction $A_1–B_1$ is heated and the junction $B_1–A_2$ is cooled, a difference in electrical potential is set up and current can be drawn from A_1 and A_2 to operate an electrical instrument or a motor. An indefinite number of such thermocouples may be used in series $(A_1–B_1–A_2–B_2–A_3–B_3–A_4 \ . \ . \ .)$, and the voltage at the terminals is the sum of the voltages of all the thermocouples. The resistances too are additive; thus the internal resistance increases and the short-circuit current decreases as the number of thermocouples increases. Thermocouples of unlike metals have voltages of 20 to 60 microvolts per degree and thermocouples of unlike semiconductors may have voltages of 1,000 microvolts per degree.

Semiconductors are made by adding selected impurities to pure crystals as described in the following chapter. The highly purified crystals do not conduct the electric current, but when small amounts of an element with a higher valence are added, their atoms become incorporated into the lattice and their extra electrons are free to move, making them fairly good conductors called semiconductors. The semiconductor with freely-moving negative electrons is known as an N-semiconductor. If an element of a lower valence is added to the crystal, electrons become attached to its atoms and there are no freely moving electrons, but the positive "holes" created by the binding of the electrons in the lattice

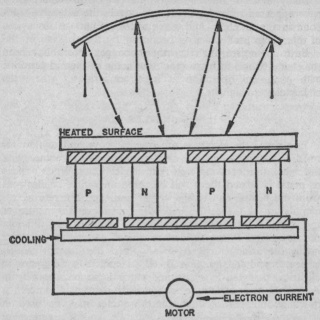

45. Arrangement of P and N junctions in a thermoelectric generator.

of the crystal are free to move. Such a semiconductor is known as a P-semiconductor. The N- and P-semiconductors are placed in series $P_1-N_1-P_2-N_2-P_1-N_3 \ldots$, similar to the A–B arrangement just described. They are illustrated in Figure 45.

The difference in rate of migration of the negative electrons and the positive holes under the temperature gradient sets up the thermoelectric voltages in these semiconductors. The thermoelectric conversion efficiency is defined as the ratio of the electrical energy delivered to the external circuit to the heat energy absorbed at the hot junction. The maximum work obtainable is limited by the Carnot cycle, as are all thermal machines that convert heat into work, according to which the efficiency is given by the relation $(T_2 - T_1)/T_2$, where T_2 is the higher absolute temperature and T_1 is the lower. There are additional limitations which make the work delivered considerably less than that calculated from the Carnot cycle. There is a loss of heat along the thermocouple from the heated end to the cold end; for this reason the heat conductivity is made as low as possible. There is also a loss of energy as heat which is produced by the passage of the electric current through the thermocouple. For this reason the electrical conductivity should be made as high as possible. The efficiency then involves two factors—the Carnot relation which applies to all thermocouples and a factor involving thermal conductivity and electrical conductivity which depends on the materials of which the thermocouple is composed.

Intensive research has been directed toward finding P- and N-thermocouple material with high thermoelectric force, low heat conductivity, and high electrical conductivity. Elements with 4, 5, and 6 electrons in their outer shells have been used most widely, including pairs of semiconductors containing silicon, phosphorus, sulfur, germanium, arsenic, selenium, tin, antimony, tellurium, and bismuth. The metals are not efficient because in them the conduction of heat and electricity takes place by the same mechanism, and it is difficult to change their ratio. In semiconductors, however, the electricity is conducted by free charges, and heat is conducted mainly by lattice vibration.

Many other factors influence the choice of thermoelectric elements. The elements must be chemically stable under the conditions of operation, including high temperatures. Unless closed in gastight containers they must not be oxidizable by air. They must have suitable mechanical strength, and the arrangement of thermoelectric units and contacts must allow for large and unequal thermal expansions.

Although larger quantities of electrical work can be produced from a given quantity of heat by introducing it at a high temperature, there are definite limits of temperature to which a thermocouple can be exposed. It should be kept well below the melting point of the thermoelectric units and accessory equipment, and below temperatures at which there is appreciable diffusion of the added impurities away from the hot end. Moreover, at sufficiently high temperatures there is a tendency for the fixed positive charges in the N-type semiconductors and the fixed negative charges in the P-type conductors to become released so that the difference in behavior of the two becomes less, thus lowering the thermoelectric force per degree.

Sometimes thermocouples are arranged with different N-materials and P-materials in series so that those at the hot end are capable of withstanding very high temperatures and those at the cold end have a high thermoelectric voltage but are not usable at the high temperature. Thus a greater thermoelectric efficiency can be obtained for a given temperature difference.

Thermocouples may be made not only of compounds of elements in the 4, 5, and 6 groups of the periodic table but also of mixed-valence material. For example, if nickel oxide is heated with an excess of oxygen, or if it is doped by the addition of a trace of a univalent element like lithium, there is a transfer of electrons to maintain electrical neutrality and a change in the mobility of the electrons which can modify the thermoelectric force. The mixed-valence materials give comparatively low thermoelectric voltages but are capable of operating at high temperatures, about 800° C.

The thermoelectric elements are set into a metal box with a thick, blackened metallic plate at the hot end to receive radiation from a focusing collector and produce a uniform temperature over the whole area in spite of the inequalities that result from imperfect focusing. The thermoelectric elements are forced against the high temperature source, sometimes with the help of a spring to exert pressure for good thermal contact and a thin sheet of mica to prevent electrical contact. The back side is water-cooled, or air-cooled with large, radiating metallic fins. The use of a selective radiation coating (described in Chapter 12) reduces heat losses and leads to higher temperatures.

THERMOELECTRIC GENERATORS

Baum lists[7] some of the compounds that have been tried for thermoelectric generators, including telurides of antimony, bismuth, germanium, and lead, and some selenides. He gives the range of working temperatures and the thermoelectric properties. He advocates the use of focusing collectors for thermoelectric generators, parabolic for concentrations of 200- to 1,000-fold and parabolic-cylindrical for concentrations of 10- to 30-fold. Baum describes some of the thermoelectric generators developed in the U.S.S.R.

Katz describes[8] the details of construction of a thermoelectric generator designed to operate with focused solar radiation, and gives estimated performances and cost calculations for a 125-watt generator. He estimates a cost of about

7¢ to 10¢ per kwhr of electricity produced from heat in such a thermoelectric generator. This thermoelectric generator (developed by the Westinghouse Electric Corporation and described by Katz) was tested with a solar focusing collector.[16] The generator was 5 inches[2] and weighed 9 lb. It was mounted at the focus of a 6-ft parabolic collector (see Plate 8). The collector shell was of fiberglass cloth and plastic laid over a plaster mold made by rotating a parabolic edge (described in Chapter 4); it was lined with aluminized Mylar. The pattern of the focused sunlight as determined photographically with moonlight is shown in Figure 46, where the numbers refer to radiation concentration ratios. The radiation hitting the target was measured calorimetrically with a blackened copper disk held at the focus and plunged into the water. It was checked by calculations based on the photographic measurements. The temperature reached 485° C. The front plate of stainless steel was nickel plated, flashed with a thin electroplated coating of copper, and then heated in air with focused solar radiation to give the black copper oxide. This selective coating (described in Chapter 12), absorbed about 85 per cent of the radiation and emitted

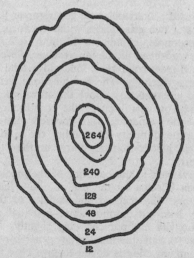

46. Patterns of focused radiation on a 12.5-cm (5-inch) square, showing areas of intensification of solar radiation.

about 25 per cent as much infrared radiation as a blackbody would. The back side of the thermoelectric generator was water cooled.

In general the focusing collector intercepted about 2 kw of solar radiation on a clear day and delivered 1 kw of heat to the target. The electricity generated was about 40 watts at first, but became less after several hours of operation. The open circuit voltage was 4 volts and the closed circuit current up to 40 amp. The efficiency of the thermoelectric generator was roughly 4 per cent, and the total efficiency of solar collector and thermoelectric generator was of the order of 2 per cent. A small motor and pump were operated to lift water. The low voltage (4 volts) is a handicap for operating motors because of the large wires needed for electrical connections and the large brush losses in the motor. In these experiments an automobile storage battery was charged in parallel and discharged in series in order to obtain a higher voltage.

Kobayashi describes 17 silicides in thermoelectric generators using N-type cobalt silicide and P-type chromium and manganese silicide. He used them at 1,000° C to generate 10 watts of electricity with an efficiency of 6 per cent and more.

Michel[18] used a thermoelectric generator of large area and a cover glass of two glass plates without a focusing collector. Each thermocouple, containing bismuth telluride, was attached to a blackened aluminum receiver. Seven watts m^{-2} were obtained from solar radiation, and a total of 120 watts from the large assembly. The hot junctions were at 140° C and the cold junctions 25° above the surrounding air.

Perrot and Touchais discuss[19] the construction of thermoelectric generators operated with focused sunlight; they call attention to the difficulty of cooling the cold end of the thermoelectric junctions, particularly in the climate of the Sahara Desert.

An improvement in the behavior of thermoelectric generators has been effected by the use of alloys instead of pure semiconductors. The thermal conductivity of these alloys is considerably less, but thermoelectric potential and the electrical conductivity are reduced only slightly. Raag has described[20] a 50-watt thermoelectric generator in which a silicon-germanium alloy is doped to give N- and P-junctions and operated at temperatures up to 850° C. These alloys have favorable mechanical properties and do not deteriorate on long usage at high temperatures.

THERMOIONIC CONVERTERS

In thermoionic converters an electron-emitting surface is heated to a very high temperature, 1,500° C or above, and electrons are "evaporated" off in a vacuum or in an atmosphere of positive ions, such as cesium ions. A cold receiving plate of metal placed only about a thousandth of an inch away collects these electrons, which are driven out across the narrow gap, and carries them around through an external wire to the electron-emitting electrode. No materials are consumed, but on long usage the surface of the emitting electrode deteriorates. Because the gap between the electrodes has a good electrical conductivity and a poor thermal conductivity, this method of generating electrical power has promising features, but there are two distinct disadvantages. The temperature has to be so high that expensive solar collectors with higher optical precision must be used, and the gap between the cooled electrode and the heated electrode is very narrow, hence the differences in temperature create problems of thermal expansion and contraction which necessitate precision alignment and close tolerances. The difficulty of the space charge built up by the stream of electrons is overcome either by having a very narrow gap in the evacuated tube or by introducing cesium vapor.

Baum reported[7] a thermoionic power generator operating at 2,600° C with an efficiency of 4 per cent and producing 11 watts cm^{-2}.

Hatsopoulos and Brosens reported[21] a thermoionic generator operating at 1,200° C and producing 0.6 watt cm^{-2} with an efficiency of 6 per cent. Operating with cesium vapor in another converter at 2,200° C, they suggested the possibility of 20 watts cm^{-2} with an efficiency of 15 per cent. They point out that only small amounts of metals such as copper, tantalum, and molybdenum are used in the construction, with a consequent low investment cost. The length of service is estimated between 10,000 and 50,000 hr.

Wilson[22] has made a complete study of thermoionic converters and points out the advantages and difficulties. He suggests that the protection of large installations against deterioration from air oxidation may be accomplished either by enclosing several electrodes in a large evacuated chamber or by using ceramic parts that are resistant to air at high temperatures.

References

1. Coblentz, W. W., Harnessing heat from the sun, *Sci. Am.*, *127:* 324. 1922.

2. Telkes, M., Solar Thermoelectric Generators, in *Solar Energy Research*, ed. F. Daniels and J. A. Duffie, Madison, University of Wisconsin Press, 1955, pp. 137–42.

3. Telkes, M., Materials for Thermoelectric Generators in *Transactions of Conference on the Use of Solar Energy: The Scientific Basis, 5:* 1–7. Tucson, University of Arizona Press, 1958.

4. Heywood, H., Mechanical Construction and Thermal Characteristics of Solar-Operated Thermoelectric Generators, ibid., pp. 8–20.

5. Momota, T., and Matsukura, Y., The Efficiency of Solar Thermoelectric Generators Composed of Semiconductors, ibid., pp. 21–30.

6. Perrot, M., Peri, G., and Robert, J., A Thermoelectric Effect with Powdered Metallic Oxides, ibid., pp. 36–42.

7. Baum, V. A., The Use of Solar Energy for Electricity Production by Direct Conversion by Means of Thermoelectric Converters and Photoelectric Cells, in *United Nations Conference on New Sources of Energy*, E 35Gr–S10, Rome, 1961.

8. Katz, K., Thermoelectric Generators for the Conversion of Solar Energy to Produce Electrical and Mechanical Power, ibid., E 35–S12.

9. Egli, P. H., *Thermoelectricity*, New York, Wiley, 1960.

10. Goldsmid, H. J., *Applications of Thermoelectricity*, London, Methuen, 1960.

11. Irving, B. C., and Miller, E., *Thermoelectric Materials and Devices*, New York, Reinhold, 1960.

12. Kaye, J., and Welsh, J. A., *Direct Conversion of Heat to Electricity*, New York, Wiley, 1960.

13. *Engineering of Thermoelectricity*, New York, Interscience, 1961.

14. MacDonald, D. K. C., *Thermoelectricity: An Introduction to the Principles*, New York, Wiley, 1962.

15. Joffe, A. F., *Semiconductor Thermoelements and Thermoelectric Cooling*, London, Infosearch, 1957. (Trans. from Russian.)

16. Breihan, R. R., Daniels, F., Duffie, J. A., and Löf, G. O. G., Preliminary Tests of a Solar-Heated Thermoelectric Converter, in *U.N. Conf. on New Sources of Energy*, E 35–S103.

17. Kobayashi, M., Thermoelectric Generator, ibid., E 35–S10.

18. Michel, R., New Solar Thermoelectric Generators—Description, Results, and Future Prospects, ibid., E 35–S55.

19. Perrot, M., and Touchais, M., Technical Research Trends at IESUA for Energy Production from Solar Radiation, ibid., E 35–S84.

20. Raag, V., Silicon-Germanium Thermocouple Development, in *17th Annual Power Conf.*, Red Bank, N.J., U.S. Army Electronics, Research and Development Laboratory, 1963, pp. 34–36.

21. Hatsopoulos, G. N., and Brosens, P. J., Solar-Heated Thermoionic Converter, in *U.N. Conf. on New Sources of Energy*, E 35–S78.

22. Wilson, V. C., The Conversion of Solar Energy to Electricity by Means of the Thermoionic Converter, ibid., E 35–S90.

CHAPTER 16

Photovoltaic Conversion

The preceding chapers have all discussed the use of solar radiation as heat. The limitations have been pointed out, such as the heat losses from equipment operating at high temperatures and the requirement for high temperatures in order to transfer heat effectively and to convert heat into work. We shall now consider the opportunities for using solar radiation as light rather than heat—in this chapter by means of solid semiconductors for the direct production of electricity, and in the following chapter by means of photochemical reactions for the storage of energy and the generation of electricity. These methods also have limitations, important among which is the fact that about half the solar radiation occurs at long wavelengths in the infrared where the energy is insufficient to bring about the photochemical and photovoltaic actions.

The photovoltaic production of electricity from the sun has interested scientists ever since the discovery of the selenium cell. At a symposium in 1953 it was stated that an efficiency of 1 per cent conversion of solar energy into electricity could be taken as a fair representation of attainability with photovoltaic cells. So rapid have been the developments in the field of solid-state physics that two years later at another symposium a silicon photovoltaic cell was reported with an efficiency of 11 per cent. Still higher efficiencies have been obtained with selected silicon photovoltaic cells, and the manufacture of these cells for satellites and space vehicles has become an industry of considerable magnitude. Photovoltaic conversion of sunlight is simple and efficient, but it is still much too expensive for general use in the production of electrical power.

PRINCIPLES

The principles of converting sunlight into electricity through photovoltaic cells are discussed by Pearson,[1] by Chapin,[2] and by Trivich.[3,4]

Photovoltaic cells, or barrier-layer cells, involve a P-N junction in a semiconductor between a positive layer which contains movable positive charges or "holes" and an N-layer which contains movable negative electrons. When light of sufficient energy enters the crystal, electrons are released and they flow to an electrode and through a wire to the other electrode where they combine with the positive holes. A barrier at the P-N junction prevents the instant recombination of electrons and positive holes and causes the electrons to go through the wire, generating useful electricity. No material is consumed, and the operation of the cell can continue indefinitely. The silicon cell will be taken as an example to illustrate photovoltaic cells because it is typical and is widely used.

Silicon has a valence of 4; in a pure crystal, the atoms are arranged in a regular and completely uniform lattice. The electrical conductivity is very low. If a 5-valence element, such as arsenic, is introduced as an impurity into the fused silicon and the liquid allowed to cool slowly, the crystal will be uniform, but some of the silicon atoms in the lattice will be replaced by arsenic atoms. Four of the five electrons of the arsenic atoms are used in the bonding of the crystals just as are the four electrons of the silicon atoms, but the fifth electron is free to move and to act as a carrier of electricity. Also when a 3-valence atom, like boron, is introduced as an impurity in the crystal lattice it takes on an extra electron, and the electron taken from the lattice of silicon atoms leaves an extra positive "hole" which is free to move. Although the pure silicon crystal is an insulator, it becomes a fair electrical conductor known as a semiconductor when "doped" with these impurities.

In the photovoltaic cell (see Fig. 47) a negative N-layer

with fixed positive charges and freely moving electrons is in contact with a positive P-layer in which the electrons are fixed but the positive holes are free to move. At the plane of contact the diffusing electrons from the N-layer meet the diffusing positive holes from the P-layer and combine. These charges become neutralized at the boundary, leaving behind positively-charged arsenic ions on the N-side and negatively-charged boron on the P-side. Whereas both layers were originally neutral, there is now a positive charge on the P-side of a barrier which reduces further diffusion of holes and a negative charge on the N-side which reduces further diffusion of electrons. Metallic electrodes are attached to these P and N parts of the crystal.

When light of sufficient energy (throughout the visible

N-Layer
with fixed
positive "holes"
in a silicon lattice.
Electrons are
free to move

Barrier layer
with fixed electrons
and positive holes

P-Layer
with fixed
electrons in a
silicon lattice.
Positive holes
are free to
move

·47. Principle of P–N photovoltaic cell. The charges in circles are not free to move; the others are free to move.

light and into the short infrared in the case of silicon) is absorbed, each unit of light (each photon) produces a negative electron and a "positive hole." In an ordinary crystal these would recombine immediately, with the net result that the light would be converted into heat. Because of the potential barrier at the P–N junction, however, the electrons produced by light in the N-layer are driven to the electrode, and the positive holes produced by light in the P-layer are driven to the other electrode. As these electrons and holes accumulate at the two separate electrodes a potential is set up, and a current of electricity flows through a wire connecting the two electrodes.

There is a tendency for the electrons and holes in each layer to combine before reaching the electrode and thus decrease the useful charges built up at the electrodes. Because the rate of this recombination is greatly increased by irregularities in the lattice caused by the presence of impurities of other elements, it is necessary to use extremely pure materials. Silicon and other materials of this high purity are made by zone refining, a method in which a narrow, moving furnace melts a small region in a long tube of crystalline material and chases impurities to one end as it moves along the tube.

Also the irregularities at the surface of a crystal catalyze the rapid recombination of electrons and holes, so it has generally been necessary to use large single crystals, rather than crystals composed of many small crystals connected in a larger crystalline mass.

The energy required to raise electrons to a sufficient energy level to enable them to move freely in the "conduction band" of the crystal depends on the chemical binding. In silicon all the visible light of sunlight and out to 11,500 Å in the infrared is sufficient to release electrons for operation of the silicon photovoltaic cell. This cut-off corresponds to an energy of 1.08 electron volts. Light of still longer wavelengths is wasted because its energy is too low to release any electrons and make the crystal conducting. The light of shorter wavelengths and greater energy releases electrons but with less efficiency because it has more energy per photon than is necessary. One photon releases only one electron, no matter how much excess energy it has.

The maximum electrical conversion takes place at about 7,000 Å, which is close to the wavelength of maximum intensity in solar radiation.

Silicon is especially favorable for the solar operation of photovoltaic cells.

SILICON PHOTOVOLTAIC CELLS

The technique for manufacturing silicon cells is well developed. Silicon, which is one of the most abundant elements in the earth's crust, is highly purified so that the concentration of objectionable impurities is reduced to less than 1 part in a million. As stated before, this purification is necessary to prevent the recombination of negative electrons and positive holes before they reach the electrodes. The cost of purified silicon was formerly \$400 lb⁻¹; in 1961 it was \$80 lb⁻¹, and still lower prices may be expected. A trace of arsenic is added in making the N-layer so that in the final crystal there is about 1 part of arsenic to 1 million parts of silicon. The material is melted in an induction furnace, and a small seed crystal of silicon is attached to the cooling surface and drawn up very slowly to make a long single crystal shaped like an icicle. It is then cut into thin sections which are "doped" with boron by placing them in a heated chamber with the vapor of boron trichloride. The temperature and time of contact are varied so that the boron diffuses into the thin section for about 10^{-4} cm from the surface and makes the P-layer. The N-layer, deeper in the crystal, remains unchanged. The P-layer on the back of the cell is etched off. Narrow electrodes are attached to the P- and N-layers by electroplating or other means (see Fig. 48). The barrier layer between the outer P-layer and the inner N-layer is produced at the end of the diffusion path of the

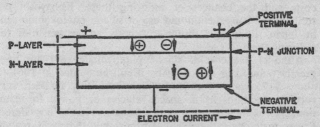

48. Arrangement of photovoltaic cell.

boron. The P-layer is so thin that the incident sunlight passes through the P-layer and penetrates beyond the P–N junction, releasing electrons and positive holes in both layers. The electrons move to one electrode, making it negative, and the holes to the other, making it positive.

In bright sunlight the voltage of a silicon photovoltaic cell is about 0.5 to 0.6 volts. The internal resistance depends on the geometry and on the electrode contacts. Several cells may be placed in series, but for maximum performances each cell must be subjected to the same intensity of light.

Calculations show that, allowing for the inactivity at the long wavelengths and the inefficiency at the shorter wavelengths, about 45 per cent of the sunlight is the maximum that can be used in releasing electrons. Perhaps only about half this energy is available as recoverable electrical energy; and also there is the loss of reflected light at the surface and the loss caused by the recombination of electrons and holes, particularly when they are released considerably above or below the P–N junction. There is some leakage of current across the junction barrier. As a result of all these losses, an efficiency of 14 per cent is about all that can be expected now, and this value has been reached in some cells.

Several reports on the uses and costs of silicon photovoltaic cells, and improvements in their construction, were reported at the United Nations Conference on New Sources of Energy at Rome in 1961. Wolf described[5] attempts to produce cheaper cells, and gave original and maintenance costs for solar silicon photovoltaic cells for communication purposes. He compared them with the costs of electric power, motor-generators, and dry cell batteries. Pearson reviewed[6] the use of solar photovoltaic cells in communications. Prince discussed[7] improvements in photovoltaic cells. Ravich discussed[8] costs and the chances of reducing them. Kobayoshi described[9] the construction and use of silicon photovoltaic cells in Japan. Rappaport discussed[10] costs and possibilities for reducing them.

Although the cost of silicon photovoltaic cells has been greatly reduced in recent years, it still amounted in 1961 to about \$175 watt^{-1} or \$175,000 kw^{-1}. Only in such very special conditions as in space vehicles or power for communications in remote areas can such a price be considered. Prices may come down still further, but they will remain high as long as the present techniques are used, involving extreme purification, growing of single crystals, and cutting with diamond saws, with the accompanying waste of materials. Perhaps cells of materials other than silicon may be cheaper, even though they are less efficient. Perhaps new techniques and new ways of using the photovoltaic cells will lower the costs. They will be discussed in the two following sections.

OTHER PHOTOVOLTAIC CELLS

Although silicon photovoltaic cells have the highest efficiencies yet obtained, many other crystals can be made with P–N junctions and good photovoltaic properties.

Rappaport lists[10,11] several materials suitable for use in the conversion of solar energy into electricity, together with their efficiencies and literature references (see Table 10).

TABLE 10. Solar Cell Materials and Best Efficiencies

Solar Cell Materials	(%)
Silicon	14
Gallium arsenide	10
Cadmium sulfide	8
Cadmium telluride	4
Indium phosphide	3
Gallium phosphide	1
Selenium	1

Cummerow has discussed[12] theories of P–N junction in photovoltaic conversion and Loferski[13] has given theoretical considerations for the choice of semiconductors for photovoltaic conversion.

The selenium cell[14] developed 80 years ago provided the first use of the barrier layer cell in converting light into electricity. Selenium cells operating with an efficiency of about 0.6 of 1 per cent are still widely used for meters and light-operated switches.

The cadmium sulfide photovoltaic cell seems to be next in competition with the silicon cell. Reynolds described[15] the construction and tests of cadmium sulfide cells before 1955. The cells gave 0.45 volts in bright sunlight on open circuit and gave 15 milliamp cm^{-2} in a closed circuit. Efficiencies of 5 to 6 per cent have been reported with single crystals.[7]

IMPROVEMENTS IN PHOTOVOLTAIC CELLS

It has been pointed out that the use of single crystals in photovoltaic cells is a serious obstacle in bringing the price low enough for general use. If an electroplated or vapor-deposited film of silicon or other material suitable for photovoltaic cells can be used, the costs can be greatly reduced. The difficulty is that these methods ordinarily produce microcrystalline material with a large area which catalyzes the recombination of electrons and holes before they can reach the electrodes. Also, the electrical resistance is increased when the electrons have to cross an interface between different crystals. Attempts have been made to roll silicon into thin films and to form films by freezing thin molten films floating on a liquid metal. Pyrolytic decompositions have also been tried.

A layer of very small spheres of silicon has been tried in place of the thin section of a single crystal. The efficiencies are lower than those obtained with single crystals but the costs could be much less.

The chances for a practical polycrystalline photovoltaic cell appear to be better with other cells than with silicon. A cadmium sulfide cell with a polycrystalline film deposited from the vapor phase has been reported with an efficiency of 4.5 per cent. Active research along these lines is under-way.[7,8,10]

Other ways of improving the photovoltaic cells include thinner films, better attachment, and better spacing for the electrodes.

A promising method for reducing costs is to focus the sunlight onto photovoltaic cells of small area. The cost of a given area of a reflecting or focusing collector intercepting sunlight is considerably less than the same area of photovoltaic cells. The difficulty of using focused radiation of high intensity is that the increased radiation per unit area of the cell causes a considerable rise in temperature, and the efficiency of the cell decreases at the higher temperatures.

High electrical energies have been obtained by Schoffer, by using intense focused sunlight up to 60 langleys min^{-1} and more.[16,17] At these radiation intensities the cells must be water cooled.

Silicon cells are used for providing auxiliary power in satellites and space vehicles, but it has been found that they undergo a serious decrease in efficiency after being exposed for long periods to such ionizing radiation of high intensity as exists in the van Allen belt in space.[18] Efforts are being made to develop cells of silicon or other elements that will be more resistant to radiation damage.

PHOTOVOLTAIC ELECTRODES IN SOLUTION

When certain electrodes with special coated surfaces are placed in an electrolytic solution and one of them is exposed to the light and the other kept in the dark, an electric potential is developed and current can be drawn from the electrodes as long as one of them is illuminated. This is an old phenomenon that merits further attention for solar energy utilization. Sancier reviews[19] the subject and gives many references in addition to those collected earlier by Copeland, Black, and Garrett.[20]

The situation is complicated by the inclusion of several different kinds of phenomena in the behavior of an illuminated electrode. Sometimes the electrode is covered with a film of material formed by oxidation or other chemical action, and P–N junctions exist near the surface. Sometimes the electrode is covered with an adsorbed dye that may release an electron when exposed to light. Sometimes there is a photochemical reaction in the body of the solution. The study of the P–N junctions in the solid electrode involves the considerations discussed in this chaper; the photochemical reactions in the liquid solutions involve the principles to be discussed in the following chapter.

REFERENCES

1. Pearson, G. L., Electricity from the Sun, in *Proceedings, World Symposium on Applied Solar Energy, Phoenix, Ariz., 1955.* Menlo Park, Calif., Stanford Research Institute, 1956, pp. 281–88.

2. Chapin, D. M., The Direct Conversion of Solar Energy to Electrical Energy, in *Introduction to the Utilization of Solar Energy,* ed. A. M. Zarem and D. D. Enway. New York, McGraw-Hill, 1963, pp. 153–89.

3. Trivich, D., Photovoltaic cells and their possible use as power converters for solar energy, *Ohio Journal of Science, 53:* 310–14. 1953.

4. Trivich, D., Flinn, P. A., and Bowlden, H. J., Photovoltaic Cells in Solar Energy Conversion, in *Solar Energy Research,* ed. F. Daniels and J. A. Duffie, Madison, University of Wisconsin Press, 1955, pp. 149–54.

5. Wolf, M., Developments in Photovoltaic Solar Energy Conversion for Earth Surface Applications, in *United Nations Conference on New Sources of Energy,* E 35–S44, Rome, 1961.

6. Pearson, G. L., Applications of Photovoltaic Cells in Communications, ibid., E 35–S40.

7. Prince, M. B., Latest Developments in the Field of Photovoltaic Conversion of Solar Energy, ibid., E 35–S65.

8. Ravich, L. E., The Film Photovoltaic Devices for Solar Energy Conversion, ibid., E 35–S56.

9. Kobayoshi, M., Utilization of Silicon Solar Batteries, ibid., E 35–S11.

10. Rappaport, P., and Moss, H. I., Low Cost Photovoltaic Conversion of Solar Energy, ibid., E 35–S106.

11. Rappaport, P., Photoelectricity, *Proc. Nat. Acad. Sci., 47:*

1303–06. 1961; *Solar Energy* (special issue), *5:* 59–62. Sept. 1961.

12. Cummerow, R. L., The Theory of Energy Conversion in P–N Junctions, in *Transactions of Conference on the Use of Solar Energy: The Scientific Basis, 5:* 57–64. Tucson, University of Arizona Press, 1958.

13. Loferski, J. J., Theoretical Considerations Governing the Choice of the Optimum Semiconductor for Photovoltaic Solar Energy Conversion, ibid., pp. 65–89.

14. Adams, W. C., and Day, R. E., The actions of light on selenium, *Proc. Royal Society, 25:* 113–17. London, 1876.

15. Reynolds, D. C., The Photovoltaic Effect in Cadmium Sulfide Crystals, in *Trans. Conf. Use of Solar Energy: The Scientific Basis, 5:* 102–16.

16. Pfeiffer, C., Schoffer, P., Spars, B. G., and Duffie, J. A., Performance of Silicon Solar Cells at High Levels of Solar Radiation. *Trans. Am. Soc. Mech. Eng. 84A:* 33. 1962.

17. Schoffer, P., and Pfeiffer, C., Performance of Photovoltaic Cells at High Radiation Levels, *Am. Soc. Mech. Eng.,* Paper 62–WA–348. 1963.

18. Dryden, H. L., and Doenkas, A. E., Solar energy in the exploration of space, *Proc. Nat. Acad. S. A., 47:* 1253–67. 1961; *Solar Energy* (special issue), *5:* Sept. 1961.

19. Sancier, K. M., Photo-Galvanic Cells, in *Trans. Conf. Use of Solar Energy: The Scientific Basis, 5:* 43–56.

20. Copeland, A. W., Black, O. D. and Garrett, A. B. *Chem. Rev., 31:* 177–226. 1942.

CHAPTER 17

Photochemical Conversion

In earlier chapters we have seen that solar radiation can readily be converted into useful work through the operation of heat engines. Since they are limited in efficiency by the Carnot cycle the temperature of operation must be high, and accordingly the collectors are costly and the heat losses large. By using the light of the sun in photochemical reactions, rather than the heat of the sun in engines, these limitations are avoided. It must be emphasized, however, that other serious limitations are encountered. Most photochemical reactions respond only to ultraviolet and visible light, since the light of longer wavelength in the infrared does not have energy of sufficient intensity to give chemical activity. Therefore less than half the solar radiation is available for photochemical conversion, and in most reactions much less than half is available.

In the preceding chapter on photovoltaic conversion we found that sunlight can be converted directly into electricity in certain solid semiconductors. In principle, the photochemical conversion of sunlight can operate in simpler, less expensive systems and has the great advantage that the photochemical products can be stored for later use. Finding a suitable photochemical reaction, however, is a very difficult problem.

Photochemistry is regarded hopefully by many solar scientists, but photochemists realize the serious difficulties involved. There are no promising laboratory photochemical reactions now for storing and using solar energy; yet most of the world's present energy sources, including all our food and most of our fuel, are the products of the photochemical combination of carbon dioxide and water. This marvelous process of photosynthesis, which we are just beginning to understand, constitutes a challenge for scientists to find ways to use sunlight photochemically in direct reactions without the living plant and without the limitations of agriculture and forestry. Although nothing significant is now in sight, there is no theoretical reason why useful products cannot be obtained photochemically with sunlight and without the requirements of good soil and climate. The basic principles of photochemistry are well established, and many of the mechanisms are understood, but much more fundamental research is needed in the quest for practical, solar-activated, photochemical reactions.

Many chemical substances can be made to react with each other on exposure to light. The reactions are governed by the principles of thermodynamics, chemical kinetics, and photochemistry. Thermodynamics is able to predict accurately whether a given chemical reaction can occur and how far it will go before reaching equilibrium. Chemical kinetics is able to predict how fast a reaction will go and to tell something of the mechanism of the reaction. Often a set of reacting substances can give several different products, all possible by thermodynamics, and the speed of the reactions then becomes the most important factor. The most abundant product will be the one that results from the fastest reaction. In order to react, molecules must become activated; in ordinary chemical reactions the activation is caused by a series of violent collisions between molecules. The energy of activation usually runs from about 10,000 to 100,000 cal mole^{-1}. Reactions that require less than this are extremely rapid and those that require more are very slow even at high temperatures. As a rough general rule most chemical reactions near room temperature will double or treble their velocity for a rise of 10° C because the number of violent collisions increases exponentially.

Some chemical reactions that do not proceed fast enough to be practical can be made to go faster by introducing light, which supplies the necessary activation energy.

PRINCIPLES OF PHOTOCHEMISTRY

General references on photochemistry are available.[1-3] One book is based on a symposium on the photochemical storage of energy,[4] devoted to photochemical possibilities for the use of sunlight.

When a beam of sunlight is passed through a vessel containing many molecules some of the light passes through unchanged, but light of certain wavelengths may be absorbed, thus giving color to the absorbing material. Light is composed of a large number of units called photons, each with a definite energy known as a quantum of energy. Only if the molecule can be rearranged to absorb an amount of energy nearly equal to that contained in a given photon does the photon have a chance of being absorbed by the molecule. Absorption of energy from ultraviolet or visible light is accomplished by displacement of an electron from its normal position in the molecule. In the infrared, the absorption of energy is accomplished by displacement of atoms within the molecule or by rotation of the molecule. Only the electron displacements involve enough energy to provide sufficient activation energy for bringing about ordinary chemical reactions. For sunlight, these extend from the red at about 8,000 Å to the ultraviolet at about 3,000 Å, corresponding roughly to 36,000 cal mole^{-1} and 95,000 cal mole^{-1}.

According to the important Einstein relation, one photon can activate only one molecule. After this activation of a molecule by a photon of visible or ultraviolet light, the following phenomena may occur.

1. The light-activated molecule may transmit its energy to other molecules by collision, increasing the translational energy of the molecules and raising the temperature. In this way the radiant energy is converted directly into heat with-

out any chemical change. This is by far the most common effect produced by sunlight.

2. The activation may break a chemical bond in the molecule and give chemical decomposition into atoms or groups of atoms.

3. The molecule may be activated to a higher energy level by displacement of an electron within the molecule, and this excited molecule may transfer its energy to a molecule of some other chemical compound with which it collides; and this second molecule may undergo chemical change. In this photosensitization a loose combination between photo-activated molecule and chemically-reacting molecule appears to be necessary. Time is required to effect the energy transfer, and the combination holds the two molecules together long enough for the transfer of energy.

4. A molecule excited by the absorption of light may fluoresce, giving off light of a different wavelength than the exciting light. The energy states of the electrons are different in fluorescent emission than in absorption.

5. The activation may have enough energy to drive an electron out of the molecule and produce ionization.

For basic experimental studies in photochemistry it is important to use light within a narrow range of wavelengths, because the chemical effects may be different with photons of different energies. Nearly monochromatic light may be produced by passage through an optical color filter or through a refracting glass prism. Interference filters of sputtered metal of specified thickness on glass are available.

It is necessary to measure quantitatively the amount of radiation absorbed by the reacting system. This may be done directly or indirectly with a blackened thermopile and galvanometer standardized against a carbon filament lamp calibrated by the United States Bureau of Standards. It is important to use a black receiving surface that responds equally to light of all different wavelengths.

The quantum yield Φ is the most important quantity in photochemical measurements. It is defined by the relation

$$\Phi = \frac{\text{number of molecules reacting}}{\text{number of photons absorbed}}$$

The amount of reaction depends on the intensity of light, the thickness of the absorbing layer, and the concentration, but a knowledge of the quantum yield permits a calculation of the amount of chemical change from the amount of light absorbed under a variety of conditions. A specific problem will be given presently to illustrate these quantum calculations.

The quantum yield is also of theoretical importance. Although there can be no photochemical reaction if there is no absorption of light, and although each photon of light absorbed activates one, and only one, molecule, the quantum yield varies greatly in different reactions because the chemical reactions that follow photoactivation are complicated. If Φ is large a chain reaction must be taking place involving many molecules; if it is small (less than unity) several possibilities may be involved such as the reversal of the photochemical reaction, loss of activation as heat, competition with other reacting molecules, or internal absorption of light by other molecules which absorb the light but do not produce the given reaction.

Typical photochemical reactions include the dissociation of hydrogen iodide by ultraviolet light to give hydrogen and iodine with a quantum yield of 1 and the combination of hydrogen and chlorine with explosive violence to give hydrogen chloride with a quantum yield of 10^6. The photoexcitation of one molecule of chlorine by one photon is followed by a long chain reaction involving chlorine atoms and hydrogen atoms. The thermal reactions that follow the primary photochemical step are often complicated. They are greatly affected by temperature, whereas the primary photo process is nearly independent of temperature. Another typical photochemical reaction is the decomposition of oxalic acid by ultraviolet or blue light, photosensitized with uranyl ion, with a quantum yield of about 0.5.

The quantitative calculations of photochemical reactions are illustrated here with a hypothetical example. Calculate the number of tons of photochemical product per acre per day produced by sunlight, assuming a molecular weight of 100, a quantum yield of 1, a photochemically-active absorption of 1/10 of the incident sunlight at an average wavelength of 5,000 Å, and 500 min of sunlight with an average intensity of 1 langley (1 cal cm^{-2}) min^{-1}.

1 acre $\times$ 43,560 ft^2 acre^{-1} $\times$ 929 cm^2 ft^{-2}
$\times$ 500 min day^{-1} $\times$ 1 cal cm^{-2} min^{-1} $\times$ 4.18

$\times\ 10^7$ ergs cal^{-1} = 8.5×10^{17} ergs acre^{-1} day^{-1}
of solar energy

One-tenth of this is absorbed and is photochemically active.

$0.1 \times 7.5 \times 10^{17}$ ergs = 8.5×10^{16} ergs acre^{-1} day^{-1}

The energy of 1 photon = 1 quantum = $\varepsilon = h\nu$ where h is Planck's constant, 6.5×10^{-27} erg seconds, and ν is the frequency of light calculated by dividing the velocity of light, 3×10^{10} cm, by the wavelength in cm. It is assumed that the average wavelength of the photochemically active light in solar radiation for this particular reaction is 5,000 Å or 5×10^{-5} cm.

$$\varepsilon = 6.5 \times 10^{-27} \text{ erg sec} \times \frac{3 \times 10^{10} \text{ cm sec}^{-1}}{5 \times 10^{-5} \text{ cm}}$$
$$= 3.9 \times 10^{-12} \text{ erg}$$

Then

$$\frac{8.5 \times 10^{16} \text{ ergs day}^{-1}}{3.9 \times 10^{-12} \text{ erg quantum}^{-1}} = 2.2 \times 10^{28} \text{ quanta day}^{-1}$$

With a quantum yield of 1, the 2×10^{28} quanta day^{-1} is equivalent to 2×10^{28} molecules day^{-1} of photochemical product.

There are 6×10^{23} molecules in 1 mole:

$$\frac{2 \times 10^{28}}{6 \times 10^{23}} = 3.3 \times 10^4 \text{ moles day}^{-1}$$

The moles of the product having an assumed weight of 100 are converted into tons as follows:

$$\frac{3.3 \times 10^4 \text{ moles day}^{-1} \times 100 \text{ g mole}^{-1}}{454 \text{ g lb}^{-1} \times 2,000 \text{ lb ton}^{-1}} = 3.6 \text{ ton day}^{-1}$$

No photochemical reaction is known that approaches this photochemical productivity in sunlight. Photosynthesis in agriculture usually has a productivity of only about 2 or 3 tons of dry plant material *per year*.

Photosynthesis

The chemical reaction of photosynthesis, by which our food and fuel are made, is

$$CO_2 + H_2O + chlorophyll + light$$
$$= H_2CO + O_2 + chlorophyll$$

The H_2CO is a fraction of a carbohydrate which contains one carbon atom. Many other reactions, largely controlled by enzymes, follow the primary photoactivation and produce fats and proteins as well as carbohydrates.

The carbohydrates and other organic plant materials are stable in air at room temperature and are readily stored, but when heated to a high temperature they burn and the reaction is reversed, with carbohydrate and oxygen of the air reacting to give carbon dioxide and water with the evolution of 112,000 cal mole^{-1} of heat. This book is not concerned with the agricultural use of sunshine, but a brief discussion of photosynthesis may help to point the way toward research in the quest for new photochemical reactions that can store and use the energy of sunlight. Excellent references are available on the subject of photosynthesis.[5–8]

Carbon dioxide and water absorb light only in the short ultraviolet and long infrared and are transparent to sunshine, but the green chlorophyll of living plants absorbs all the visible sunlight below 6,800 Å and becomes activated. It passes its energy over to the water which then releases a hydrogen atom for reaction with carbon dioxide. The energy intensity of red light is only 40,000 cal mole^{-1}, and the energy required for making a mole of H_2CO is at least as much as the 112,000 cal mole^{-1} evolved when the H_2CO is oxidized in the reverse reaction. Three photons of red light, or about two of blue light, must act together in order to provide the energy needed for producing one molecule of the carbohydrate H_2CO. But it is not ordinarily possible for two or more photons to activate a single molecule; the lifetime of the activated state is very short and the activation energy of the excited molecule is lost before the second photon is absorbed. The energy requirement is met by the release of several hydrogen atoms from the water by a succession of excited chlorophyll molecules. The carbon dioxide is thus reduced in steps, finally giving a carbohydrate.

Many complicated chemical reactions follow the primary activation, and therefore the overall reaction is greatly influenced by an increase in temperature. Important conclusions can be drawn from data on the use of flashing intermittent light followed by periods of darkness. In light of low intensity the rate of photosynthesis is controlled by the intensity of the light, but in bright light the rate is controlled by the rate at which the reacting material, carbon dioxide, can be fed into the site of photosynthesis and the rate at which the thermal reactions can take place. These increase with an increase in temperature.

The efficiency of photosynthesis under optimum conditions in the laboratory is about 1 molecule of carbohydrate (containing 1 carbon atom) produced for every 8 photons *absorbed*. It is about the same at all wavelengths from 4,000 to 6,800 Å, which is the range of absorption of chlorophyll. These measurements[9,10] were made with chlorella, using monochromatic light of measured intensity, and the rate of the reaction was obtained by several different methods including microchemical, electrochemical, and pressure measurements of the carbon dioxide and oxygen. The energy of 8 moles of photons of red light is 320,000 ($= 8 \times 40,000$) and the minimum theoretical energy requirement is 112,000, giving an efficiency of about 30 per cent. Warburg and others have reported efficiencies of 75 per cent but most American workers accept a value of about 30 per cent. Some energy must be lost in chemical side reactions and reverse reactions, which follow the primary photochemical reaction.

This efficiency of 30 per cent is remarkably high. An agricultural crop in the temperate zone produces about 2 or 3 tons of dry organic material per acre per year, giving a storage efficiency of about 0.2 of one per cent of the annual sunlight. Some of the reasons for the low yields (much less than the 30 per cent conversion in laboratory experiments) are that the growing season is only one third of the year, that the carbon dioxide in the air is 0.03 per cent instead of the 3 per cent used in the laboratory, and that the far red and infrared radiation (amounting to more than half the solar radiation) is not absorbed by chlorophyll. Furthermore the whole surface of the land or water is not covered with chlorophyll; but perhaps the most important reason is that the high photosynthetic efficiency is not maintained in light as intense as sunlight. The enzyme-controlled thermal reactions cannot then keep up with the primary photochemical process.

The mechanism of photosynthesis and the possibilities for improving it and finding other similar reactions are fully treated by Rabinowitch.[8,11] He points out that one of the chief reasons for lower efficiency is the presence of back reactions or reverse reactions and that in the growing plant the photochemical products are kept separate in the plant tissue. The chloroplasts where photosynthesis occurs have alternate layers of materials that are wet by water and that repel water, and the chlorophyll molecules are probably located at the interfaces in such a way that the products of the photochemical reaction can be kept separate. Also the intermediate products are quickly converted into other products which cannot then participate in the reverse reaction.

Rabinowitch has pointed out that in photosynthesis the supply of carbon dioxide has been the limiting factor and there has been no need in nature to evolve enzymes capable of giving more rapid utilization of the photochemical products in the thermal reactions which follow the primary photochemical step. Now that man can increase the supply of carbon dioxide, the bottleneck in increased photosynthesis is the rate of using the photochemical products in the later thermal reactions. It should be possible to develop enzymes that will give more rapid thermal reactions in the photosynthetic process and thus increase the efficiency of photosynthesis in bright light. Through selection and plant breeding it has been possible to develop plants with specific desired characteristics such as color, strength of stem, and resistance to disease. It should be possible through selection and plant breeding to develop algae and plants that will give much higher photosynthesis efficiencies in intense sunlight and high carbon dioxide concentration than present species give.

In view of the much greater photosynthetic efficiencies obtained in the laboratory than in ordinary agriculture, efforts have been directed toward the mass culture of algae.[12-15] By growing algae under optimum conditions in ponds or plastic tubes with full nutrient fertilization, and with a high carbon dioxide content well above that in air, the photosynthetic yields have been increased about 20-fold over those obtainable in ordinary agriculture. The cost of production is high, however, because of the large capital investment and operating costs of the equipment (containers for the algae, pumps for circulating the water containing the algae, cooling units for removing heat, centrifuges for collecting the algae, and means for adding extra carbon dioxide). Fisher and also Tamiya estimated that dry chlorella algae can be produced for about 25¢ lb^{-1}. This is too high for use as fuel but not too high for food or for a source of chemicals and medicinal products.

There are many difficulties in the mass production of algae. The temperature must be kept low enough for their proper growth. There is promise in the use of algae, obtained from hot springs, which have been selectively adapted to growth in hot water. The algal suspensions are readily contaminated by other organisms, many of which consume the algae and do not themselves bring about photosynthesis. The harvesting of the algae is a problem because they are not easily filtered and the separation by centrifuging is expensive. Carbon dioxide is provided either by the burning of fuel or as a by-product from industry or by heating limestone. Tamiya in Japan has continued extensive development of the large-scale growth of chlorella and has been operating large ponds comprising over an acre. It is possible in algae growth to alter the ratio of carbohydrates, fats, and proteins and there is hope that algae may be an acceptable food in certain parts of the world.

Myers[16] has been active in basic research on growing algae for food or fuel.

Kok[17] obtained yields of algae in which the newly produced organic material stored 20 per cent of the absorbed light and released it on combustion. This corresponds to about 10 per cent efficiency with total solar radiation.

Attention has also been directed to the growth of higher plants. They do not have the advantage of algae that every cell is a photosynthesizing cell, but they do not require a centrifuge for harvesting, and the newly photosynthesized material can readily be collected mechanically. Some of the factors involved in the production by photosynthesis of large quantities of organic material have been summarized by Thimann,[18] Mangelsdorf,[19] and Pirie.[20] Pirie has advocated the use of water hyacinths which grow in such profusion in tropical countries that they present a problem in water transportation in small rivers and bays. They store large quantities of energy, and are easily harvested. Pirie points out that higher plants of this kind can be put under pressure to extract the water and the dissolved edible materials for food; the insoluble residue, containing a high content of cellulose, can be used for fuel.

Stahman[21] had found that a certain type of alfalfa can give by extraction 20 per cent of edible proteins of high nutritive value. The remaining material can be used for fuel. There is difficulty in obtaining sufficient proteins for healthy nutrition in many tropical areas, partly because of the spoilage of milk and meat but chiefly because the communities cannot grow enough cereal and vegetable food to feed animals. The animals give less than 20 per cent of the energy of the original agricultural crop, which in turn stores only a few tenths of 1 per cent of the sunlight. The animals themselves consume over 80 per cent of it in living their own lives.

Meier has proposed[22] the use of photobiological methods for obtaining gaseous fuels. Goleuke and Oswald[23] have made a significant contribution to the generation of power from solar energy using methane produced by the anaerobic fermentation of alga. The methane is used to operate a conventional internal-combustion engine. They have carried out extensive laboratory and pilot-plant tests on the growth of algae in municipal sewage and its fermentation to methane and believe that on a large scale electricity can be produced by this method for 1¢ or 2¢ per kwhr. One of the large costs in the mass culture of algae is that of fertilizing nutrients, but they are available without cost in sewage. In fact, their removal is an asset in waste disposal. The enrichment of carbon dioxide comes from the aerobic fermentation of the sewage by bacteria and from the burning of the methane in the engines. The algae are grown in large ponds which are stirred occasionally. They are harvested either by centrifugation or by precipitation with aluminum salts and filtering, and then treated to give about 5 per cent solids and 95 per cent water. This material is subjected to anaerobic fermentation for about three weeks; half the organic material is then converted into methane gas and stored. The residues containing mineral nutrients can be returned for the growth of new algae.

The methane gas is used to operate an internal-combustion engine and the by-product heat is used for heating the fermenting material. The storage of methane gas makes possible the continuous production of electricity through the night and through cloudy weather.

In the experimental work the maximum energy conversion of sunlight into algae was 3 per cent and the conversion of algae into methane was about 66 per cent, making a total efficiency of 2 per cent from sunlight to easily combustible and storable fuel.

It is estimated that a one acre algae pond could give 15 kw of electricity. In regions of bright sunlight and ample available sewage, with reasonable technical improvements a cost of 1.1¢ kwhr^{-1} appears to be possible for large-scale plants.

The process of photosynthesis is remarkably effective, but it is complicated in the physical structure of the plant cells and in the chemical reactions and intermediate steps that follow the primary photochemical excitation. A reaction involving organic phosphates is probably involved. Our understanding of the steps has been greatly increased through the use of isotopic tracers and radioautography.[24]

It is natural that research efforts should be directed toward the photochemical behavior of chlorophyll outside the growing plant, both as a chemical extract of pure chlorophyll and as a constituent of chloroplasts separated mechanically from the dead cell. The behavior of chlorophyll under radically different conditions can be studied, and the way might be opened to photosynthesis *in vitro* without the restrictions of the living plant.

Livingston[25] has studied the photo behavior of chlorophyll, emphasizing fluorescence measurements in the presence of different quenching agents and absorption measurements made immediately after intense flash photolysis of the chlorophyll.

The Hill reaction[26] is an interesting one, similar to photosynthesis, that can be carried out in the laboratory without the living plant. The chlorophyll is contained in dead chloroplasts or fragments of chloroplasts, and oxygen is produced as in photosynthesis, but the chemical conditions are not right for reducing carbon dioxide to carbohydrate. Instead an electron acceptor (or oxidant), A, more powerful than carbon dioxide is used, such as ferricyanide or other reducible inorganic ion or organic molecule such as a quinone. The reaction is

$$4A + 2H_2O + \text{light} \; (+ \text{chloroplasts})$$
$$= 4A^- + 4H^+ + O_2 \; (+ \text{chloroplasts})$$

and the wavelength response and the quantum yield for oxygen in the Hill reaction is about the same as for photosynthesis with carbon dioxide.

Marcus[27,28] has studied a large number of potential Hill-reaction oxidants and concludes that not only must the oxidation–reduction standard electrode potentials be sufficient but the oxidant must have an optical absorption spectrum with effective absorption in the same spectral region as that of chlorophyll. This similarity in absorption spectra is necessary for easy transfer of energy from electronic excitation.

PHOTOCHEMICAL PRODUCTION OF ELECTRICITY

The stored energy of photochemically-produced chemical compounds may be made available for use in two different ways. The dark reaction which is the reverse of the photochemical reaction may regenerate the original material by ordinary chemical reaction involving the breaking and forming of chemical bonds with the evolution of heat. If the reaction involves oxidation or reduction the reaction may be carried out by the transfer of an electron with the evolution of heat. If the reacting materials are placed in an electrochemical cell with the oxidant around one electrode and the reductant around the other, however, it may be possible to transfer the electron not directly from molecule to molecule but from the oxidizing molecule to electrode A, to connecting wire, to electrode B, and then to the reducing molecule. The overall reaction is the same, but the electrochemical transfer has the great advantage that while the electron is going through the connecting wire it generates a magnetic field and can do work; and it also permits using the chemical energy of the reaction to effect chemical changes in other materials at other electrodes in the electrical circuit.

It is possible to have a storage battery in which the unstable materials around the electrodes are produced not by an electric charging current but by photochemical reactions in the battery. Electrical energy is obtained when the photochemically produced unstable materials react to discharge the battery electrically. The great difficulty is that the direct chemical and the electrochemical transfer of electrons are in competition with each other, and the distance to the electrodes must be small and the electrochemical reactions rapid if the electrochemical transfer through the external conducting wire is to take place.

Rabinowitch has stated the conditions necessary for the electrochemical storage of light.[29-31] He has given as an example the reaction

$$\text{Thionine} + 2Fe^{++} \underset{\text{dark}}{\overset{\text{light}}{\rightleftharpoons}} \text{leukothionine} + 2Fe^{+++}$$

When an aqueous solution of thionine and ferrous ions is illuminated by light the ferrous ion reduces the purple-colored dye thionine (i.e. transfers an electron to it) to give colorless leukothionine and ferric ion. When the light is removed the reaction reverses over a period of several minutes and the purple color of the dye returns. The operation can be repeated through an indefinite number of cycles. If two electrodes are placed in the solution which is then illuminated, it is possible to obtain a voltage between the electrodes up to 0.4 volt, because of the difference in concentration of oxidized and reduced materials. When the electrodes are connected by a wire, the electrons pass from the leukothionine to the Fe^{+++} ion through the connecting wire, and the thionine with its purple color is restored. In this way some of the light energy is stored for a while and then made available as electrical energy.

Another similar photogalvanic, reversible reaction that can store light energy and release it as electrical energy is the photo reduction of mercuric chloride by ferrous ion:

$$Fe^{++} + HgCl_2 \underset{\text{dark}}{\overset{\text{light}}{\rightleftharpoons}} Fe^{+++} + HgCl + Cl^-$$

Research should be directed toward finding more of these photogalvanic reactions and cells with suitable configurations and barriers and stirring mechanisms. It is necessary to increase the fraction of the energy of the dark reaction, which takes place electrochemically with the production of useful electricity, and reduce the fraction which takes place thermally with the evolution of heat.

In the Hill reaction oxygen is evolved, but there is no storage of energy in the photochemical products as there is in photosynthesis. The addition of an electron to the hydrogen ion of water could theoretically make possible the production of hydrogen gas which could be used as a storable fuel; and at first sight it would not appear to require more energy and greater electrode potential than required for the production of carbohydrate from carbon dioxide. Marcus[28] has found, however, that visible light does not have sufficient energy to produce hydrogen, because an additional 35,000 cal is required for the total reaction in addition to the 44,000 cal required to release hydrogen atoms from water.

In another type of cell, one electrode is surrounded by a fluorescent material and subjected to intense light, giving rise to potential differences between the electrodes and thus producing electrical energy.

PHOTOCHEMICAL STORAGE OF ENERGY

At the symposium on photochemistry in the liquid and solid states held at Dedham, Massachusetts, in 1957, the committee formulated the following criteria for selecting photochemical reactions of possible value in using solar energy.[82]

1. The photochemical reaction produced by sunlight must be endothermic (absorbing energy) with a high quantum yield.

Most photochemical reactions are exothermic with the evolution of energy. The absorption of light simply makes them go faster by supplying activation energy. There is no tendency for the reaction to go in the opposite direction in the dark. Only photochemical reactions that absorb energy and increase the thermodynamic energy content are capable of reacting in the opposite direction when the light is removed, thus providing a means for storing and releasing photochemical energy received from the sun.

2. In order to use the stored photochemical energy the reaction must be reversible, and the reverse reaction must be fast enough to be practically useful but not so fast that the reverse reaction is completed during the time of exposure to the light.

3. For the direct conversion of solar energy into electrical energy the electrons are transferred photochemically from a position of lower energy to a position of higher energy. If they return to the position of lower energy instantly no energy can be stored.

If they return to a lower energy level by radiation, collision, or release of chemical energy they evolve heat. If the electrons in the light-activated molecules can be transferred to positions of lower energy in other molecules by passage through electrodes and a connecting wire before the activated molecules can react chemically, it should be possible to use the energy of the reverse or thermal reaction for producing electrical work rather than heat. The electron passing through the wire may be made to give off heat, to operate an electric motor, to charge a storage battery, or to produce by electrolysis new chemical products that can combine later with the evolution of heat.

4. The reactants, or an added photosensitizer, should absorb light throughout most of the visible spectrum to use photochemically as much as possible of the total solar radiation. There is almost no chance that the infrared half of the sunlight can be used photochemically because the energy per photon is too low to bring about chemical reactions.

5. The energy stored in the photo products should be large—at least 50 to 100 cal g^{-1}. If the photochemical energy can be made available as electricity rather than heat, the practical requirement can be less than the 50 cal g^{-1}.

6. The photo reactants should be inexpensive, even though they are used through many cycles of photochemical reaction followed by the reverse thermal reaction in the dark.

7. Liquids and solids are preferred as reactants because of their smaller size, but reactions involving gases are also worthy of consideration.

There are several ways in which the energy produced in these photochemical reactions may be stored and used.

1. The photo products may be separated and stored indefinitely for use at a later time.

If the reverse reaction is appreciable, automatic ways may be required for separating the photochemical products. A gaseous product may be insoluble and automatically evolved from a liquid solution containing the reactants; or solid products may be precipitated from solution. The products may be prevented from reacting with each other by separating them through absorption or adsorption, or chromatographic adsorption. In another method the photochemical products can be separated by dissolving each in a different liquid solvent, using solvents that do not mix with each other.

In case water or oxygen or some other replaceable material is one of the photo products, it may be allowed to escape because the reverse reaction may take place later with a fresh supply of water, or of oxygen from the air.

2. In case the photo products require a high activation energy for recombination they may remain in contact with each other because of the slow rate of reaction. The carbohydrate and oxygen produced by photosynthesis is an example. The thermal, reverse reaction may be initiated by raising the temperature of a small part of the photo products and the evolution of heat produced by the reaction then keeps the reaction going at the higher temperature. Also a photochemical reaction might be found in which the products would not react with each other until a catalyst is introduced.

3. Sunlight can be used as work more effectively if the stored energy is released as electrical energy rather than as heat. There is then no need for a heat engine with its low efficiency and extra expense.

4. If the reactants respond only to the short wavelengths of sunlight in the ultraviolet and blue, the range of usefully absorbed light may sometimes be extended to longer wavelengths by making structural changes in the molecule. The absorption bands of organic dyes can be shifted toward the red by incorporating heavier atoms or groups of atoms into the molecule.

Photosensitizers may also be used to extend the range of photochemically active absorption. Examples are chlorophyll in photosynthesis, uranyl ion in the decomposition of oxalic acid, and specially-adsorbed red dyes in the sensitization of photographic plates to red light.

5. The photo products may be kept separate and stored by using a two-phase system such as a pair of immiscible solvents or the two parts of an electrochemical cell.

6. Photochemical storage of sunlight can be carried out in solids as well as in liquids, solutions, and gases.

Excited molecules and free radicals may sometimes be preserved when formed in rigid glasses in which chemical and ionic changes may be delayed.

Photo-excited molecules with electrons in the singlet state may lose their energy so fast (10^{-8} sec) that it cannot be used for the storage of energy. The lifetimes may be of the order of 10^{-9} sec. The kinetics of the problem have been discussed by Noyes.[83] Some photo-excited molecules with electrons in the triplet state may have lifetimes of the order of 10^{-3} sec, making easier the storage and transfer of solar energy. Progress has been made in understanding the excited states of some complex, polyatomic molecules like anthracene. Chemical reactions such as oxidations and dimerizations can sometimes compete with the deactivation of these excited molecules. The kinetic problems are discussed, with specific examples, by Livingston.[34]

PHOTOCHEMICAL REACTIONS

Very few photochemical reactions are known that meet the requirements described in the preceding discussions. Yet there is no theoretical reason why they cannot be found. Calvert discusses[35] the possibilities of the photochemical use of sunlight and cites several examples.

As stated before, most of the known photochemical reactions are not useful because they are not reversible at a later time—the sunlight is not stored as chemical energy, it simply accelerates an irreversible reaction.

The photodissociation of iodine (I_2) molecules into atoms absorbs most of the visible light of the sun with a considerable amount of energy, but the iodine atoms recombine so fast that the energy cannot be retained. It is immediately evolved as heat during the exposure to light.

The dissociation of brown NO_2 into nitric oxide and oxygen takes place in ultraviolet and blue light; the recombination is fairly slow but still too fast to be useful for the photochemical storage of energy.

In principle the photolysis of nitrosyl chloride[36,37]

$$2NOCl + light = 2NO + Cl_2$$

is an attractive possibility. Nitrosyl chloride either in the gas phase or in carbon tetrachloride absorbs throughout most of the visible part of solar radiation and dissociates at all the wavelengths with a quantum yield of nearly 1. The products can be readily separated because though the chlorine remains dissolved in the carbon tetrachloride solvent, the nitric oxide gas is insoluble and immediately escapes from solution and may be stored in tanks. The nitrosyl chloride may be readily regenerated at room temperature or slightly above with the evolution of heat. The process can be repeated continuously through an indefinite number of cycles. Thus the reaction meets most of the criteria for photochemical reactions for using sunlight. However, some of the recombination of chlorine and nitric oxide occurs during the photo dissociation and a steady state would be reached. Therefore it is necessary to use a flowing process in which the solution of nitrosyl chloride remains in the light for a limited time before the solution is regenerated. Another unfavorable feature is the fact that, in the photo dissociation, chlorine atoms are first formed from the molecules of NOCl and the atoms recombine immediately to give chlorine molecules with the evolution of heat. and this heat energy cannot be stored. The thermal recombination of nitric oxide and chlorine molecules with the evolution of 137 cal g^{-1} is only about one fourth as large as the energy required for the photochemical dissociation.

In reactions like this it would be much more useful if the photo products are combined in an electrochemical cell to give electricity rather than heat.

Another similar reaction that might be studied is the photo dissociation of nickel carbonyl to give carbon monoxide (poisonous) and metallic nickel. The products can be recombined under suitable conditions at 50° C with the evolution of 29 cal g^{-1} of heat.

Photopolymerizations and photoisomerizations provide another group of reversible reactions suitable for consideration in the photochemical storage of sunlight. The heats of reaction are usually low, however, and most of the reactions respond only to ultraviolet light, which is too low in intensity in sunlight to be useful.

The reaction

$$\text{anthracene} \underset{\text{dark}}{\overset{\text{light}}{\rightleftarrows} } \text{dianthracene}$$

absorbs 50 cal g^{-1} when illuminated with ultraviolet light at 3,600 Å. The anthracene may be dissolved in benzene or other solvent and the depolymerization is slow enough for storage at room temperature but rapid enough for use at somewhat higher temperatures.

The photoisomerization of maleic acid stores 70 cal g^{-1} and the reversal is slow; the photoisomerization of stillbene stores 57 cal g^{-1}, but these reactions respond only to ultraviolet light.

Surveys of many of the photochemical reactions recorded

in the literature and their quantum yields and range of wavelengths for activation are available,[38–40] but none of these reactions appears to be satisfactory for the photochemical storage of sunlight. New endothermic photochemical reactions should be searched for and studied.

The photochemical dissociation of metallic oxides might be studied in the search for suitable reactions for the storage of sunlight energy. Some of the oxides decompose at fairly low temperatures to give oxygen and the free metal. Mercuric oxide (HgO) was decomposed with focused sunlight over two centuries ago, not by photochemical means but simply by raising the temperature to give a different thermodynamic equilibrium constant. Perhaps some oxide may be found that will decompose photochemically and reform at room temperature in the dark by combining the metal with the oxygen of the air. The oxygen liberated photochemically would not have to be stored because there is an ever-present supply in the air.

Efforts should be made to find reversible chemical dissociations that can be carried out with infrared radiation. Ordinary chemical reactions which involve the breaking or rearrangements of bonds require more energy mole^{-1} than can be supplied by infrared radiation, but if a suitable reaction requiring 40,000 cal or less for thermodynamic energy and kinetic activation were available it might be possible to make use of the infrared half of solar radiation photochemically. Chemical addition compounds with weak bonds, compounds held together with hydrogen bonds, organic and inorganic complexes, and salt hydrates are among the materials that might be studied.

PHOTOCHEMICAL REACTIONS OF SOLIDS

There are possibilities in the use of solids as well as gas, liquids, and solutions. Possibly there are more unexplored reactions.

The photo dissociation of silver bromide or chloride to give the halogen gas and silver has been studied by Marcus. These products are separated and can be stored and recombined later electrochemically or thermally. The range of response to sunlight can be extended further into the red to cover the whole visible spectrum by sensitizing with dyes.

It is possible to photosynthesize hydrogen peroxide from water using particles of zinc oxide and other oxides. Usually light of short wavelength is required. The hydrogen peroxide is a product containing extra energy that can be released thermally or electrochemically. The reaction depends greatly on the very high purity of the crystalline zinc oxide and the addition of specific promoters. Apparently the electrons and positive holes produced by the light migrate to the surface where they can undergo oxidizing reactions and reducing reactions with molecules adsorbed on the surface of the oxide particles.

There is another rather unlikely way of storing the energy of sunlight in crystals.[35] With radiation of very high energy such as X-rays or gamma rays it is possible to dislodge electrons in semiconductors, some of which become trapped in imperfections of the crystal lattice. They can be released later with the evolution of light, producing the phenomenon of thermoluminescence. The energy stored and released in this way is less than 0.01 per cent of the incident radiation, and the energy required is much greater than that available in sunlight. However, some intermolecular or intramolecular change that can be brought about by sunlight (10 to 70 kcal mole^{-1}) may possibly be found in crystals of complex organic molecules. Such stored chemical energy might then be released later by raising the temperature.

REFERENCES

1. Noyes, W. A., Jr., and Leighton, P. A., *The Photochemistry of Gases,* New York, Reinhold, 1941.

2. Rollefson, G. K., and Burton, M., *Photochemistry,* Englewood Cliffs, N.J., Prentice-Hall, 1939.

3. Daniels, F., and Alberty, R. A., *Physical Chemistry,* Chs. 18 and 23. New York, Wiley, 1961.

4. Heidt, L. J., Livingston, R. S., Rabinowitch, E., and Daniels, F., *Photochemistry in the Liquid and Solid States,* New York, Wiley, 1960.

5. Rabinowitch, E., *Photosynthesis and Related Processes,* New York, Interscience, 1945 and 1951.

6. Hollaender, A., *Radiation Biology,* Vols. 1–3. New York, McGraw-Hill, 1954 and 1955.

7. Photochemical Processes, in *Transactions of Conference on the Use of Solar Energy: The Scientific Basis,* Vol. 4. Tucson, University of Arizona Press, 1958.

8. Rabinowitch, E., Photochemical utilization of light energy, *Nat. Acad. Sci., 47:* 1296–1303. 1961; *Solar Energy* (special issue), *5:* 52–58. Sept. 1961.

9. Daniels, F., Energy Efficiency in Photosynthesis, in Hollaender, A., *Radiation Biology*, New York, McGraw-Hill, 1956, *3:* 259–92.

10. Yuan, E. L., Evans, R. W., and Daniels, F., Energy efficiency of photosynthesis by chlorella, *Biochim. Biophys. Acta, 17:* 187–93. 1955.

11. Rabinowitch, E., The Photochemical Storage of Energy, in *Trans. Conf. Use of Solar Energy: The Scientific Basis, 4:* 182–87.

12. Burlew, J. S., *Algal Culture from Laboratory to Pilot Plant*, Publ. 600, Washington, D.C., Carnegie Institution of Washington, 1953.

13. Fisher, A. W., Jr., Economic Aspects of Algae as Potential Fuel, in *Solar Energy Research*, ed. F. Daniels, and J. A. Duffie, pp. 185–89. Madison, University of Wisconsin Press, 1955.

14. Fisher, A. W., Jr., Engineering for Algae Culture, *Proceedings World Symposium on Applied Solar Energy, Phoenix, Ariz., 1955*, pp. 243–54. Menlo Park, Calif., Stanford Research Institute, 1956.

15. Tamiya, H., Growing Chlorella for Food and Feed, ibid., pp. 231–42.

16. Myers, J., Algae as an Energy Converter, ibid., pp. 227–30.

17. Kok, B., The Yield of Sunlight Conversion by Chlorella, *Trans. Conf. Use of Solar Energy: The Scientific Basis, 4:* 48–54.

18. Thimann, K. V., Solar Energy Utilization by Higher Plants, *Proc. World Symposium on Applied Solar Energy*, pp. 255–59.

19. Mangelsdorf, P. C., The World's Principal Food Plants as Converters of Solar Energy, in *Trans. Conf. Use of Solar Energy: The Scientific Basis, 4:* 122–29.

20. Pirie, N. W., The Use of Higher Plants for Storing Solar Energy, ibid., pp. 115–21.

21. Stahman, M., Private communication.

22. Meier, R. L., Biological Cycles in the Transformation of Solar Energy into Useful Fuels, in *Solar Energy Research*, ed. F. Daniels and J. A. Duffie, pp. 179–84.

23. Golueke, C. G., and Oswald, W. J., Power from solar energy via algae-produced methane, *Solar Energy, 7:* 86–92. 1963.

24. Calvin, M., and Brassham, J. A., *The Photosynthesis of Carbon Compounds*, New York, Benjamin, 1962; *The Path of Carbon in Photosynthesis*, Englewood Cliffs, N.J., Prentice-Hall, 1957.

25. Livingston, R., The Photochemistry of Chlorophyll *in Vitro*, in *Trans. Conf. Use of Solar Energy: The Scientific Basis, 4:* 138–44.

26. Hill, R., Oxygen evolved by isolated chloroplasts, *Nature,* 139: 881–82. 1937.

27. Marcus, R. J., Chemical conversion of solar energy, *Science,* 123: 399–405. 1956.

28. Marcus, R. J., *The Hill Reaction as a Model for Chemical Conversion of Solar Energy*, Publ. PB 161,462, Washington, D.C.

29. Rabinowitch, E., Photochemical Utilization of Light Energy, in *Solar Energy Research*, pp. 193–202.

30. Ibid., pp. 1301–03.

31. Rabinowitch, E., Photochemical Redox Reactions and Photosynthesis, in Heidt et al., (see below) *Photochemistry in the Liquid and Solid States*, p. 84.

32. Heidt, L. J., et al., *Photochemistry in the Liquid and Solid States*, New York, Wiley, 1960, pp. 3–4.

33. Noyes, R. M., Kinetic Complications Associated with Photochemical Storage of Energy, ibid., pp. 70–74.

34. Livingston, R., The Role of the Triplet State in the Photochemical Auto-Oxidation of Aryl Hydrocarbons, ibid., pp. 76–82.

35. Calvert, J. G., Photochemical Processes for Utilization of Solar Energy, in *Introduction to the Utilization of Solar Energy*, ed. A. M. Zarem and D. D. Erway. New York, McGraw-Hill, 1963, pp. 190–210.

36. Neuwirth, O. S., The photolysis of nitrosyl chloride and the storage of solar energy, *J. Phys. Chem., 63:* 17. 1959. Also Heidt et al., *Photochemistry in the Liquid and Solid States*, pp. 16–20.

37. Marcus, R. J., and Wohlers, H. C., Photolysis of nitrosyl chloride, *Solar Energy, 4* (2): 1–8. 1960.

38. Daniels, F., A table of quantum yields in experimental photochemistry, *J. Phys. Chem., 42:* 713–32. 1938.

39. Marcus, R. J., Survey of electron transfer spectra of inorganic ions, *Solar Energy, 4* (4): 20–23. 1960.

40. Heidt, L. J., et al., *Photochemistry in the Liquid and Solid States*, p. 4.

CHAPTER 18

Storage and Transportation of Power

In Chapter 8 we discussed stored heat, and stated that it could be used later as a source of mechanical or electrical power. In this chapter we shall consider the more difficult problem of the storage of power through mechanical, electrical, and chemical means. The subject has been discussed at two recent symposia on the use of solar energy.[1,2]

All our present fuels are easily stored—coal, oil, gas, and wood. One of the great advantages of the photochemical conversion of solar radiation is the fact that it produces chemical materials which can be stored until they are used. The photochemical conversion of sunlight and the chemical storage of its energy were discussed in the preceding chapter.

MECHANICAL STORAGE OF POWER

Mechanical energy can be stored in a variety of ways. One of the simplest is to pump water to a reservoir at a higher level and let it flow down through a water turbine when power is needed. In some locations large reservoirs can be easily built on high plateaus or on hills, and they provide effective low-cost storage of power on a large scale. An example is to be found at Austin, Texas, where a steam plant pumps water from below the dam in a river to the reservoir above the dam, when the demands for electric power are small. At a later time when the demands for power are large, both the steam plant and the hydraulic plant are operated to supply electricity. A similar hydraulic reservoir for electric power is being built in Missouri. There are many others. Pumping water with a water turbine is perhaps 90 per cent efficient in large units, but small pumps of fractional kilowatts pumping a few gallons of water per minute have a low efficiency of perhaps 30 per cent. This type of storage is not satisfactory for small-scale operation.

If all the available land is flat, and the water has to be stored in large reservoirs on tall frames or towers, the cost of storage is excessive. In such cases it may be cheaper to dig a hole in the ground and place the reservoir at ground level and the pump and turbine at the bottom of the hole. In locations near the ocean or a deep lake, it might be possible to place the pump and turbine in an enclosure well below the surface of the water. The storage of appreciable quantities of power in hydraulic reservoirs requires very large installations. For example, to store 1 kwhr of energy in a reservoir at an elevation of 1 m (3.28 ft) requires 367,000 kg of water or 96,900 gal or 12,900 ft^3.

In principle, mechanical work can also be stored by raising weights to a higher level and letting them fall. The weights, attached to a rope wound around an axle of a rotating wheel, may fall from an elevated platform or from ground level into a hole in the ground. This principle has been used effectively to operate grandfather clocks and small mechanical units but is hardly practical for the storage of large amounts of energy. It would take 2,650 sacks of sand, each weighing 100 lb (45.6 kg), falling through 10 ft (3 m), to produce 1 kwhr of mechanical energy. Other mechanical devices for storing power include the coiling of a spring (as in a watch), the operation of a low-friction flywheel, and the compression of air in strong metal tanks. For small amounts of power these devices may sometimes be useful, but they are not suitable for large quantities of power.

ELECTRICAL STORAGE OF POWER

The storage battery is highly developed and very efficient. There is a lead–sulfuric acid storage battery in practically every automobile in the world. The battery consists of an electrode of lead and an electrode of lead oxide immersed in sulfuric acid. The electrochemical reactions are

$$Pb + PbO_2 + 2H^+$$

$$+ 2HSO_4^- \underset{charge}{\overset{discharge}{\rightleftarrows}} 2PbSO_4 + 2H_2O$$

When the electrodes are connected the electrons flow from the lead electrode through an external circuit to the lead oxide electrode and do useful electrical work. The electrode reactions are

$$Pb - 2 \text{ electrons} = Pb^{++};$$
$$Pb^{++++} + 2 \text{ electrons} = Pb^{++}$$

Lead sulfate and water are produced. When a higher voltage is applied and these electrons are made to flow through the external circuit from the lead oxide electrode to the lead electrode, the reactions are reversed. Lead and lead oxide are produced on the electrodes.

The lead storage battery requires careful attention and must be kept filled with distilled water and not allowed to stand long in a discharged condition because the lead sulfate crystals become difficult to remove. The voltage of each cell is about 2 volts, and the automobile batteries for operating the motor and starting the internal combustion engine have a current drain of 50 amp and more. They are compact and rugged. The plates are close together and they are roughened to increase the surface area and reduce the internal resistance. The frequent recycling, electrodeposit of solids, and the close-fitting parts result in a useful life of only about two years. Reserve lead storage batteries for power stations do not have to meet such severe conditions and they may last for 10 years or more.

For the storage of solar energy without the demand for portability and heavy currents, the batteries might be made more cheaply, but the fact that they would be subject to much deeper discharges would shorten their lives. Every day the batteries would be largely discharged, whereas automobile batteries rarely deliver more than a small fraction of their stored energy. Because automobile batteries are mass produced, and industry has had long experience in their manufacture, the present prices are reasonably low.

Evans gives[3] specifications and cost estimates for storage batteries. He states that they deliver about 20 watt-hr lb^{-1}, amounting to 50 lb per kwhr, and occupy about 0.4 ft^3 per kwhr. Assuming a price of \$110 $kwhr^{-1}$, a 10-year life, and depreciation of the capital investment at 4 per cent, he arrives at a cost of \$13.50 $year^{-1}$ to supply the capacity for storing 1 kwhr of electricity. The same costs apply to large installations as well as small ones.

Many different types of electrical storage batteries have been developed, but none is so cheap as the lead–sulfuric acid battery. Other types such as the iron–nickel alkaline battery and the nickel–cadmium battery are more efficient and require less careful operation and upkeep. An intensive development of new types of storage batteries has been encouraged in industrial laboratories by the military branches and the space agency of the United States government.

One of the advantages of storage batteries is the fact that they can be charged in parallel at low voltages from solar-operated photovoltaic or thermoelectric units and then discharged in series at a higher voltage. For operating motors and other electrical equipment, it is much better to use the electricity at high voltages and low currents. The electrical connecting wires have to be excessively large for carrying a current of high amperage.

A standard electrical distribution network or grid could theoretically be used on a large scale for the storage of solar-generated electricity. If many electrical power stations were joined together, the solar power stations (of the future) could put their electricity into the grid while the sun is shining and reduce the use of fuel in the other conventional power stations. When the sun was not shining the other power stations could take over the load.

Fuel Cells

Fuel cells that convert chemical reactions into electricity offer attractive possibilities for storing solar energy. Primary batteries, such as operate flashlights, consume the materials and then the battery is thrown away. Storage batteries can be recharged for further use with an electric current which reverses the reaction and regenerates the reacting materials. Fuel cells are electrochemical cells in which fresh, reacting materials are fed into the cell continuously as the original material is used. The structure of the cell and the electrodes remain unchanged while more chemicals are added. There is very active research in many countries on fuel cells and many millions of dollars are being invested in it by industrial laboratories in the United States. This activity is encouraged by the high efficiency of performance of fuel cells. As much as 50 to 60 and even 70 per cent of the chemical energy has been converted directly into electricity, whereas with heat engines the maximum efficiency is about half as much. There is no limitation to efficiency such as is imposed by the Carnot cycle for heat engines, there are no moving parts, the construction is simple, and the capital costs are rather low.

Fuels cells have serious problems, however, and their large-scale use has not yet come, in spite of early optimism. Most of the fuel cells operate with gases, and catalytic electrode surfaces are necessary, such as platinum for hydrogen and hydrocarbons, and silver for oxygen. One of the most important economic considerations is the length of life. In most operating cells at present the electrodes tend to become inactive through poisoning or disintegration of solid surfaces after hundreds of cycles, and the life of some of them is less than a year. The catalytic surfaces can be renewed rather easily. It has been estimated, however, that if fuel cells ever replaced dynamos for the large-scale generation of electricity, the world's supply of platinum would be exhausted after a few hundred thousand kilowatts of fuel cells had been built, and a substitute catalyst would have to be found. Then there is the problem of getting the reacting chemicals to the active sites on the electrodes and removing the spent chemicals so the cell does not become clogged and inoperative. Probably these difficulties can be overcome by further research, and each year sees important advances. Several symposia and books are available on fuel cells.[4-6]

The hydrogen–oxygen fuel cell is the oldest and the most advanced. In its simplest form it consists of hydrogen gas in contact with one inert electrode and oxygen or air in contact with the other inert electrode. Both electrodes have catalytic surfaces. The electrodes are kept separate from each other and immersed in a solution of sodium hydroxide or other electrolyte. The reaction is

$$2H_2 \text{ (gas)} + O_2 \text{ (gas)} = 2H_2O$$

This cell is of special interest for solar energy applications because it provides an obvious and effective way of storing solar energy. Electricity is generated with photovoltaic cells, thermoelectric units, or heat engines and dynamos, and hydrogen is produced by the electrolysis of water. The hydrogen can be transported and stored and used in a fuel cell to regenerate electricity with a high efficiency.

The development of fuel cells depends not only on thermodynamics and electrochemistry but also on chemical kinetics. Often the principal bottleneck in the operation of the fuel cell is the slow rate of reaction at the electrodes. A whole new field of research on electrode kinetics is opening up and much basic research is needed to give an understanding of the electrode processes. Catalytic surfaces, high temperatures, and high concentrations of the reactants are necessary, but these variables need more basic study. In order to have the electrode reactions proceed fast enough to be practical, it is often necessary to operate at temperatures so high that water cannot be used as a solvent, and fused salts such as phosphates may be used.

Gases are frequently used as the reacting materials; they are introduced through porous electrodes of inert metals such as nickel or graphite. It is important to keep these pores from filling up with the products of the reaction. Frequently a porous barrier is necessary to prevent mixing of electrolytes or reactants.

One kind of hydrogen–oxygen fuel cell developed largely by Bacon[4,7] operates at 200° C and at hydrogen pressures of 20 to 40 atmospheres (300 to 600 lb inch[-2]). Another kind operates nearly at atmospheric pressure and from 20 to

70° C. Both use aqueous solutions of potassium hydroxide. Fuel cells of 1 kw to several kw have been demonstrated but are not yet available in the general market.

The electrolysis of water is a necessary part of the storage and use of solar energy with fuel cells. Electrolytic cells for making hydrogen have been highly developed. On the basis of hydrogen and oxygen per faraday or per ampere-hour they are nearly 100 per cent efficient. On the basis of energy consumption and watt-hours, however, they are about 70 per cent efficient. The operation can be simplified and the storage of oxygen eliminated by using air instead of oxygen, but the efficiency of the fuel cell is then less.

Bacon describes[7] the requirements for the electrolyzer, hydrogen storage units, and fuel cells, and gives cost estimates. He believes that the overall efficiency is not now apt to be over 50 per cent but improvements may be expected. He estimates an overall capital investment of about $325 kw[-1] for a 100-kw installation. Plants of smaller capacity are more expensive per kilowatt.

Bacon includes a study of different means of storing hydrogen—in low-pressure gas holders, in high-pressure steel tanks, and in underground caverns. He favors storage in long steel pipes at pressures of about 100 atmospheres. In 1961 Bacon believed that the development of fuel cells had not yet progressed far enough for the storage of solar energy in economically less developed countries.

Evans[3] has also made a careful study of fuel cells for solar energy use. For small units he estimates the cost of the electrolyzer to be $25 year[-1] for 1 kw and 50¢ year[-1] for the storage of hydrogen for 1 kwhr, using high-pressure steel tanks. He estimates an annual cost per kilowatt (not the cost of the capital investment as estimated by Bacon) of $75 for power levels of 1 kw. He suggests that the cost might come down to $30 after further research.

Other fuel cells in addition to the hydrogen–oxygen fuel cell are under active investigation. Great efforts are being directed toward fuel cells that use petroleum hydrocarbons, and successes have been achieved.[8]

Fuel cells of molten silver, operating at high temperatures, have been reported.[9] An interesting development is a biological fuel cell in which organic material is acted upon by bacteria to produce electricity.

A new kind of fuel cell has been studied in the laboratory,[10] in which waste organic matter is oxidized by electrolytic ions in acid solution and the ions are then fed into a fuel cell. The voltages are very low (less than 0.1 volt) but there are important advantages which are being investigated. The technical operation of the cell has been established, but the engineering and economic difficulties are not yet known. If such a cell could be made to produce electrical energy with grass or garbage or waste paper, oxidized indirectly by air, a new way of using solar energy might become available. The cell is a concentration cell with ferrous ions around one inert electrode and ferric ions around the other, each at a concentration of about one-half molar. A membrane with large pores hinders the diffusion and the thermal convection of the ions to the other electrode compartment, while permitting the diffusion of hydrogen ions and other current-carrying ions. Electrons are transferred through the wire from the electrode in contact with the ferrous ions to the electrode in contact with the ferric ions until each compartment contains a 50–50 mixture of ferrous and ferric ions and the voltage falls to zero. Before the cell is completely run down the solutions are removed; half is oxidized to ferric ions with air and the other half is reduced by organic matter to ferrous ions, and the solutions are replaced in their respective electrode compartments. The operation can be made continuous with a constant flow of solutions between the electrochemical cell and the chemical-reprocessing vessels. No solids are formed at the electrodes, as there are in most batteries, and the only change is chemical oxidation and reduction in a homogeneous solution. The battery should be capable of an indefinite number of cycles of charging and discharging.

The solutions are concentrated in iron salts and in sulfuric acid, which makes the internal resistance low. Many cells are arranged in series, all placed in polyethylene compartments. The electrodes (|) are highly-conducting sheets of polyethylene impregnated with graphite. Coarse barriers (⋮) separate the cells, having ferrous ions on one side and ferric on the other; thus

$$- \boxed{ \quad \xrightarrow{\text{electrons}\longrightarrow} \quad } +$$
$$\mid Fe^{++} \;\vdots\; Fe^{+++} \mid Fe^{++} \;\vdots\; Fe^{+++} \mid$$

External connectors are needed only for the two end electrodes.

The great difficulty lies in the slowness of the chemical

reactions. The solutions are kept boiling with focused sunlight, and the ferric sulfate oxidizes cellulose and waste organic material in a few hours, becoming reduced in the reaction to ferrous ions. The oxidation of the ferrous ion to ferric by air is difficult, but it can be accomplished in a few hours with the help of a platinum catalyst. Other catalysts are being sought. This indirect oxidation-reduction fuel cell, without the problems of gas electrodes or formation of crystalline solids on the electrodes, has interesting possibilities.

Another promising way of using fuel cells is to regenerate them thermally in a closed cycle. Two chemicals react at the electrodes of a cell, generate electricity, and give new products. Instead of being thrown away or regenerated by electricity, they are reconverted into the original chemical compounds, ready to generate electricity again, by heating with focused solar radiation.

A good example of the thermally regeneratable fuel cell is the lithium hydride, operating at 350° C. It is described by Werner and Ciarlariello.[11] The cell has one electrode of hydrogen gas and one of lithium. The reactions at the two electrodes are

$$2\,Li \rightarrow 2Li^+ + 2e$$

and

$$H_2 + 2e \rightarrow 2H^-$$

The electrons from the lithium pass through the external wire to the hydrogen electrode and do electrical work. The two ions, Li^+ and H^-, combine in the solution to form lithium hydride, LiH. To regenerate the cell the lithium hydride is heated to 900° C with focused solar radiation, whereupon it dissociates into lithium metal and hydrogen gas which are stored until needed to operate the cell. The cycles of cell operation and thermal regeneration can be continued indefinitely.

The voltage of each cell is 0.3 volt. A design for a 10-kw generator is described,[11] and the efficiency of conversion of intercepted solar energy into usable electrical energy is expected to be around 13 per cent. This is a high efficiency in comparison with that obtainable by heat engines, thermoelectric units, and photovoltaic cells, and the cell has the great advantage that it can store the energy and deliver the electrical work at any later time.

Werner and Ciarlariello give physical chemical data for several other hydride systems also; but the lithium hydride appears to offer the best properties for a fuel cell. They point out that the free energy change in the chemical reaction must not be too large because the temperature range required for reversibility will then be too great, and it must not be too low because then the voltage of the cell will be too low.

McCully has reported[12] a thorough thermodynamic investigation of possible thermally regeneratable electrochemical cells of oxides, hydrides, halides, carbides, and nitrides in temperature ranges obtainable with focusing solar collectors. He believes it is possible to choose reversible systems that can convert 11 per cent of the heat absorbed at the higher temperature into electrical work. He describes two promising cells, one of silver oxide and manganese oxide and the other of antimony and tin chlorides. The cost of the cells would be high.

HYDROGEN FUEL

Hydrogen obtained from solar energy will probably be an important fuel of the future. Hydrogen can be produced easily by the electrolysis of water using electricity generated by photovoltaic cells, thermoelectric or thermoionic converters, or dynamos operated by heat engines. Attempts to produce hydrogen directly by the photolysis of water or by the use of chlorophyll in a modified scheme of photosynthesis have not been promising thus far. The water needed for the electrolytic production of hydrogen is available everywhere. Even in the desert it can be extracted from the air by silica gel or other water-absorbing material and released by heating with focused sunlight. The capital investment for the electrolytic cells is low, the cells have a very long life, and over 70 per cent of the theoretical amount of hydrogen is produced. Complicated machinery and skilled operators are not necessary.

The most efficient way to use hydrogen for useful work is in the fuel cells previously described. Hydrogen can also be used for the operation of internal-combustion engines. There are no serious difficulties in using hydrogen instead of petroleum hydrocarbons, but further research is needed. On a volume basis hydrogen has a low heat of combustion (274 BTU ft^{-3} compared with 912 BTU ft^{-3} of methane or natural gas gas) but on a weight basis a pound of hydrogen has 2.4 times as much heat of combustion as a pound of methane.

Hydrogen can also be used as a fuel to burn with air for heating boilers for steam engines or turbines; or it might be used without a boiler by burning directly with air to supply high-temperature steam within a turbine.

The storage of hydrogen for operating fuel cells or engines is a problem deserving considerable research effort. It may be stored in large closed tanks or even in caves by the displacement of water. It can be stored in plastic bags at atmospheric pressure or in steel cylinders under pressure. Bacon[7] believes that storage under pressure in long steel pipes is the best method. Hydrogen could be stored under pressure in large abandoned mines, as natural gas is now stored.

Storage as a liquid is possible, and is in fact being used now for propelling rockets and space vehicles, but the temperature of storage is very low and extensive insulation is required.

Storage in palladium metal is attractive but too expensive. One volume of palladium will hold 800 volumes of hydrogen at room temperature and atmospheric pressure. The weight absorbed increases with the pressure. Hydrogen could be forced into palladium under pressure as generated in the electrolysis cell, without the help of mechanical pumps. It could be withdrawn later as desired at atmospheric pressure. Metallic uranium will also absorb considerable quantities of hydrogen at room temperature and release it when heated to about 300° C.

There are many organic and inorganic reactions with hydrogen that can be reversed by changing the temperature or the pressure. Research is needed to find suitable reactions for hydrogen storage that involve inexpensive chemicals, large absorption of hydrogen, and quick response to changing pressure and temperature.

Hydrogen is transportable in tanks, or in pipelines just as natural gas is now transported. The present practical limit for distributing electrical power by high-voltage transmission lines is about 300 or 400 miles, but there is no limit in distance for transporting gaseous fuel with the help of booster pumps. The consideration of the solar production of hydrogen is for small-scale operations or for future economics, because in large chemical industries it is possible to produce hydrogen from cheap petroleum at a cost of 35¢ per 1,000 ft³.

The possibility of using hydrogen for the operation of such moving vehicles as automobiles and tractors should be explored. Automobiles have been operated with fuel gas of carbon monoxide contained in plastic bags mounted on the roof. It might be feasible in some areas to operate vehicles with hydrogen contained in pressure tanks or in balloons anchored to a moving tractor. One kwhr of electricity, electrolyzing water at 1.7 volts, can produce 10.5 moles of hydrogen gas occupying 252 liters or 8.9 ft³. If the hydrogen is used to operate an internal-combustion engine at 10 per cent efficiency, ten times the volume of hydrogen would be required, i.e. 89 ft³ would be required to give 1 kwhr of work. If it were used to operate a fuel cell with an efficiency of 60 per cent, 14.8 ft³ of stored hydrogen would be required for 1 kwhr of work. It would be possible to electrolyze water for several hours with electricity produced by solar energy and store the hydrogen in a balloon to operate a tractor or truck for a short time. The operation would be inefficient but would make operations possible without the expenditure of cash for petroleum fuel, and it might help reduce the number of work animals on a farm and thus release food for human consumption.

Hydrogen-containing compounds in the form of liquids or solids would be much more convenient for the storage and transportation of hydrogen fuel than gaseous hydrogen. Solid palladium containing hydrogen has already been mentioned, as has the possibility of reversibly hydrogenated organic or inorganic compounds. There are also other compounds to be considered. Ammonia is a definite possibility for a future fuel.[13,14] At room temperature the liquid has a vapor pressure of about 10 atmospheres. It is made by combining hydrogen with atmospheric nitrogen under pressure with a catalyst at an elevated temperature. Known as the Haber process, this is carried out on a very large scale all over the world, and liquid ammonia is transported in tank cars and tank trucks. It is used extensively as a liquid fertilizer. Ammonia gas is readily converted into hydrogen and nitrogen by heating, and the hydrogen diluted with nitrogen can be used in heat engines. Ammonia could be used directly in internal-combustion engines. It is a poor fuel in comparison with hydrocarbons and petroleum, but it is a better fuel than almost any other substitute for petroleum products.

Research should be undertaken on the use of ammonia in fuel cells. Very concentrated solutions of electrolytes in ammonia can be readily made, as described in Chapter 13, and the solutions have a high electrical conductance. Moreover in these solutions the ammonia has a low vapor pressure, down to 1 atmosphere and less. A fuel cell with concentrated ammonia in solution at one electrode and air at the other is a definite possibility.

Another transportable liquid fuel that can be made from hydrogen is methanol.[13,14] Techniques are available now for combining hydrogen and carbon dioxide under pressure with the help of a catalyst. The carbon dioxide could be obtained from the air even though it is present to the extent of only one part in 3,000, or it could be obtained by heating limestone above 800° C with a solar furnace. Methanol can be used to operate internal-combustion engines, to produce steam for turbines, and possibly to generate electricity by oxidation with air in a fuel cell.

There are still other electrochemical ways for storing electricity generated by the sun. Instead of electrolyzing water to produce hydrogen fuel for reaction with the oxygen of the air, the electric current might be used for the electrodeposit of metals which could be used in primary electric batteries. When the batteries are run down, the metals, such as zinc or aluminum, may be regenerated by electroplating from the spent battery solutions.

ECONOMICS OF POWER STORAGE

The cost of stored electrical or mechanical energy is considerably greater than the cost of the energy produced directly, because of the inefficiency of the storage and the later release of the stored energy.[1]

The total cost T of 1 kwhr of electrical energy delivered from storage can be expressed in the following terms:

$$T = \frac{P}{e_S e_D} + \frac{M}{n} + \frac{I}{n} + \frac{C}{ny}$$

where $P =$ cost of 1 kwhr of electricity produced initially by the sun; $e_S =$ efficiency of storage; $e_D =$ efficiency of delivery; $M =$ cost of maintaining and operating storage per year;

$n =$ number of kwhr delivered from storage per year; $I =$ annual interest charges on capital investment; $C =$ capital investment for storage and delivery of energy; and $y =$ number of years of life of storage unit.

The storage unit can be composed of several parts, each with a different life. Therefore C/y can be regraded as a summation of the cost of each part divided by the length of its life.

This formula can be illustrated with specific examples. It is assumed that solar-produced electricity costing 5¢ kwhr^{-1} charges at 12-volt lead–acid storage battery at 10 amp for an average of 8⅓ hr day^{-1}. Thus 1 kwhr is delivered to storage per day, or 365 kwhr year^{-1}. The efficiency of delivery to storage is assumed to be 90 per cent and the efficiency of recovery from storage 80 per cent, so the number n of kwhr delivered from storage is $365 \times 0.9 \times 0.8 = 263$. The cost of the storage battery C is assumed to be \$25 or 2,500¢, and the useful life y is 2 years. The cost of maintenance and operation M is neglected and the interest charge is assumed to be 10 per cent. Then

$$T = \frac{5}{0.9 \times 0.8} + \frac{250}{263} + \frac{2500}{2 \times 263} = 12.6¢$$

The prices assumed here are in fair agreement with the findings of Evans[3] but lower than those of Bacon.[7]

In a second illustration, it is assumed that the solar energy supplies electricity at 12 volts and 10 amp for 8⅓ hr day^{-1} providing 1 kwhr, which is used to electrolyze water with an efficiency of 70 per cent. The stored hydrogen and oxygen then operate a fuel cell and produce electricity with an efficiency of 60 per cent. The kwhr year^{-1} delivered from storage are then $365 \times 0.7 \times 0.6$ or 153. It is assumed that the electrolyzer, the fuel cell, and the storage tank for the hydrogen and oxygen will cost twice that of a storage battery, i.e. \$50, and that they will operate for 5 years. However, it is assumed that the electrodes with their catalytic surfaces will have to be replaced at a cost M of \$2 year^{-1}. Then

$$T = \frac{5}{0.7 \times 0.6} + \frac{200}{153} + \frac{500}{153} + \frac{5000}{5 \times 153} = 23¢$$

More exact costs of fuel cells are discussed thoroughly by Bacon[7] and by Evans.[8]

These formulas show that the efficiency of storage and delivery and the length of life of the equipment greatly influence the cost. If the storage is to be effected through pumping water to a higher reservoir, the formula shows the great advantage of going to larger units with higher pumping efficiencies. If storage and recovery are to be effected by later operation of a heat engine with a Carnot-cycle limitation of perhaps 10 per cent, the small value of e_D makes the total cost T extremely high.

One kwhr of energy from a storage battery will operate four 50-watt electric lamps for 5 hr, or will pump 61,000 liters or 16,000 gal of water to 10 ft (3 m) if the combined efficiency of motor and pump is 50 per cent. If one 50-watt lamp were to be operated for 3 hr each evening, using 150 watt-hr, the cost according to the example just given would be $0.15 \times 12.6¢$ or $1.9¢$, assuming that the very small unit of 0.15 kwhr day^{-1} has the same efficiency and the same relative cost as a unit of 1 kwhr.

REFERENCES

1. Daniels, F., Energy Storage Problems, in *United Nations Conferences on New Sources of Energy*, E 35Gr–Gen. 2, Rome, 1961. Also, *Solar Energy*, 6: 78–83. 1962.

2. Landry, B. A., The Storage of Heat and Electricity, *Proc. Nat. Acad. Sci.*, 47: 1290–95. 1961. Also, *Solar Energy* (special issue), 5: 46–51. Sept. 1961.

3. Evans, G. E., Electrochemical Energy Storage for Intermittent Power Sources, in *U.N. Conf. on New Sources of Energy*, E 35–Gen. 3, Rome, 1961.

4. Young, G. J., *Fuel Cells*, New York, Reinhold, 1960; Vol. 2, 1963.

5. *Fuel Cell Technical Manual*, New York, Publication Dept., Am. Inst. Chem. Eng. 1963.

6. *Proc. Annual Power Conference*, U.S. Army Signal Research and Development Laboratory, Red Bank, N.J., P.S.C. Publications Committee, 1960–64.

7. Bacon, F. T., Energy Storage Based on Electrolyzers and Hydrogen-Oxygen Fuel Cells, in *U.N. Conf. on New Sources of Energy*, E 35–Gen. 9, Rome, 1961.

8. Liebhafsky, H. A., and Cairns, E. J., The hydrocarbon fuel cell, *Chem. Eng. Prog.*, 59 (10): 35–37. 1962.

9. General Electric Research Bulletin, Summer, p. 4, 1963.

10. Christiansen, J., Fiez, I., and Daniels, F., Forthcoming publication, Solar Energy Laboratory, University of Wisconsin.

11. Werner, R., and Ciarlariello, T., Metal Hydride Fuel Cells as Energy Storage Devices, in *U.N. Conf. on New Sources of Energy*, E 35–Gen. 14, Rome, 1961.

12. McCully, C., The Chemical Conversion of Solar Energy to Electrical Energy, ibid., E 35–Gen. 6.

13. Busch, C. W., Future Portable Energy Systems, M.S. Thesis, University of Wisconsin, 1962.

14. Lauck, F. W., Busch, C. W., Uyehara, O. A., and Myers, P. S., Portable Power From Non-Portable Energy Sources, *Society of Automotive Engineers*, Paper 608A, National Power Plant Meeting, Philadelphia, 1962.

CHAPTER 19

Conclusions

We have seen that the total solar energy reaching the earth is much greater than the energy requirements of all the world's population and that technologically it could be used to replace the energy now being supplied by fuels and electricity. But it will not be used at present except in a few special cases because the cost of collection and the investment required for solar devices are high. However, our present fossil fuels—coal, gas, and oil—are irreplaceable and they are being consumed at an increasingly rapid rate. Eventually they will become more expensive, relative to other goods and services. Furthermore, research and development, and eventually mass production of solar equipment, will lower the cost of the conversion of solar energy to a point where it can compete economically with fossil fuels. This competition will come gradually, first in selected areas where fuel is scarce and sunshine abundant. As emphasized earlier, solar energy is not suitable for use in cold cloudy regions or in large cities, where the acres of sunshine per person are not nearly enough to supply the needs. Solar energy is particularly suitable for use in sunny rural areas where there are few potential users, living far apart, and where the cost of distribution of electricity by transmission lines is high.

In a few areas the use of solar energy can be considered

immediately, and in many more areas only a slight advance in solar energy technology is needed to make it economical in the near future.

In Chapter 3 we discussed the amounts of solar radiation that are available and the instruments for measuring it. We found that better records are needed in many areas for making decisions on the economic advisability of installing solar devices. Good progress is being made in such records.

The biggest barrier to rapid expansion of solar energy use is the high cost of collectors of solar radiation, both flat-plate collectors for moderate temperatures and movable focusing collectors for high temperatures. These collectors are described in Chapter 4.

Solar radiation is so low in intensity that collectors of very large areas are required, and large areas of any material are expensive. High temperatures are desired in order to achieve practical heat transfer operations and high thermodynamic efficiencies. In the past, glass has been the chief material for the collector covers. One or two layers have been used for heating and distillation. Glass mirrors have been used for the focusing collectors required for higher temperatures. But now plastics are available that are nearly as good in many respects and are nonshatterable, easily transportable, and initially much cheaper. The use of plastics is one important development that should greatly reduce the time before there is a wider use of solar energy. Solar collectors of plastic materials are available now and directions for their use have been given throughout the book, but there is still research needed to produce focusing collectors of higher precision and cheaper construction and to make flat-plate collectors of less expensive fabrication and greater durability.

As described in Chapter 5, solar cookers equivalent to a ½-kw electric heater are available. They can be manufactured in quantity or they can be made locally. Field tests have been made in Mexico. The cost of $12 to $25, the frustration of cloudy weather, and particularly the fact that women do not like to cook outdoors in the sunshine are deterrents to the social acceptance of these cookers. The acceptance would probably be much greater if a small portable storage unit of 1 kwhr of heat can be developed that could be exposed to sunlight, with occasional focusing, over a 2-hr period during the day and then carried to an insulated box in the house for cooking a meal in the normal kitchen environment several hours later. The development of such a heat storage unit is difficult but not impossible.

Solar water heaters for domestic use, discussed in Chapter 6, are already widely used. There are hundreds of thousands of them in areas where fuel is expensive. Apparently they can compete with expensive electrical heating but not with heating by natural gas. They range from large permanent household installations to inexpensive, hand-operated units costing only a few dollars. They will probably expand rapidly in use and could be widely accepted in isolated areas and for summer vacation cabins.

The use of the sun for drying agricultural crops is as old as agriculture. As described in Chapter 7, greater efficiency in operation, higher yields, and improved quality of the crop can sometimes be achieved through the use of modern solar collectors, usually made of plastic sheets. The capital costs are not large. Electrical motors are usually needed for blowing the air. An interesting field for exploration is the accelerated solar drying of lumber and other products in small units in isolated places.

The storage of heat in pebble beds, water tanks, and chemicals is discussed in Chapter 8. Pebble beds used with air circulation is the cheapest method, while the method using chemicals is the most expensive and the most efficient in space utilization. A small electric motor is required for circulating the air or water. A considerable effort is needed to find better ways of storing heat in chemicals at high temperatures and of preventing the supercooling of liquids in which the release of stored heat involves crystallization.

The solar heating of houses, discussed in Chapter 8, has developed very slowly, in spite of the fact that about one fourth of the world's annual consumption of fuel is used for space heating, and the substitution of solar heating could be a large factor in conserving our fossil fuels. But at present the capital investment is too great and the available sunshine in the colder climates too small for wide acceptance. Auxiliary heating with fuels is necessary in most cold climates to avoid the high cost of excessively large heat-storage capacities if the sun is to be the only source of heat. Then there is the architectural handicap of large flat collectors. Probably less than twenty solar-heated buildings, with heat storage, have been built and tested in the world; they are fully described in the literature and form a good background for further advances. There is good opportunity for solar-heated houses in sunny climates. The best opportunity, and one in which practically no work has been done, seems to be in the solar heating of one-room low-cost houses in sunny rural areas using inexpensive plastic collectors and rock beds for heat storage. The fact that such houses rarely have electric power for blowing air is a difficulty and constitutes a challenge for finding other ways to circulate air.

Distillation of seawater is one of the obvious applications of solar energy with great potentialities. The distillation can be carried out easily with simple equipment. As shown in Chapter 10, the problems are economic. Solar distillation with its low capital investment and its opportunity for small-scale operations has distinct advantages over other methods where small units of a few gallons per day are needed. Where electrical power and fuel are not available at reasonable prices, solar distillation should be competitive with other methods of distillation. Efficiencies of 30 per cent are fairly readily obtainable but effective use of more than half of the sun's energy in recoverable distilled water is difficult to obtain. In large fuel-operated stills it is possible to use multiple stills in which the condensing steam evaporates additional water, producing very high yields with many times the theoretical amount based on a single distillation. Such multiple stills are not easily adapted to solar operation. For large-scale distillation the capital investment and the area of land necessary for the solar still become very large. Most stills require expensive flat land, but tilted stills for hilly land with southern exposures are worthy of special attention. Though most solar stills have been made of glass, newly developed plastics with resistance to solar deterioration and with wettable surfaces point to the possibility of large use for solar distillation. In Chapter 10 the construction and tests of small solar stills and family stills are given particular attention. They should be competitive in small units even where fuel is cheap.

Solar furnaces with precision focusing are capable of reaching temperatures of 2,000° and 3,000° C and higher. Chapter 11 gives a brief summary of this field. Such solar equipment is expensive and its use depends on clear skies, but it is very valuable in high-temperature research, particularly in cases where other types of furnaces are objectionable because of contamination.

Selective radiation surfaces are promising. They absorb most of the sun's radiation but give only a small fraction of the radiation emitted by an ordinary black surface. They make possible a considerably higher efficiency in heating by solar radiation. The preparation and use of these special surfaces is described in Chapter 12.

The principles and operations of cooling with the sun are given in Chapter 13. Although there is practically no solar refrigeration or solar air conditioning in the world at present, it seems likely that both may become well established within a decade. The demand is great in sunny countries where the cost of electricity for conventional cooling units is very high. There is a real need for cooling in many regions where there is no electrical power. The production of ice and the cooling of buildings have been carried out technologically, and there are no serious difficulties. In countries where electricity and fuel are abundant and cheap, solar cooling will have difficult competition with present mass-produced electric-powered cooling devices, but it has the possibility of large savings in operation costs. Interesting experiments with ammonia and water have been described, and a new chemical system for solar cooling, sodium thiocyanate and ammonia, has been tested and seems promising. It is expected that solar cooling will follow two different lines—small, hand-operated discontinuous solar coolers and large continuously-operated coolers. The small units are cheaper, but they may be impractical for operation by the individual, technically untrained householder. Larger units could be operated by skilled technicians and the ice distributed to nearby families. Other chemical systems should be explored, and a considerable effort in engineering design and testing of both the small units and the large units is needed.

Heat engines, using steam, vapor, and hot air, are studied in Chapter 14. Small steam engines are inefficient, and it seems unlikely that solar steam engines will soon be important. Progress has been made in finding new chemicals such as chlorobenzene with thermodynamic properties which are particularly favorable. Hot-air engines have a high efficiency and appear to be quite hopeful. Although the Stirling hot-air engine is old and no longer important for operation with fuel in competition with internal-combustion engines, it may be important for producing work from focused solar radiation.

There are three ways of converting solar radiation directly into electrical power—heat engines are discussed in Chapter 14, thermoelectric generators in Chapter 15, and photovoltaic generators in Chapter 16. The hot-air engine is now the cheapest, and very small engines have been successfully operated with the sun, but difficulties have been experienced with larger engines. Undoubtedly these difficulties will be overcome.

Thermoelectric generators have no moving parts and are simple in principle and operation. Their efficiencies have been increased 10-fold in recent years through new developments with highly purified and specially treated semiconductors. The outlook for thermoelectric generators is handicapped by the fact that many thermoelements lose efficiency after long-time use at the high temperatures where the thermodynamic relations are favorable. One important advantage of thermoelectric generators is that their efficiency of conversion of heat into work is nearly as good in small units as in large ones and many can be operated in series to give higher voltages. Thermoionic generators hold promise of effective power conversion at reasonably low cost if focusing collectors of sufficiently high optical precision can be made cheaply enough. This situation has not yet been reached; the presence of oxygen in air is a difficulty.

Thanks to intensive research and large government subsidies for space exploration, effective photovoltaic cells are now available. Silicon photovoltaic cells capable of long life at efficiencies of 8 per cent and more can be bought off the shelf. But they are very expensive for ordinary use—over $100 watt^{-1}. There is a chance that the cost may be greatly reduced if a practical way can be found to make efficient polycrystalline cells to replace the present cells which are cut from a single crystal. A phenomenal 10-fold increase in the efficiency of photovoltaic cells in the mid-1950s was brought about by advances in the theory and practical production of P–N junctions in semiconductors.

Photochemistry is an important field for research in the search for new ways to use the sun's energy. The principles and ground rules for new photochemical reactions are given in Chapter 17. The conversion of sunlight into work or electricity does not require a difference in temperature. No really practical photochemical reaction is yet available for storing the energy of the sun or converting it into work, but there is no theoretical reason to deny the possibility. We know that all our food and present fuels have been made through photosynthesis.

In Chapter 18 the storage of energy is considered, using electrical, mechanical, and chemical systems. An effective method of storing energy is necessary for many uses of solar energy, since the sun is available only during the day. Here also, as in all the branches of solar energy use, it is highly important to explore new possibilities through research and to increase our store of basic knowledge which will lead more quickly to finding favorable systems. Then there is the equally important task of engineering design and testing to develop practical workable systems which can compete economically with other systems.

The chief limitations to use of the sun's energy, at least in sunny areas, are economic rather than technological. There has been so little experience with solar devices that reliable cost estimates are not available.

Limited ventures in solar energy research by industrial companies in the United States have not been successful thus far. The potential markets have not yet developed, and when they do materialize they will probably come first in foreign markets among the rapidly developing countries where there are difficulties in international payments. These countries should endeavor to build up their own industries to make equipment for using the sun's energy, but the industrialized countries will still export the manufactured materials such as plastics and special products. The possibility of making materials to cover square miles of land should be an incentive.

The economics of solar energy has been discussed by Löf[1] and by Kastens.[2]

The world's reserves of fossil fuel are very large, and authorities differ on the estimates of the time that will elapse before the cost of coal, oil, and gas will be a serious problem.[3-6]

Nuclear fission of uranium and thorium will take over for centuries an increasing fraction of the world's energy load. If nuclear fusion should become available for power, the large-scale energy problem could be met with nuclear fusion of the deuterium of the oceans.

Solar energy is present in sufficient abundance on the earth to supply all energy needs, but like fossil fuels its practical availability is limited to specific localities. Beyond the limit of a few hundred miles with electric transmission lines, it must be converted into chemicals that can be stored and transported. We have seen that these chemicals will probably include hydrogen, ammonia, and methanol. None of these can compare with our present hydrocarbon fuels in efficiency and cost, but they can in principle be made with solar energy from inexhaustible materials—water, nitrogen, and carbon dioxide.

During the past decade, progress in the direct use of the sun's energy has been slow but steady. The solar scientists and engineers, working in different fields of activity and in different countries around the world, have been drawn together for better cooperation through several international symposia and through the Solar Energy Society and its publications. Even the unrealistic enthusiasts have come to realize that there are no quick and easy solutions to the intermittency of the sun and the high cost of collecting its energy.

It is clear to all that much basic research in science and engineering is needed before solar energy can be widely successful in competition with our present sources of energy. But it is clear, also, that much basic research has already been done—for example, in solid-state physics for improving photovoltaic cells, and in the industrial production of inexpensive sun-resistant plastics with desirable properties. The sudden demand for solar-operated devices for the exploration of outer space came as a surprise, and it will be interesting to see what further surprises lie ahead in the coming decade. It seems likely that the next few years will see the utilization of solar energy in many sun-rich, fuel-poor areas of the world and that the ground work will be laid for general advances well before the inevitable decrease in our fuel reserves requires alternative sources of energy.

REFERENCES

1. Löf, G. O. G., Profits in solar energy, *Solar Energy, 4* (2): 9–16. 1960.

2. Kastens, M., Economics of Solar Energy, in *Introduction to the Utilization of Solar Energy,* ed. A. M. Zarem and D. D. Erway, New York, McGraw-Hill, 1963, pp. 211–38.

3. Putnam, P. C., *Energy in the Future,* Princeton, N.J., Van Nostrand, 1956.

4. Putnam, P. C., Expected World Energy Demands, in *Solar Energy Research*, Ed. F. Daniels, F. and J. A. Duffie, Madison, University of Wisconsin Press, 1955, pp. 7–11.

5. Ayres, E., and Scarlott, C. A., *Energy Sources, The Wealth of the World*, New York, McGraw-Hill, 1952.

6. Schurr, S. H., Energy, *Scientific American, 209* (3): 110–26. Sept. 1963.

Appendix

CONVERSION FACTORS

To Change	Into	Multiply By
(ft)	(inches)	12
(m)	(cm)	100
acres	ft^2	43,560
acres	m^2	4,047
atmospheres	cm of mercury	76.0
atmospheres	lb inch^{-2}	14.7
BTU	cal	252
BTU	joules	1,055
BTU	kcal	0.252
BTU	kwhr	2.93×10^{-4}
BTU ft^{-2}	langleys (cal cm^{-2})	0.271
cal	BTU	3.97×10^{-3}
cal	ft-lb	3.09
cal	joules	4.184
cal	kcal	0.001
cal min^{-1}	watts	0.0698
cm	inches	0.394
cc or cm^3	inches^3	0.0610
ft^3	liters	28.3
inches^3	cc or cm^3	16.4
ft	inches	12
ft	m	0.305
ft-lb	cal	0.324
ft-lb	joules	1.36
ft-lb	kg-m	0.138
ft-lb	kwhr	3.77×10^{-7}
gal	liters	3.79
gal	qt	4.00
g	lb	0.00220
hectares	acres	2.47
hp	kw	0.745
inches	cm	2.54
joules	BTU	9.48×10^{-4}

CONVERSION FACTORS (*continued*)

To Change	Into	Multiply By
joules	cal	0.239
joules	ft-lb	0.738
kcal	BTU	3.97
kcal	cal	1,000
kcal min^{-1}	kw	0.0698
kg-m	ft-lb	7.23
kg	lb	2.20
kg	tons	0.00110
kw	hp	1.34
kwhr	BTU	3,413
kwhr	ft-lb	2.66×10^6
kw	kcal min^{-1}	14.3
langleys (cal cm^2)	BTU ft^{-2}	3.69
langleys min^{-1} (cal cm^{-2} min^{-1})	watts cm^{-2}	0.0698
liters	gal	0.264
liters	qt	1.06
m	ft	3.28
m	inches	39.4
m	miles	6.21×10^4
miles	ft	5,280
miles	m	1,609
lb	g	454
lb	kg	0.454
lb inches^{-2}	atmospheres	0.068
qt	liters	0.946
cm^2	ft^2	0.00108
cm^2	inches^2	0.155
ft^2	cm^2	929
ft^2	inches^2	144
ft^2	m^2	0.0929
inches^2	cm^2	6.45
m^2	ft^2	10.8
m^2	miles^2	3.86×10^{-7}
miles^2	acres	640
miles^2	ft^2	2.79×10^7
miles^2	m^2	2.59×10^6
tons	kg	907
tons	lb	2,000
watts cm^{-2}	langleys (cal cm^2) min^{-1}	14.3

CONVERSION FACTORS (*continued*)

To Change	Into	Multiply By
yd	ft	3.00
yd	cm	91.4
°Fahrenheit	°Centigrade	subtract 32 and multiply by 5/9 or 0.555
°Centigrade	°Fahrenheit	multiply by 9/5 or 1.800 and add 32
cal cm^{-2} sec^{-1} °C^{-1}	BTU ft^{-2} hr^{-1} °F^{-1}	7,380
BTU ft^{-2} hr^{-1} °F^{-1}	cal cm^{-2} sec^{-2} °C^{-1}	0.000135

Index

265

SIERRA CLUB BOOKS
Eloquent tributes to the irreplaceable natural beauty of this country.

Available at your bookstore or use this coupon.